D1250644

Television Versus the Internet

CHANDOS

INTERNET SERIES

Chandos' new series of books are aimed at all those individuals interested in the Internet. They have been specially commissioned to provide the reader with an authoritative view of current thinking. If you would like a full listing of current and forthcoming titles, please visit our website www.chandospublishing.com or e-mail info@chandospublishing.com or telephone +44 (0) 1223 499140.

New authors: we are always pleased to receive ideas for new titles; if you would like to write a book for Chandos, please contact Dr Glyn Jones on e-mail gjones@ chandospublishing.com or telephone number +44 (0) 1993 848726.

Bulk orders: some organisations buy a number of copies of our books. If you are interested in doing this, we would be pleased to discuss a discount. Please e-mail info@chandospublishing.com or telephone +44 (0) 1223 499140.

Television Versus the Internet

Will TV prosper or perish as the world moves online?

BARRIE GUNTER

CHANDOS
PUBLISHING

Oxford Cambridge New Delhi

Chandos Publishing
Hexagon House
Avenue 4
Station Lane
Witney
Oxford OX28 4BN
UK
Tel: +44 (0) 1993 848726
Email: info@chandospublishing.com
www.chandospublishing.com

Chandos Publishing is an imprint of Woodhead Publishing Limited

Woodhead Publishing Limited
80 High Street
Sawston
Cambridge CB22 3HJ
UK
Tel: +44 (0) 1223 499140
Fax: +44 (0) 1223 832819
www.woodheadpublishing.com

First published in 2010

ISBN:
978 1 84334 636 4

© B. Gunter, 2010

British Library Cataloguing-in-Publication Data.
A catalogue record for this book is available from the British Library.

Typeset by RefineCatch Limited, Bungay, Suffolk
Printed in the UK and USA.

Printed in the UK by 4edge Limited - www.4edge.co.uk

682 88/93 0

Contents

List of tables	*ix*
Preface	*xi*
About the author	*xv*
1 Audience evolution patterns	**1**
Growth of media supply and television viewing	3
Growth of the Internet	4
Implications of media expansion	7
The position of television in society	9
Changing patterns of consumption	10
Does one medium cannibalise another?	14
Models of displacement	16
Increase–decrease relationship	19
Competition or synergy?	25
Ensuring access, diversity and quality	26
Concluding remarks	31
2 The importance of television and the Internet to media consumers	**35**
How important is television to people today?	35
The importance of digital	36
The importance of channels	44
Are we satisfied with television channels?	48
The importance of programme service values	52

The importance of programme genres 58

Behavioural evidence of what is important to media consumers 61

The importance of the Internet 63

Concluding remarks 65

3 The functional overlaps of television and the Internet 67

The importance of media motives 68

The attraction of the Internet 70

Conditional displacement 74

Overlapping functional displacement of television by the Internet 76

Non-overlapping functional displacement of television by
the Internet 79

Concluding remarks 83

4 The future of television as an information source 85

The valued attributes of television news 86

Television versus the Internet 89

Importance of different information sources 90

Importance of different news sources: Internet users
versus non-users 95

The future for television news 95

Time devoted to television news 97

Levels of use of online news 99

Receptivity of new news sources 102

News source displacement 102

Credibility of offline versus online news 107

Importance of news brands 110

Concluding remarks 111

5   The future of television as an entertainment source   113

    Perceived importance of different entertainment sources   114

    The Internet as an entertainment source   117

    Video viewing online   118

    Online video viewing versus television   128

    Video game playing   132

    Concluding remarks   133

6   Future audiences, future services   137

    Television versus the Internet: continuing distinctions   138

    The promise of digital   140

    Future audiences   143

    Final thoughts   163

References   167

Index   183

List of tables

1.1 Audience share for public service broadcast (PSB) channels in all and in multi-channel homes   13

2.1 Perceived importance of television programme genres   60

2.2 Audience shares of channel genres in UK multi-channel TV homes   62

Preface

The television marketplace has become increasingly competitive since the early 1990s. Technological developments have driven the growth of television channels and opened up new platforms for the transmission of programmes and much other content as the emergence of digital communications has begun a process of rapid transformation of the traditional media landscape. The conversion of pictures and sounds into binary codes means that content can be compressed to the extent that it is possible to convey significantly more content to media consumers, including television viewers, within the same waveband space (Negroponte, 1995). The switch to digital will, say its proponents, reap economic benefits for the television industry (as well as for other media sectors), facilitate production of better quality programmes, create better quality reception, and bring greater choice for viewers (Parliamentary Office of Science and Technology, 2006).

The rapid growth of the television marketplace facilitated by digital technology has also raised concerns in some sectors of broadcasting about its implications for their future operations. In the United Kingdom, it has triggered debates about the future of public service broadcasting (PSB) and led to questions being raised about the business models and regulatory restrictions of government-funded and commercially-funded PSB operators (Ofcom, 2004, 2007a, 2009d). While this debate is relevant to any analysis of the overall importance of television, more far-reaching changes to the medium are being driven by the relentless growth of the Internet which is emerging as a platform of significance for the delivery of television programmes and movies and is changing the way media consumers seek to select audio-visual content for their entertainment and information (Hammersley, 2006).

Major commercial broadcasters have felt the strain in particular as advertising revenues have dropped. The emergence of multi-channel television platforms has meant that viewers have far more channels to choose from and this has reduced the audience share of the channels that pre-dated these platforms. As the penetration of multi-channel platforms has spread, so the share reductions of the major channels in the UK, that all have public service broadcasting (PSB) requirements placed upon them, have become increasingly acute. This development has led to important debates about the future of PSB, how it should be funded and whether it is viable in its current form, or at all, in the future. The emergence then of the Internet as a new information and entertainment source has created a further threat to television with fears that audiences for the medium in general will be seriously eroded.

Its defenders have pointed out that so far there are no signs that television is on the way out. Looking back at the audiences for the medium over time indicates that they have changed little. Over a ten-year period from the mid- to late-1990s, the average amount of time people watch television has shown mild fluctuations but certainly no progressive downward trend. Moreover, the evidence frequently cited in support of the cannibalisation of television audiences by the Internet is generally founded on self-report data the accuracy of which can be called into question (Alps, 2008).

That television is moving through a period of rapid change is undeniable. Technological developments have encouraged the multiplication of TV channels, TV signals can be received via different technology platforms and programme viewing is no longer restricted only to standard TV sets. Governments around the world are switching from analogue to digital forms of transmission to further expand the amount of content that TV signals can carry. In the United States, for example, the digital switchover occurred between 2006 and 2009 and in the United Kingdom was set to occur in a rolling programme across the country between 2008 and 2012 (Conformity e-News Breaks, 2006; DCMS/BIS, 2010). All these changes have created a great deal more competition for viewers within the traditional TV marketplace. At the same time, competition for eyeballs has also grown from outside that traditional marketplace with the emergence of the Internet. The roll-out of the broadband Internet has had the greatest impact because online technology has been created that can readily convey the same content as television.

The rapid penetration of online applications that supply information, entertainment and communications channels has resulted in ever-growing numbers of people devoting more and more of their time to the Internet and the World Wide Web. The Internet has proven to be especially popular with young people who have adopted its applications to a far greater extent than their elders, though even the latter have now begun to take up online activities in significant numbers (Gunter, Rowlands and

Nicholas, 2009). Does the appeal of the Internet mean that people are turning away from television? If this is the case, what future does television have? Or have scaremongers who claim that television is not long for this world got it all wrong? Rather than eating away at television's audiences, can the Internet provide an alternative route through which television can evolve and prosper in the future?

As well as being a competitor to television for users, the Internet has also emerged as an alternative platform for the distribution of programmes (see Hammersley, 2006). The use of video content online has become a factor driving the growth of use of the Internet (Bulkley, 2010) while at the same time, the level of interactivity associated with online applications has also begun to surface with digital television technology. Advanced digital interactive technologies will convert the television set from a passive receptacle of standard format programmes into a communication centre through which viewers will be able to send as well as receive content (Gunter, 2005a). This will open up all kinds of new possibilities whereby television can be used, much as personal computers, as transactional devices.

These developments signal a movement away from traditional forms of television viewing, dominated by linear programme schedules contained within television channels where the timing of transmission is determined by the producer or sender, towards a more interactive, non-linear system within which the consumer can decide what to watch and when (Swedlow, 2000; Maad, 2005).

This on-demand environment presents both challenges and opportunities for established broadcasters. New suppliers of television services have emerged within the online world who are competing directly within multi-channel packages conveyed via television sets. Some of these Internet-based services such as Zattoo provide video streams of existing television channels and others, such as Babelgum, Blinkbox, Joost, and SeeSaw provide access to a range of genres of programming and movies that can be downloaded or streamed on-demand. Furthermore, these online services tend, more often than not, to be available free of charge to users.

In addition, the major broadcasters have themselves begun to establish their own on-demand services available over the Internet and in due course via Internet-enabled television sets. In the UK, public service broadcasters such as the BBC have joined forces with telecommunications operators to provide online video and interactive services (Cooper, 2010). Even broadcasters' traditional offline competitors such as newspapers have entered the video production market on the Internet with video content used to support news stories on their web sites (Bulkley, 2010). Once these developments really take hold, the entire shape of traditional television viewing could change and could render the linear television channel arrangement outmoded. If this scenario represents an accurate description of the way the Internet will drive television to evolve, it will have significant implications for the future of public service and commercial broadcasters that will have to re-think their current business models. Some commentators have argued that on-demand services still tend to be used as enhancements to conventional channel-based viewing on television as viewers go to on-demand frequently to catch up on programmes they missed on first transmission in channel schedules (Alps, 2010). Nonetheless, even this 'catch-up' viewing entails a different kind of engagement with video content and a different style of television viewing.

This book will explore these questions by considering the evidence concerning the user bases or audiences for television and the Internet. Are these audiences the same? Do people make a choice between these two media or do they use them both at different times and for different reasons? Can television utilise the Internet in profitable ways to enhance its market position? Will television have to evolve from its current state to provide the kinds of content reception services to which people have become accustomed in the online world? If it does need to change to survive, will this also mean a radical new configuration of content and the disappearance of 'channels' with fixed, pre-determined programme schedules?

About the author

Barrie Gunter is currently Professor of Mass Communication and Head of the Department of Media and Communication, University of Leicester. Previously he was Professor of Journalism Studies, Department of Journalism Studies, University of Sheffield. Before moving to the academic world in 1994, he worked as an audience researcher in the broadcasting sector and was Head of Research at both the Independent Television Commission and Independent Broadcasting Authority. He is a psychologist by training with degrees from the University of Wales (BSc), University of London (MSc) and University of East London (PhD). He has published 50 books and more than 300 refereed journal papers, book chapters, non-refereed articles, and technical reports in the fields of media, marketing, and psychology. His major current research interests include the study of digital media developments and their impact upon consumer, social and political behaviour and upon the use of 'old' media.

The author may be contacted at

www.le.ac.uk/mediacom/

Audience evolution patterns

New communications technologies have opened up significantly enhanced choices for media consumers in obtaining entertainment and information. This development has not simply been reflected in the growth of television channels facilitated by digital transmission technology, but also in the range of other technologies – fixed and mobile – through which electronic content can be received. Multi-channel TV packages have spread far and wide and the majority of viewers in the UK had adopted them even before the digital switch-over. In consequence, television audiences have fragmented and the major channels that have been broadcasting the longest have experienced significant erosion of their audiences with important implications for their future viability. The emergence of the Internet and its dramatic penetration of the population have added to the complexity of the communications and media environment. Is television as a medium under threat as the Internet pulls users towards it for reasons that could displace the relevance of television in their lives? Is the Internet cannibalising television audiences, or is that claim over-stated?

The convergence of previously distinct technologies such as sound and visual broadcasting, computing, and telecommunications has meant that the same pieces of kit can be used to send and receive content and that that content can be sent and received in a number of forms – audio, picture and text. Hence, mass communications and interpersonal communications can be accommodated by the same technological apparatus. Historically, these communications forms and systems were carried by different technologies with different types of organisation providing these distinctive communications services. Technological convergence has meant that such distinctions are disappearing. It also means that communications organisations are changing to become multi-media businesses rather than single-medium businesses. Telecommunications companies, for example, no longer conceive of themselves simply as providers of a communications infrastructure; they now recognise the importance to their business future of also becoming content providers. Broadcasters can generate revenue not simply through the sale of airtime to advertisers or sale of programmes to other broadcasters, but also by engaging their audiences interactively via the telephone. All these actors are evolving as businesses in response to the opportunities and challenges presented to them by the growth of digital communications technologies. The traditional business models of these industries are being revised as well as consumers becoming empowered by digital technology to expect personalised services on-demand (Berman, 2004).

The expansion of reception technologies also means that media consumers are no longer restricted to receiving entertainment and information via fixed technologies such as their household television and radio sets. Personal digital assistants have built-in telephone and content reception technology. They can be used not only to send voice or text messages one-to-one, but also to receive still and moving images and music. Personal computers (PCs) and laptops can be used for word processing and data analysis, but also represent communications technologies through which multi-media content (audio, visual and text) can be sent and received. When used to download music, films and news via the Internet, PCs compete directly with television for people's attention. These developments have opened up a wide range of new content reception opportunities for media audiences. The use of increasingly interactive communications technologies has also conditioned new media-related behaviours. Media consumers are significantly more empowered to control the way they consume information and entertainment content and have become accustomed to having not only more choice of content, but also direct influence over the time and place of consumption (OECD, 2008).

Perhaps the most significant development in this context from the mid-1990s has been the emergence and rapid penetration of the Internet. The Internet has been perceived as a direct threat to the longer established media such as newspapers, radio and, perhaps most of all, television (Adoni and Nossek, 2001; Holmewood and Hughes, 2009). One perception is that the time occupied by being online will be subtracted in the case of most media consumers from the time they devote to reading newspapers, listening to radio or watching television. The focus of this book is concerned with the influence of the Internet on the way television is used. Does Internet use displace television viewing? Or can the Internet actually benefit television (and other mass media)?

Growth of media supply and television viewing

Increasingly, national audits of households across the UK have revealed that more and more people own more and more communications equipment (Ofcom, 2009a, 2009b). Nearly all households possess at least one television set, and many have more than one. Virtually all households have both landline and mobile telephones and half of all households have personal computers with Internet access. Rapidly growing numbers of British households are signing up to broadband telecommunications networks enabling the faster transfer and larger and larger volumes of multi-media content.

Hence, the UK is experiencing a changing communications environment that has embraced the introduction of new media and the upgrading of established older media. Radio and television services are being technologically upgraded to digital transmission to enhance the quality and volume of content carried. Even newspapers, traditionally consumed in hard copy, are increasingly available in electronic form via the Internet (Ofcom, 2007c).

Even when considering just television, recent times have witnessed radical changes to the nature of the home entertainment it can provide. A handful of television channels have been superseded by multi-channel packages that may offer dozens or even hundreds of channels. On cable and satellite television systems, viewers can order programmes virtually on demand, while broadband technology can allow viewers to order individual programmes for delivery to them whenever they want.

Older media generations were brought up in a world where they had only a handful of television channels and radio stations to choose from and where telecommunications were used only to contact other individuals in one-to-one conversations. The 1980s witnessed a growth in television hours on established television channels and some growth in the number of channels that were available to everyone and via cable and satellite transmission systems for those willing to pay extra. Video recorders also became widespread in households by the later years of this decade. But the range of content choice and degree of control available to media consumers even then was significantly less than in the post-2000 era.

Throughout the 1990s media technologies continued to evolve and diversify. Perhaps the most significant development to occur during this decade was the emergence of the Internet for general public use and consumption. Other developments of comparable significance in terms of their speed of adoption were the rapid spread of multi-channel television packages and mobile telephones. By the end of the first decade of the twenty-first century, virtually everyone in the UK (99%) had some form of basic TV access to the five analogue, terrestrially-transmitted TV channels, while nearly as many (98%) could gain access to digital satellite TV. Digital terrestrial TV services which are free of charge were available to nearly three out of four homes (73%). Other multi-channel platforms including digital cable TV (49%) and Internet protocol television (IPTV) (39%) were available to large minorities (Ofcom, 2009a).

Growth of the Internet

A number of studies have indicated that the Internet market has experienced rapid growth around the world. This growth has been manifest in the penetration of the Internet, the extent to which people claim to use it, and digital log tracking of traffic levels of web sites. By the close of the first decade in the twenty-first century there were 361 million Internet users worldwide, a growth of 380 per cent since 2000. Internet penetration was highest in North America (74%), Australia/Oceania (60%) and Europe (52%) (InternetWorldStats, 2009). In the UK, Internet penetration among people aged 15 and over grew from 30 per cent in 2000 to 76 per cent in 2009. This followed similar growth in ownership at home of personal computers/laptops (46% to 76%). It is worth noting that multi-channel television penetration also increased significantly over this period (36% in 2000 to 90% in 2009) (Ofcom, 2009c).

It is worth taking a closer look at Internet-related data because adoption rates have varied across different sectors of the population. Changing Media (2007) reported steady growth year-on-year in the proportion of the UK population that uses the Internet. In a report produced for the BBC Trust, this agency reported data from a number of UK research sources that showed a fairly consistent increase in the proportion of UK households with Internet access from 50–57 per cent in 2004 to 60–67 per cent in 2007. In the same report, further research conducted by leading market research company Ipsos MORI (2007) was presented that indicated that over one in two people in the UK (55%) claimed to have access to the Internet in 2004 and that by 2007 this figure had risen to nearly two-thirds (65%) of the population. Further figures were reported from research by Eurostat in 2007 that showed the percentage of 16 to 74 year-olds in the UK that had access to the Internet at least once a month over three months increased from around one in two (49%) in 2004 to nearly two-thirds (65%) in 2007 (Changing Media, 2007).

Internet penetration has not reached the same levels for all sectors of the population. In the UK, Changing Media (2007) reported that Internet users tended to be better educated, more affluent and were disproportionately represented by people living in London. There were also marked age differences in the use of the Internet. The youngest adult age groups were the biggest online aficionados. Data that were presented from the Office of National Statistics (ONS), however, revealed that all age groups exhibited year-on-year growth in Internet use between 2006 and 2007: 16–24s, 83% to 90%; 25–44s, 79% to 80%; 45–54s, 68% to 75%; 55–64s, 52% to 59%; and 65+, 15% to 24%. Although exhibiting the lowest level of use, the oldest members of the population also exhibited the biggest year-on-year increase.

The data from the ONS were corroborated by research from the Oxford Internet Institute (OII; Dutton and Helsper, 2007). The OII data derived from 2005 and 2007 and were based on large nationwide surveys in the UK. The age-bands used here were different from those used by the ONS, but Internet penetration levels were similar where age-band comparisons could be made between the two sets of data. Once again, Internet use fell steadily with the age of respondents, but increased throughout between 2005 and 2007: under 18s, 90% to 94%; 18–24s, 78% to 86%; 25–34s, 69% to 78%; 35–44s, 69% to 77%; 45–54s, 65% to 78%; 55–64s, 53% to 58%; 65–74s, 31% to 37%; and 75+, 20% to 24%.

According to Eurostat data for 2006 reported by Changing Media (2007) both women and men used the Internet on a daily basis to an equal extent (50% in each case) among people aged 16 to 24 years. Among older users aged 24 to 54 years and 55 to 74 years, however, men (54% and 26% respectively) were more likely than women (40% and 13% respectively) to go online every day.

Research from the Oxford Internet Institute confirmed that home access was most prevalent among Internet users but also indicated that this occurred to a much wider extent (89% in 2003; 94% in 2007) than indicated by Ofcom (Dutton and Helsper, 2007). The OII research revealed the greatest magnitude of location increase between 2003 and 2007 was to go online in someone's house (from 10% to 30% of UK Internet users).

The extent of its penetration outlines the potential of the Internet to compete with television. The more people there are who go online, the greater is the number of households in which the Internet potentially could displace TV viewing. The mere presence of the Internet in households, however, reveals nothing about the extent to which it might be used within specific households. The greater the amount of time people devote to online activities, the more likely it is that their online behaviour could eat into their waking time budget and displace other activities.

Data produced by the Office of National Statistics indicated that by 2007, two-thirds of all Internet users (67%) claimed to go online every day or almost every day. One in four (24%) claimed to go online at least once a week, and fewer than one in ten (9%) said they went online less often than once a week (Changing Media, 2007). These 'reach' figures for online behaviour give some idea of the popularity of the Internet, but still fall short of the data we need to fully appreciate how time-consuming online activities can be. Even those who claim to go online every day could vary widely in the amount of time they usually stay online.

Research produced by the EIAA 2006 Mediascope study collected data about online behaviour from the UK, Germany, France, Spain, Italy and the Nordic countries. UK Internet users reported that they remained online for between eight and 18 hours per week. Over a three-year period of monitoring, this study found that reported hours per UK Internet user spent online in a typical week increased progressively across 2005 (10.7 hours), 2006 (11.3 hours) to 2007 (12 hours) (see Changing Media, 2007).

These self-report data are indicative of time spent online but may also be susceptible to inaccuracies of memory on the part of survey respondents. Even more robust data on Internet use can be derived from continuous monitoring of Internet users' behaviour. Industry assessment agencies such as Nielsen NetRatings specialise in producing such data. Ofcom (2007c) reported data from Nielsen that showed that on average nearly half of UK Internet users (48%) used the Internet at least once during a one-month observation period in April 2007, and spent an average of 30.5 hours online during that spell. This research demonstrates the need to consider how the Internet is used from a number of perspectives.

Confirming findings reported earlier in this chapter, the oldest Internet users, aged 65 and over, were least likely to have gone online at all during April 2007 (16%). The youngest adults, aged 18 to 24 years (65%) were far more likely to have gone online at all, as indeed were those aged 25 to 34 (51%), 35 to 49 (47%) and 50 to 64 (44%). Surprisingly, the oldest Internet users exhibited the heaviest usage of the Internet once they were online (41.6 hours during April 2007), outstripping even the 18 to 24s (37.9 hours). This does not mean that Internet use displaced television viewing to a greater extent among the oldest users than among younger users, although it does open up the possibility that that could happen. It is equally feasible that retired people have more time in general to use all kinds of media and that they can accommodate a greater than average amount of Internet use without sacrificing any of their television viewing. There could be a far greater likelihood of Internet use displacing TV viewing among younger age groups that may have far less time to devote to any media consumption, especially at home, because of the greater demands on their time from work and family life.

One particularly important aspect of Internet growth has been the popularity of online video watching. In the United States, more than 158 million Internet users watched online videos during one month in July 2009 (81% of the Internet population). They averaged 135 videos each, occupying over eight hours (Strangelove.com, 2009). In the United Kingdom, Internet audience research revealed that eight in ten Internet users (80%) viewed online videos in January 2009, amounting to an average of 9.5 hours per viewer (ComScore, 2009b). This phenomenon will be revisited later in this book. These figures serve to illustrate its prevalence and the time it now occupies among significant numbers of people.

Implications of media expansion

The explosion of electronic content and media services, the rapid development of communications technologies and blurring of industry boundaries have created an exciting and complex media environment which for many media consumers is confusing (Buckingham, 2006; Gunter, Rowlands and Nicholas, 2009). To make the most of this environment, a higher level of media literacy is needed across the population (Frechette, 2006; Gunter et al., 2009). Programming a video recorder, utilising interactive television services, surfing the web, using e-mail and sending text messages via mobile and fixed technologies, and downloading content from distant computer servers all require a degree of technological competence. While such competency is growing, there remain many people who experience serious problems even at relatively basic levels of utility. Indeed, for many people, technology anxiety may result in avoidance of more sophisticated media services. Nervousness and perceived lack of competence to use interactive digital television services, mobile phones and personal computers is most prevalent among the over 65s, but also troubles one in ten to one in five people from younger age groups (Ofcom, 2009c).

Communications technologies have been regarded by governments as playing critical roles in relation to the economic, cultural, social and political fabric of society. A legislative and regulatory environment is needed that can ensure the UK's internal media market is a vibrant and competitive one in which major players can grow big enough to compete effectively on the international stage (BIS/DCMS, 2009). Communications industries must be able to converge to capitalise on their different strengths in bringing together distinctive technologies to deliver new kinds of services that offer consumers more choice and control. A vibrant industry can also be expected to generate revenues to facilitate investment in the high quality outputs and services.

The media should reach all sectors of society and represent the diverse social and cultural mix of society. In the case of television, there should be programme services that cater for the interests, needs, and tastes of different minority groups as well as the mass. Diversity should not be delivered at the expense of quality. While services should offer more choice, they should also seek to attain the highest quality possible in terms of production value and in not offending people or by breaching normal standards of taste and decency. In the latter context, people as citizens and as consumers should be protected against offence and against over-priced access to services. While the expansion of media services will give media consumers more choice, this may come at a financial cost. Leading media organisations that may seek to control production, distribution and reception technologies and processes will gain the power to determine the price the consumer market must pay to gain access to content. Market competitiveness will depend in part on market diversity – that is, a market in which there are a number of different providers of services in competition with each other for customers. Government controls over media ownership and market dominance are therefore needed to safeguard consumer interests in this way. At the same time, any regulatory framework must perform a balancing act between freedom of speech and freedom to trade and consumer protection. These points have all been recognised by government in the UK in setting out its stall for communications legislation (BIS/DCMS, 2009).

Within a political context, it is important that the major media provide a diversity of viewpoints as well as of services. As a major source of information, this provision is especially significant in the case of television. The central focus is on people as citizens rather than as consumers. Citizens comprise the electorate and the electorate underpins democracy by playing an active part in the selection of government. Citizens need to be kept adequately and accurately informed about world events and, more especially in relation to their democratic role, about political developments, government and opposition parties' policies and government performance.

The range of quality of information supplied by the media as news sources thus has paramount importance. These points apply to television perhaps more than any other medium. This is because television has regularly been nominated by the public as its main source of news. There is an expectation, on the part of the public, that television can be depended upon as a truthful, comprehensive and impartial news provider.

The position of television in society

To ensure that the political, social and cultural interests of the public are safeguarded, it has been the custom in Britain to ensure that part of its television system remains free of the pressure of the commercial marketplace. In fact, when broadcasting in the form of radio was initially launched in this country with the establishment of the BBC, it was regarded as a cultural resource the primary purpose of which was to enrich the lives of those who consumed its outputs (Curran and Seaton, 1997). This value system was carried over to television broadcasting not only as championed by the BBC but also by the initial commercial broadcasters. Public service broadcasting (PSB) principles were designed to ensure that broadcasting served to provide diverse and high quality programme services that informed and edified as well as entertained audiences. These services were required to observe principles of impartiality in news reporting, especially on matters of political and industrial significance in Britain and of taste and decency across all forms of programming (Briggs, 1961, 1979).

In a limited broadcasting system, with few television channels and radio stations, the policing of public service broadcasting principles was relatively straightforward. In the modern broadcasting environment, with many hundreds of broadcast operators, this process has become more complicated. A lynchpin of the public service broadcasting tradition was that the broadcast spectrum could accommodate only a small number of channels. This scarce resource therefore had to be used wisely and responsibly (Briggs, 1979; Curran and Seaton, 1997). Technological developments during the latter part of the twentieth century changed all this. Digital transmission technology, over the air and via wired-up systems, created a significantly expanded capacity for the carriage of television channels. The founding rationale of 'scarce resource' no longer applied. In addition, media consumers became more sophisticated and more demanding. The idea that the broadcasters alone would decide what was good for their audiences became replaced by one in which the media consumer has sovereignty (Ofcom, 2004).

Media consumers have also shown that they are prepared to pay extra for the content they wish to consume (Klein, Kargar and Sinclair, 2004b; Ofcom, 2006d). While the costs of television viewing traditionally comprised the purchase price of the set and any add-ons (e.g. video recorder) and the licence fee, in the modern media environment, most television services can now be accessed only at additional cost, either in the form of a periodic subscription fee attached to specific channel packages or in terms of pay-per-view whereby the consumer pays a fixed fee for a particular product (e.g., a movie or major sports event).

A further important technological development has been that a traditionally 'passive' medium, in terms of mode of reception, was converted into a more dynamic medium. The advantages of interactivity in media reception, whereby the consumer controls what is received, when it is received, and whether it is retained or thrown away, became apparent with the emergence of the Internet. Personal computers represent a form of technology in which the user actively engages with the hardware and its accompanying software to determine precisely the content that is consumed. Digital technology holds the promise of a similar form of content reception for television. It is expected that new generation television sets to emerge in the first decade or two of the twenty-first century will have the same interactive capabilities as personal computers.

All these developments will mean that the traditional form of television viewing, whereby selections are made at the channel level and then at the programme level, will be replaced by a reception environment in which television consumers will select from libraries of content the particular items they wish to consume. In that environment, the traditional notion of public service broadcasting may need to change. Indeed, it may be difficult for it to survive in the form in which it has been known since the earliest days of broadcasting.

Changing patterns of consumption

The environment for television viewing is extremely volatile. In part, the explanation for this might be that the Internet has exposed viewers to fresh opportunities for getting entertainment and information as well as new sets of gratifying activities to occupy their leisure time. Part of the reason can also be linked to the changing nature of viewing itself contingent upon technology advances that have given viewers more choice and control.

The patterns of TV viewing have changed in response to the rapidly evolving digitised television environment. Whereas viewing was dominated by a small handful of TV channels 20 years ago, in the twenty-first century it has become fragmented. Ofcom (2009a) reported, for example, that in 1982, shortly before the launch of Channel 4, ITV (now ITV1) enjoyed a 50 per cent share of the total TV audience in the UK, BBC1 captured a 38 per cent share and BBC2 managed a 12 per cent share. In 2008, ITV1 achieved an audience share across all UK TV homes of just over 18 per cent, BBC1 managed nearly 22 per cent and BBC2 achieved just short of 8 per cent.

Thus, those channels that once monopolised the airwaves now face a much more competitive market for viewers alongside a progressively growing multitude of other channels on the burgeoning multi-channel platforms. There is consistent evidence that all five public service broadcast channels – BBC1, BBC2, ITV1, Channel Four, and Five – have collectively, and in some cases individually, experienced significant erosion in their shares of the total television audience in the face of growing competition from commercial, multi-channel packages.

Audience share losses experienced by the longer-established terrestrial channels with public broadcasting remits do not really pinpoint whether they have lost popularity in general or whether audience losses were associated with particular types of programme output. Multi-channel television packages offer volume and diversity of content through a wide range of thematically specialised channels. Diversity is therefore achieved across channels, even though within specific channels the only diversity to occur, in most cases, is that which occurs within a genre. In contrast, each public service channel attempts to offer genre diversity in its own right.

The extent of audience loss incurred by the five terrestrial television channels within multi-channel homes has been found to vary across programme genres. In its analysis of audience trends between 1998 and 2003, Ofcom (2004) reported that network news on the terrestrial channels was a particularly big loser. Audience reach for the news on BBC, ITV1, Channel 4 and Five fell, across this period, from 74 per cent to 55 per cent. There were further significant declines for current affairs (50% to 22%), serious factual programmes (45% to 20%) and arts and classical music broadcasts (30% to 7%).

Some programmes emerged as more vulnerable than others to audience losses in the face of competition from the multi-channel environment. Ofcom (2004) reported, for example, that the long-running religious series, *Songs of Praise*, saw its audience share fall by 66 per cent in multi-channel homes compared with homes that could receive only the five terrestrial channels. In comparison, the highly popular music talent competition series, *Pop Idol*, experienced a drop of 16 per cent. Thus, it is clear that in a more competitive television viewing environment in which audiences have many more channels to choose between, audiences for even the most popular shows on BBC, ITV, Channel 4 and Five will suffer, but some programmes are better able to survive this competition than others.

Such findings, where they represent consistent trends over time, may reveal vulnerabilities in the schedules of the public service broadcasters. There is also a need to consider carefully what such trends mean for the future of publicly-funded television or of television that is commercially funded but which nevertheless must repay what historically was regarded as its privileged position by providing special interest programmes. In other words, commercial public service broadcasters are required to tread a fine line between making and transmitting programmes that will attract mass audiences and generate significant advertising revenue and ones that, while attracting relatively small audiences, cater to a diverse array of minority tastes and may therefore often be unprofitable. Where this volatility within the television market becomes compounded with other changes, such as the rapid growth of the Internet as a leisure-time resource, this may raise wider questions about what the future holds for the medium.

Table 1.1 indicates that the major public service broadcast TV channels in the UK (BBC1, BBC2, ITV1, Channel 4 and Five) collectively lost audience shares between 2003 and 2008. For all of these channels, this trend was true of their audience share in all TV households in the UK while this trend was apparent only for ITV1 in multi-channel TV households. The other channels either maintained their multi-channel audience share or, as with BBC1, saw it improve marginally. In a multi-channel environment, all these channels suffered audience share losses compared with the 'all homes' share figure. What is perhaps more interesting to note is that the difference between the 'all homes' and 'multi-channel homes' share figures declined over time for all five channels (Ofcom, 2009a). Clearly, as the penetration of multi-channel packages has grown the 'dividend' of the analogue terrestrial-only environment for these channels has diminished. The PSB channels have partially reclaimed some of their 'lost' viewers via spin-off services on multi-channel packages that carry the major brand (e.g., BBC3, BBC4, ITV2, ITV3, and so on), though these additional services do not provide complete compensation for the losses of the major channels (Ofcom, 2006b, 2009a).

| Table 1.1 | Audience shares for public service broadcast (PSB) channels in all and in multi-channel homes | | | | | |

	2003 %	2004 %	2005 %	2006 %	2007 %	2008 %
All PSB Channels	76.5	73.6	70.4	66.7	63.5	60.8
BBC1						
All homes	25.6	24.7	23.3	22.8	22.0	21.8
Multi-channel homes	19.3	19.5	19.3	20.0	19.9	20.4
Difference	*6.3*	*5.2*	*4.0*	*2.8*	*2.1*	*1.4*
BBC2						
All homes	11.0	10.0	9.4	8.8	8.6	7.8
Multi-channel homes	7.0	6.7	6.9	6.9	7.1	7.0
Difference	*4.0*	*3.3*	*2.5*	*1.9*	*1.5*	*0.8*
ITV1						
All homes	23.7	22.8	21.5	19.7	19.2	18.4
Multi-channel homes	19.3	18.9	18.4	17.5	17.6	17.2
Difference	*4.4*	*3.9*	*3.1*	*2.2*	*1.6*	*1.2*
Channel 4						
All homes	9.6	9.8	9.7	9.8	8.6	7.8
Multi-channel homes	6.9	7.3	7.9	8.2	7.4	6.8
Difference	*2.7*	*2.5*	*1.8*	*1.6*	*1.2*	*1.0*
Five						
All homes	6.5	6.6	6.4	5.7	5.2	5.0
Multi-channel homes	4.7	5.1	5.3	4.9	4.6	4.7
Difference	*1.8*	*1.5*	*1.1*	*0.8*	*0.6*	*0.3*

Source: Ofcom, 2009a/BARB.

Public service broadcasting channels continued to attract relatively substantial audiences though they also experienced significant losses of audience share in multi-channel TV environments. In addition, there is competition from outside the medium. TV channels not only face fierce competition for viewers' loyalty within multi-channel TV platforms, but also from other communications technologies through which individuals can obtain information and entertainment. These other technologies include a range of offline and online content including computer games and the Internet.

Research has indicated that media can lose audiences to other media when both sets of media serve similar audience needs and gratifications. Where one medium offers services that are functionally equivalent to those offered by another medium, those two media can come into direct competition for audiences. Where two media cater to different audience needs and gratifications, and are therefore functionally dissimilar, this is much less likely to happen (Dimmick and Rothenbuhler, 1984a, 1984b; see Chapter 3 for more detailed discussion). The Internet, for instance, has the potential to inform, educate and entertain its users and, as such, could potentially challenge all areas of television broadcasting for audience patronage.

As communications technologies evolve over the coming decades, the Internet could pose a growing challenge to television. As we will see, the Internet can also open up new opportunities for 'old media' such as television to reach media consumers. In the UK, for instance, by 2009 digital television was available to virtually everybody (98%) via satellite, to most (73%) via terrestrial transmitters, and to nearly half (49%) via cable. It was also available to four in ten people (39%) via Internet protocol television (Ofcom, 2009a).

It is important to note that some media are mutually exclusive in terms of their utility, while others are not. Hence, it is perfectly possible, and frequently likely, that we may read our newspaper while watching television. We can switch attention between the two media and conduct both activities in the same room. In contrast, using a personal computer – another audio-visual medium – is unlikely to occur in parallel with watching television. These two pieces of kit are usually situated in different rooms and in any case both demand similar forms of attention from us.

Does one medium cannibalise another?

Growth in competition within the TV marketplace has exerted a significant impact on the market share of major channels that once enjoyed audience dominance. In the United Kingdom, as we have already seen, with public service broadcasting (PSB) requirements placed upon them, BBC1 and 2, ITV1, Channel 4 and Five have found their audience shares severely squeezed in multi-channel environments. The audiences for these channels have been significantly eroded by the presence of multiple additional channels in multi-channel television packages. It is not simply competition within the television market that has become more acute, but additional competition for the time of viewers from the Internet. How serious this competition will prove to be is a matter that is still unravelling. Although the Internet has been portrayed as a rival to offline media, it can prove to be an ally when adopted by those media as an alternative platform for content delivery. What the Internet does offer to media consumers, however, is a different way of accessing content that is more flexible and consumer-centred than the traditional fixed-schedule arrangement of television channels.

With the growth of the Internet through which video materials can be streamed, what are the implications for the use of television as a medium? Certainly, under a simplistic displacement model, time devoted to watching television could be re-directed, at least in part, towards surfing the web. Under such conditions, will regular traditional forms of TV viewing diminish? If so, could this produce yet more competition for PSB operators (and indeed for other TV channels) on top of that already being experienced by them when produced within multi-channel TV packages?

One reason for presuming that the Internet might erode television audiences derives from historical evidence of displacement of old media by new media. As a new medium, television itself was once regarded as posing this kind of threat to the even older, established media – newspapers and radio. The empirical evidence for this displacement effect, however, was not consistent (see Chapter 3). It was usually measured via people's self-reports about their media consumption obtained in questionnaire-based surveys. While cross-sectional surveys conducted with respondents at one point in time generally yielded little evidence of television's displacement of other media, longitudinal surveys with panels of respondents over time did produce some displacement evidence (Cummings and Kraut, 2002).

One observation has been that if the Internet becomes an increasingly attractive source of entertainment and information, and also introduces people to new forms of communication with which they wish to spend more and more of their time, other activities will have to give way. Television could be a significant victim in this scenario given that not only might the Internet compete for use of time, it could also offer an attractive functional alternative to television anyway for entertainment and information.

Not everyone has been convinced by the simple time displacement hypothesis here. It could also be a misrepresentation to label the Internet as a single medium. It offers a wider range of content and applications which invite usage for many different reasons (Kraut et al., 1996; Kraut et al., 2004). There has even been evidence that Internet use and television viewing are positively related which suggests that online behaviour could promote some viewing (Cole et al., 2000).

Some researchers have noted that new technologies such as the Internet accessed via a computer screen do not invariably serve to supplant use of television, but could occur alongside viewing. Increasingly, young people who are introduced to computers at an early stage of development demonstrate the ability to divide their attention between more than one mediated activity at a time (Livingstone and Bovill, 2001). This phenomenon has been acknowledged in time use surveys where respondents are invited to provide records of their primary and secondary activities during specific time periods (Robinson et al., 2000).

Models of displacement

The notion of one medium displacing another is not a new concept triggered by the growth in popularity of the Internet. Early enquiries into displacement effects between mass media can be dated back to the first half of the twentieth century when questions were asked about the impact of radio broadcasting on newspaper consumption (Lazarsfeld, 1940). Displacement effects attracted further attention from media researchers during the 1950s, 1960s and 1970s with the growing prevalence of broadcast television. At the time, television was regarded as a potential threat both to newspapers and radio (see Belson, 1961; Mendelsohn, 1964; Provonost, 2002; Robinson, 1981).

The major network terrestrially-transmitted television channels dominated the airwaves in the early years of the medium. Then television-related technology developments posed threats first to these established television services with the arrival of cable television (Kaplan, 1978; Sparkes, 1983) and then the conventional nature of viewing following the emergence of video-recorders (Harvey and Rothe, 1985; Henke and Donohue, 1989). Some researchers indicated that rather than being a threat, cable television could actually broaden and enhance the appeal of television as a medium (Grotta and Newsom, 1982).

By the 1990s, computer-mediated communication evolved from being a specialist technology confined to expert user-groups to a widely available platform conveying a diverse array of applications of relevance to the general public. The most prominent manifestation of this new technology was the Internet. As new interactive technologies were rapidly adopted, questions were asked about whether it posed a serious threat to the consumption of all other media (Finholt and Sproull, 1990; James, Wotring and Forrest, 1995; Robinson, Barth and Kohut, 1997).

The Internet provides entertainment and information content and also serves as an interpersonal communication medium. Each of these applications can use up time. The notion that the appearance of a new medium can reduce the time people spend with an existing medium has been embodied in the idea of media displacement. There are different schools of thought about displacement. One model presumes that there is a zero-sum relationship between the amount of time allocated to two or more media. As one medium commands more of people's time, less time is therefore devoted by them to other media in the same media marketplace.

This basic idea derives from the bio-ecological theory of the niche (Dimmick and Rothenbuhler, 1984a, 1984b). This theory was developed to explain how different groups compete for finite resources within an environment. Where resources are limited, groups may have to engage in competitive endeavours to secure resources for their own members. Where one group achieves dominance within an environment it may be able to command more resources than a less powerful group. The weaker group may be left with the choice of accepting a smaller 'market share' and getting by with that or of leaving that environment completely. Weaker groups might also sometimes be subsumed by more powerful groups and trade autonomy for survival.

If the media environment is regarded as an 'ecology', similar principles could be applied to explain what would happen when a number of different media find themselves competing for media consumers within the same marketplace. The most simplistic notion is that as the proportion of the available market attracted to one medium increases, the proportion devoting its time to another medium should decrease. Hence, a new medium entering an established market could destabilise it by drawing consumers away from the other media that already populate that marketplace. In other words, there would be what has been termed an 'increase–decrease' relationship between new and old media.

An alternative position is that a zero-sum relationship is not the only possibility. In an environment with limited resources, competing factions could reach an arrangement whereby they cooperate to share out the finite resources that are available to the benefit of both competitors (Dimmick and Rothenbuhler, 1984a). In the media marketplace, this 'increase–increase' scenario might mean that competing parties could enter into relationships to their mutual benefit in terms of attracting media consumers. As we will see later, the Internet has been used by newspapers, radio stations and television broadcasters to convey their content.

A third model of displacement that has been examined in connection with competition between communications media is 'functional displacement'. It is not simply a matter of one medium reducing the overall amount of time people spend with a second medium. This outcome is underpinned by whether the two media perform the same or similar functions for their users. If two media both supply entertainment to their consumers, but one of them is judged by consumers to be the superior supplier, that one will command a larger market share. If the two media cater to different functions, however, for example one medium provides information and the other entertainment, then there may be room for both of them because they attract distinctive markets defined by function (entertainment supply versus information supply). Thus, the Internet might displace television if the two are in direct competition for consumers motivated by the same needs.

One school of thought concerning the Internet then is that if it occupies time, that time must be subtracted from other activities. Research reported by Nie and Erbring (2000, 2002) supported this simple displacement hypothesis. In households from which they collected data across the United States, time spent online meant less time devoted to a range of offline activities including socialising with family and friends. Online behaviour was also related to reductions in use of other media. This type of evidence has not received consistent support from other time use studies. Research in Switzerland, for instance, found that Internet users often used e-mail extensively and that this was, in turn, associated with maintaining richer social connections to others rather than withdrawal from them (Franzen, 2000).

In evaluating the evidence, it is important to consider methodological features of displacement studies. Some investigations have obtained data about time use at one point in time, while others have collected data over time from the same panel of individuals. There has been mixed support from these different approaches for a displacement effect of use of the Internet on watching television. There has been cross-sectional research support for a negative relationship between the amount of time devoted to television viewing and use of the Internet (Nie and Erbring, 2000; Adoni and Nossek, 2001; Dryburgh, 2001; Williams, 2001; Robinson et al., 2002). This finding has also been corroborated by some longitudinal data (Kraut et al., 2005). Elsewhere, however, this relationship was found to be weakened or to disappear completely in the face of controls for multiple demographic variables (Cole and Robinson, 2002). Other studies have reported no link between time spent with the Internet and amount of time devoted to watching television (Veenhof, 2006).

Another method-related problem concerns the degree to which the circumstances under which online behaviour was measured departed from the everyday living conditions of those being observed. This was certainly an issue in respect of the research by Nie and Erbring. These researchers encouraged their participants by offering them web TV access as payment for taking part. Participants then supplied self-reported data about their daily activities on a questionnaire administered weekly via the web TV set. The provision of new technology as part of the study could have created an artificial set of circumstances for participants, albeit in their natural living environments. Novelty effects could have arisen that produced unusual patterns of behaviour (see Kestnbaum et al., 2002).

In a continuation of their research, Nie and Hillygus (2002) attempted to reduce the self-reporting workload of their participants by restricting the amount of time per day on which activity reports were requested. Participants could select at random any six hours per day on which to report. Consequently the study did not represent a full account of daily behaviour or use of time. Further, data were collected once a week instead of every day which meant that recall inaccuracies were more probable (Lesnard, 2005).

It is worth taking a closer look at the relevant evidence on overall use of the Internet and television watching. It is important to have confidence that daily behaviours and use of time are accurately and effectively represented before jumping to conclusions about displacement effects between the use of different media. Later chapters will consider evidence for more specific displacement effects between the Internet and television associated with particular types of use of these technologies.

Increase–decrease relationship

Research evidence on the impact of alternative technology platforms on TV viewing has so far produced mixed findings. There are two main types of evidence presented about the impact of using one medium such as the Internet on the use of another medium such as television. In one case, media users are surveyed and asked whether they think their use of the Internet has resulted in a reduction in the amount of time they devote to television. A second type of evidence relies upon examining the magnitude and direction of correlations between self-reported frequencies or quantities of consumption of different media. Thus, does greater reported use of the Internet correlate with reduced viewing of television (and vice versa)?

Self-attributed media habit changes

One type of evidence that has been used to demonstrate that the Internet is displacing television viewing comprises self-attributed behaviour shifts reported by survey respondents. In this case, respondents are asked to report subjectively whether they believe that their use of the Internet has eaten into how much they watch television. Often this judgement about television viewing is embedded within a list of other activities that might also have been affected by time spent online. This type of question has produced evidence that people who use the Internet often perceive that they have changed how much time they devote to other activities as a result. Television viewing is one activity frequently endorsed as being displaced by online behaviour. This finding emerged from one online survey of UK Internet users in which more than four in ten (42%) said they had decreased the amount of time they watched television since becoming linked to the Internet (Gunter et al., 2003).

In the United States, Kayany and Yelsma (2000) asked a small sample of families whether they felt that their television viewing had increased, decreased or stayed the same following their adoption of online media into their lives. In general, there was perceived stability of viewing, but more respondents claimed that viewing had dropped than increased since they had started using online media. There was no evidence, however, that there was a tendency for heavy Internet users to reduce their viewing to a greater extent than light Internet users.

Rose and Roisin (2001) asked Internet users which activities they spent less time with due to the time they spent online. Thirty-three per cent said they were watching TV less, followed by magazines (25%), newspapers (23%), and finally radio (16%). This perceived effect on television viewing may be explained by the additional fact that peak Internet usage time was at night, which was also peak television viewing time. Radio, in contrast, tended to be used during the daytime when the Internet was less likely to be used. Such self-attributed changes in behaviour, however, do not necessarily reflect with accuracy the actual behavioural adjustments that occurred in respect of television viewing in the presence of more time spent online.

Further research in the United States reported that while most Internet users in 2003 believed that their television viewing was unaffected by their use of the Internet, a significant and growing minority (38%; up from 33% in 2001) estimated that they spent less time with television because of going online (Cole et al., 2004). Another significant finding to emerge from this survey was that experienced users who had been going online for at least seven years were much more likely than relatively new users with less than one year's experience (43% versus 20%) to report spending less time with television because of the Internet. Furthermore, the experienced users exhibited a growing propensity, between 2001 (35%) and 2003 (46%), to say that their Internet behaviour was displacing their viewing.

A survey of UK Internet users aged 15 and over asked respondents to estimate the impact upon a range of other activities of the time they spent on online social networks. The great majority (77%) said that using social networks had no impact on their watching television. However, one in six (17%) believed that this online activity reduced the time they spent with television while a small minority (5%) claimed that it increased their viewing time. Reduced television viewing attributed to use of social networks was more widespread among female than among male respondents and was most pronounced among teenage girls aged 15 to 19 years (Entertainment Media Research, 2008).

Self-reported media use

Studies based on one-off surveys of self-reported media use have yielded findings that indicate a displacement effect of the Internet on TV viewing (Kayany and Yelsma, 2000; Nie and Hillygus, 2002). Other similar research has contradicted these findings (Cole et al., 2000). The use of large-scale fusion research that matched respondents from separate TV viewing and Internet using panels produced no evidence of displacement effects (Nielsen Media Research, 2006). Heavy Internet users also tended to be heavy TV viewers.

Earlier American time use research has produced mixed results on the displacement of television watching by use of the Internet. One time-use study that obtained data on the allocation of time to a range of activities reported evidence that time devoted to television was less among established Internet users than non-Internet users. This research also differentiated between primary activities and secondary activities allowing the possibility that individuals can engage in more than one activity at the same time, but one of these is generally likely to command the most attention (Robinson et al., 2002). In terms of TV viewing as a primary activity, non-users of the Internet averaged significantly more reported hours per week (15.2) than did long-term Internet users (11.5 hours). Turning to TV viewing classified as a secondary activity, the difference between non-users (5.1 hours per week) and Internet users (5.6 hours per week) was a reversal of the primary activities data, but the difference on this occasion was non-significant.

Another study reported that initial observed differences in reported amounts of television watching by non-users and users of the Internet disappeared in the presence of multiple statistical controls for demographic variables such as education, gender, income and marital status. Initial base observations indicated that Internet users watched television on average for fives hours less per week than did non-Internet users. After controls for variables associated with demographics on both Internet use and television viewing, however, this difference dropped to one and a half hours – a non-significant difference (Cole and Robinson, 2002).

Research in Israel examined the possible displacement effects of reported use of new information and communications technologies on old media, including books, cinema, newspapers and television. This survey took place in the relatively early days of the Internet in 1997. The data indicated that respondents who owned computers with Internet access reported greater consumption of books, other print media and cinema films than did non-owners. Computer owners were less likely to include heavy television viewers among their numbers than were non-owners. The fact that television and not other media was negatively related to Internet-linked computer ownership was interpreted as an indication of possible functional displacement of the older medium by the newer one (Adoni and Nossek, 2001).

In contrast, Canadian research using data from Canada's General Social Survey which incorporated a one-day time-use diary found no evidence that Internet users spent significantly less time watching television each week than did non-users of the Internet (Veenhof, 2006). This finding, however, failed to confirm earlier Canadian data (Dryburgh, 2001; Williams, 2001).

Some researchers have argued that longitudinal approaches are probably better than one-off surveys at detecting inter-technology displacement effects (Kraut et al., 2005). The latter researchers obtained data from a national US panel and examined not simply overall Internet use but also online behaviour disaggregated in terms of types of use. Two survey waves were conducted six to eight months apart. Twenty-one different Internet and TV functions were measured using a frequency scale.

On a cross-sectional comparison from the first survey wave, Kraut and his colleagues found that heavier Internet users also watched more television. Longitudinally, TV viewing increased over time, but did so to a lesser degree for heavier Internet users. A simple comparison between Internet users versus non-users revealed no differences in TV viewing levels. Although TV viewing levels generally increased over time, this was not true for all respondents. Reduced amounts of TV viewing were more likely to occur for heavier than for lighter Internet users. No evidence emerged that use of the Internet for entertainment purposes reduced the use of TV for the same reason. There was, however, a reduction in TV viewing associated with use of the Internet to communicate with strangers. These findings indicate that the relationship between TV viewing and Internet use is not straightforward. There are individuals who use both media frequently, while there are others for whom use of the Internet for certain purposes might displace some of their TV viewing.

Research by the European Interactive Advertising Association (EIAA) (2007) reported that European Internet users on average spent 12 hours per week online. This survey was conducted via telephone in 11 countries across Western Europe. Young Internet users, aged 16 to 24 years, spent even more time online. Tracking their use of different media over time, the EIAA research found that while average hours spent online increased markedly between 2004 (10.3 hours/week) and 2007 (14.7 hours/week), average amounts of TV viewing for 16 to 24s also increased over that same time period (12.6 hours/week to 13.4 hours/week). Radio listening and newspaper reading were also both largely unchanged in the time they occupied. Nevertheless, when Internet users in general were asked whether they spent less time doing other things as a result of using the Internet, virtually all (97%) acknowledged some activity displacement. Four in ten European Internet users (40%) claimed that they watched less television because of the Internet. The latter percentage was even higher among the 16 to 24s (48%).

Findahl (2008) reported data for Sweden on relationships between Internet use and use of newspapers and television. He examined subjective judgements (i.e., self-attributions) about the impact of the Internet on use of other media and correlation coefficients between self-reported frequencies of use of different media. Self-attribution data were available from several surveys conducted between 2000 and 2007, while reported frequencies data were available from 1996 to 2006.

The proportion of Internet users saying that using the Internet resulted in them watching less television declined over all respondents from

31 per cent in 2000 to 22 per cent in 2005 and then to 21 per cent in 2007. Among young adults aged 18 to 29 years in 2007, however, the proportion saying the Internet caused them to watch less television was 37 per cent. This finding encouraged Findahl to take a closer look at age differences in the nature of relationships between Internet use and television watching. On comparing people who claimed to be Internet users and non-users in 2007, he found that the latter watched more television on average each week (14 hours 38 minutes) than did the former (12 hours 28 minutes). When comparisons were made between age groups, however, in two cases Internet users watched less television than did Internet non-users, and in two cases Internet users watched *more* television. With a further three age groups there was no significant relationship between Internet use and television watching.

Mannell, Zuzanek and Aronson (2005) conducted a time-use survey among teenagers in Canada with a sub-sample also completing an experience sampling method study. The latter involved respondents entering their current behaviour in a daily diary of events at each point at which they were prompted by an audio paging device that they carried around with them. It was possible with these data to quantify the amount of time spent on different activities, including watching television, using the Internet and playing with computer games. A regression analysis indicated that the more time respondents spent on computer and video gaming, the less time they spent watching television (and being physically and socially active). Computer-game playing also produced high levels of 'flow' experiences meaning that they were more challenging and potentially fulfilling than watching television. There was no evidence of a significant link between use of the Internet and watching television.

Research for the UK found that in 2007 Internet users differed from non-users in the hours they reportedly spent with other media, including television (Dutton and Helsper, 2007). In this case, non-users of the Internet reported watching television an average of 24 hours per week, compared with 16 hours of viewing reported by Internet users. There was little difference between Internet non-users and users in the amounts of time they reportedly spent each week listening to radio (10 hours versus eight hours), reading books (five hours in both cases) or with newspapers (four hours versus three hours). These data say nothing about whether use of one medium had a direct impact on the use of another medium. Once again, though, these differences between Internet users and non-users are indicative of a potential Internet displacement effect on television.

The fact that television viewing was distinctive among the different media behaviours examined here that was substantially lower among

Internet users than among non-users also suggests that some form of functional displacement might be occurring. In other words, the Internet might cater for overlapping media consumer needs with television. Alternatively, any use of the Internet might require an individual's attention to a specific technology – a computer interface – that cannot be readily shared with watching a TV screen. It might also indicate that home use of the Internet occurs during time periods that overlap with customary TV viewing times. Use of other media might be limited to different day parts (e.g. radio listening in the car when out of home, reading a newspaper or book while commuting to work, etc). Functional displacement issues are examined in Chapter 3.

Competition or synergy?

With the onset and rapid uptake of broadband technology, the capacity of the Internet to carry video content without degradation of reception quality has rendered the online environment a more appealing medium for video consumption. Broadband information conveyance speeds meant that it became possible to distribute large files via the Internet and that download times have become more manageable. In consequence, the Internet has witnessed a rapid growth in traffic linked to video consumption. Internet users can not only access large quantities of video material online, they can also engage in its production (see Gunter et al., 2009).

The establishment of online video-based entertainment and information markets, however, has opened up fresh opportunities for broadcasters. Rather than the Internet representing a rival, it presents a new platform for the distribution of video content originally produced for terrestrial or satellite transmission purposes. More and more television viewers are willing to go online to access programme catch-up services or video archives. As viewers have migrated online, so television operators have followed.

Established broadcasters have experienced new competition from the online world from Internet television services provided by companies that traditionally operated outside broadcast markets – most especially telecommunications operators – that now offer television services over broadband Internet. However, the established broadcasters themselves have been able to move into this market as well and have produced services of their own via the Internet or have utilised new online operators as new distributors for their broadcast content. Thus, the net effect of the Internet may not be to erode television broadcasters' audiences, but rather to present new opportunities for reaching audiences (Whelan, 2008).

Ensuring access, diversity and quality

The prospects of television as a distinctive medium may improve with the emergence of digital technology. However, it will also require some re-learning of normal television viewing practices. Television still represents the premier medium to relax with for most people (i.e., a 'lean back' medium), while use of a personal computer is perceived to be more effortful (i.e. a 'lean forward' medium). The Internet, however, offers a richness of content and, assuming the user can navigate the 'web' effectively, gives the consumer greater control over reception. The quality of reception on the Internet, though, has not always matched that of television. Even with broadband, it can take time to download large quantities of audio-visual material. Digital television will present the opportunity for television to match the Internet in terms of content volume and the higher level of reception control that comes with interactivity. More technologically advanced TV sets and accessories will provide Internet access via the set and a return path link will open up two-way communications options, facilitating the use of interpersonal audio, text and video messaging via the television set.

Such a technological evolution of a traditionally passive medium will create more competition still for conventional styles of television viewing and hence also for the public service channels. This position is still some way off. In the early years of the twenty-first century, around one in five people with digital television used interactive services (Towler, 2003). The usability of these facilities is a critical factor underpinning their penetration of the viewing population (George and Lennard, 2007). Nonetheless, this early interactive television behaviour marks the beginning of the end of television as a one-way only content receptacle. In consequence, viewers could become conditioned to expect not simply diversity of channels or programmes, but also diversity of reception within programmes, with interactive services being used to provide alternative angles to a sports context, different endings to a drama, or different perspectives on a news story.

Digital technologies are expected to meet an apparently insatiable consumer demand for content and to stimulate competition between media platform providers. The convergence of communications technologies will, at the same time, open up fresh avenues through which media consumers can gain access to audio-visual content over the Internet or through mobile telephony. With the emergence of new technology platforms for the reception of audio-visual materials, however, there may be a need for ingenuity and creativity to be applied to the development of new forms of production, designed specifically for these communications media. This point refers to the possibility that presentation formats that work well in one media technology environment (e.g. television) may not invariably work well in a different media technology setting such as the mobile phone. Differences in the nature of the reception technology, particularly its interface with the consumer, and in the usual consumption context (e.g. in home versus out of home), may mean that entertainment and information delivery formats may need to be customised to the medium. A media consumer might be happy watching a short audio-visual download of a music video of several minutes duration on a small screen on a mobile device, but would not choose this technology for viewing a full-length motion picture. It is also important to recognise differences between media consumers in the ease with which they will adopt and use new communications technologies and enhancements to older technologies such as interactive facilities on television (George and Lennard, 2007).

Despite the prospects for greater choice and consumer control afforded by the technological advances of digital television, real benefits will only accrue for society if everyone or virtually everyone has access to new media services. There is ample evidence that new communications technologies tend not to spread evenly throughout societies. Some social groups adopt communications innovations more readily than others (Gunter et al., 2009). This phenomenon has been summed up by the term 'digital divide' (see Norris, 2001). The media rich get richer and the media poor are left further behind. The cost of adoption can be an important factor. The economically disadvantaged, for example, may be less likely to subscribe to new technologies and the services they deliver if the costs of reception equipment and service subscription are prohibitive (Norris, 2001).

Lee and Leung (2006) conducted a study of media displacement effects among Internet users that distinguished between information and entertainment uses. They also tested a number of different measures of media consumption. Many displacement investigations measure the absolute amounts of time, expressed in hours per day or per week, that survey respondents claim to spend with named media. Such measures, however, could give a misleading impression of displacement of use of one medium by the emergence of a new medium across individuals whose media consumption time budgets already vary dramatically. For instance, one individual might spend 10 hours a day on media consumption, while another devotes just five hours a day to doing this. If a new medium became available to them and both devoted one hour a day to it, in absolute terms there would be no difference between them. However, if that one hour a day was expressed as a proportion of the total time each day they devote to any media consumption, there would be a marked difference between these two people. In one case, the one hour would represent just 10 per cent of his or her daily media consumption time, while for the other individual it would represent 20 per cent of their media time.

In a survey of Hong Kong households that achieved a sample of nearly 700 respondents, media use was measured in terms of minutes a day spent with each listed medium (including television, radio, newspapers, magazines, books, comic books, electronic games, video recording devices, and music recording devices) and Internet users were asked to estimate how frequently they accessed the Internet for news, information and entertainment. Each of these terms was further defined for respondents to ensure that they were operating from a common frame of reference in content definitions.

When the absolute time measure was used the use of television and telephone, comic books, e-mail, computer, electronic games, video and music recoding devices were positively associated with the amount of time reportedly spent using the Internet. When the proportion of media time measure was used instead, use of the Internet was associated with less reported use of television, radio, newspapers, magazines, telephone, video recording devices, books and music recording devices. Not surprisingly, greater use of the Internet, in terms of proportion of media time devoted to it, was associated with more time spent using a computer, e-mail and e-games.

Lee and Kuo (2002) examined relationships between Internet use and six activities in Singapore: TV viewing, newspaper reading, radio listening, sports and exercise, interaction with family and socialising with friends. In all, 1,251 students were contacted for participation in 1999 and some of these were surveyed both then and again in 2000. Respondents were asked how many hours and minutes in a typical week they spent on using the Internet and on other media and non-media activities. Of the 817 interviewed in the first wave, 73 per cent were Internet users. Of the 711 interviewed in the second wave, 87 per cent were Internet users. Results showed that an increase in Internet use depressed TV viewing, but was related to increased newspaper reading, radio listening and socialising with friends. There was no impact on physical activities or interaction with family members.

Stoneman (2006) examined methodological issues in time-use research as applied to the study of use of the Internet and the extent to which online behaviour displaces a variety of different offline behaviours, including use of other media. In particular it tackles research published earlier by Nie and Erbring (2000) and by Gershuny (2002, 2003). It places some emphasis on whether Internet use is displacing TV viewing. Television itself, as a new medium, was accused of displacing other activities including social contacts with others (see Himmelweit, Oppenheim and Vince, 1958; Schramm, Lyle and Parker, 1961; Williams, 1986). The Internet is the latest new medium against which such accusations are being levelled (Rice and Haythornthwaite, 2002). The interactive nature of the Internet, however, has meant that it is used for social purposes such as maintaining open channels of communication with other people. The Internet is not simply a communications medium, however. It also provides access to vast archives or repositories of information and entertainment content.

Among the key weakness of much displacement research is that it has been based on one-off surveys that take a single cross-sectional look at the online and offline behaviour of respondents. It has also relied heavily upon self-report data in which respondents indicate, by recall from memory, how much time they devote to different activities each week or each day. Such data, of course could be unreliable because respondents may be unable to recall their daily behavioural routines at this level of detail with any great accuracy.

Cross-section analyses fail to allow for behavioural developments that take place over time. In understanding how specific patterns of behaviour emerge, it is essential to examine the way they emerged and this requires repeat measurement at more than one point in time, whether the data obtained are based on self-report or direct observation.

Even if time estimates as such are taken at face value, it is important to differentiate between people who devote small and large amounts of their time to specific activities such as using the Internet. This point becomes especially important in longitudinal research that examines behavioural changes over time and is also very significant in the context of measuring how one activity could time-displace another activity.

Some Internet displacement research has found that Internet use per se is not enough to guarantee changes to patterns of behaviour elsewhere in a person's life. People who report using the Internet less than five hours a week, for instance, may reveal little change in other behaviours, while those stating that they go online more than 10 hours a week may display reductions in some offline behaviours (Nie and Erbring, 2000).

The Nie and Erbring research was challenged, however, for measurement error in its assessment of the time respondents claimed to spend on different activities and its cross-sectional nature that meant that the study could draw no inferences about how behaviours might change over time (Gershuny, 2002). These limitations can be overcome by giving respondents daily diaries to complete instead of providing activity time estimates via a questionnaire and by surveying the same respondents more than once over time. Even this revised methodology has a crucial limitation. Any change in the nature of an activity over time could be explained in terms of existing levels of experience with different activities being compared. Thus, a low-level Internet user may be less likely to display such significant changes in their online behaviour as a high-level Internet user because the latter may be a more experienced Internet user who goes online for a wider range of purposes. The low-level user, lacking that experience, must first become more familiar with the medium before his or her use of it really takes off.

A subsequent panel study that obtained time-use data via diaries over the 1999–2001 period among a sample in the UK found that on the whole increased Internet use was related to reduced time spent on hobbies and on watching television. For women, however, while the latter findings were confirmed, there was a positive link between using the Internet and going out (Gershuny, 2002).

Stoneman (2006) argued that because a new medium such as the Internet may experience a novelty effect, the way it is used early on may be different from the patterns of usage that become established in the longer term. When examining relationships that exist between Internet use and other behaviours over time, therefore, respondents who were less or more experienced Internet users at the outset cannot be regarded as being the same because they start from different online behavioural baselines. Any subsequent cumulative effects of Internet use on levels of engagement in other activities could differ between these groups and need to be examined and explained separately.

Another issue in displacement research is 'reverse causation'. Cross-sectional and longitudinal survey designs both yield correlations between variables, whether these associations occur at one or more than one point in time. A co-variation between two variables may indicate that they are inter-related, but the direction of causality – whether from variable A to variable B or in the reverse direction – is not unequivocally established.

To unravel this problem, Stoneman took panel data on time use obtained in three separate surveys with the same respondents and used regression analysis to find out whether spending more time online resulted in subsequent reduction in time spent socialising with friends. He found evidence that this relationship did exist. He then reversed the position of these variables to find out whether reducing time with friends resulted later on in more time being spent online. No support was found for this link. It was also found that more time spent watching television was related to spending less time contacting friends or engaging in recreational activities also likely to promote social contact. No evidence emerged that spending more time online produced subsequent reduction in television watching.

Concluding remarks

There is often a presumption that when a new medium enters the market, others will have to give ground to make way for it. This is not the only feasible outcome, however (see Livingstone, 2003). An expanded repertoire of media could also produce expanded overall use of media (Stanger and Gridina, 1999). Given that time is finite, this would mean that other activities would eventually have to be displaced. These might include social and physical pursuits, time at work, or sleep.

A new medium, however, could supplement rather than supplant an old medium. This outcome might be true of television and the Internet. It might be misleading in any case to classify the Internet as a 'medium' when it really comprises a bundle of different communications and media forms which overlap in their nature with the attributes of other media (e.g., television, radio, newspapers, telephony, etc.). If this is true, then the Internet could enhance other media by providing them with a new platform on which to reach media consumers (Bolter and Grusin, 1999).

Whether a new medium can significantly displace an old medium not simply for specific individuals but on a macro-level across an entire media marketplace might also depend upon the overall extent to which the newcomer penetrates the marketplace. In research into diffusion of innovations, adoption of new technologies has been observed to follow a consistent pattern whereby initial adoption occurs gradually and reaches only a minority of consumers in a population. At a specific point, however, once an optimal critical mass of people had adopted it, a new technology can spread very rapidly among later adopters and quickly reach the majority (Rogers, 1995). The switch from slow to dramatic rates of adoption has been called the 'tipping point' (Gladwell, 2000).

Observations across a range of technologies, including new communications and media systems, have indicated that this point is usually reached once penetration has reached between ten per cent and 25 per cent of consumers in a market (Rogers, 1995). In the case of the Internet, this critical penetration point was reached in developed countries in regions such as Europe and North America at varying points during the first decade of the new millennium. However, it is perhaps more important in this context to consider the adoption levels of specific Internet-related activities or communications systems, particularly those that have functional similarities to television (see Gunter, Rowlands and Nicholas, 2009).

With television, the Internet might not only enhance this older medium but also change the way it is used. Digital technology is far more dynamic and interactive than analogue technology. Thus, if the Internet provides a new platform for accessing information and entertainment of the type that has also been obtained via television and also demonstrates new ways of accessing such content through which media consumers have more control over the nature of reception, new television viewing behaviours could become conditioned. Old style television watching could be regarded as outmoded unless it too evolves.

The Internet engages people differently from conventional television technology. Television offers a more rigid content structure framed by fixed schedules of programmes branded by differently named television channels. This structure is available on the Internet as well within Internet protocol television packages. In addition, extensive online programme archives and repositories can be accessed and selections made for immediate viewing on-demand. Some of these repositories provide temporary archives that are replenished within a relatively short time-cycle of one week or one month (e.g., catch-up services provided by major broadcasters), while others offer archives in which programmes are deposited indefinitely. Channel formats become redundant in this world as media consumers construct their own personalised programme schedules.

Many leading broadcasters – and growing numbers of minor ones – are migrating programmes into Internet accessible repositories. In that sense, they are contributing to these new developments and the new demands that will emerge from them among media consumers. It is difficult to put a time estimate on how long it will be before channel formats become outdated but there is a clear movement towards the conditioning of viewing behaviours that will eventually produce this outcome. This change does not spell the end for television, however, merely a new beginning.

On a final point, audience data for the UK have indicated that there were no signs during the latter part of the first decade in the twenty-first century that television viewing as a whole was in decline. The average amount of time devoted per day across all television channels and all viewers aged four and over remained unchanged between 2004 and 2008 at 3.7 hours. This stability in time spent viewing characterised all age groups from the very young to the very old (Ofcom, 2009d). Thus, while use of the Internet has grown over time in terms of demographic spread and volume of time occupied, time devoted to conventional television use has not altered. This evidence is not sufficient to allow us to dismiss any possibility that Internet use could have selectively displaced television for some people in regard to specific applications or functions. The importance of television relative to the Internet and the functionality of the two media are topics examined over the next two chapters.

2

The importance of television and the Internet to media consumers

The basis of any loyalty to television can be expected to stem from people's perceptions of how important it is to them. How much is television valued by its viewers? Are there particular aspects of television that are important to viewers? Similar questions will also be asked about the Internet. This chapter will present evidence from a number of sources, both academic and industry-based, on how important television is perceived to be in general and about the importance attached to specific aspects of the medium's outputs. What happens also if the medium is taken out of people's lives? Do they miss it? Evidence on these questions will be presented from technology deprivation research in which people are temporarily starved of access to television and computerised technology including video games and the Internet.

How important is television to people today?

Television is highly valued by most people who watch it. It is not just television in general that people value, but also specific parts of its output. Despite crises of confidence on the part of major public service broadcasters and recognition across the commercial broadcasting sector that their world has become a more competitive place in the twenty-first century than it ever was in the twentieth century, there is plenty of evidence that television remains important to the general public. It is certainly true that the longest-established TV networks have seen their audience shares eroded across the 1990s and into the 2000s. Yet, television overall commands as much attention from people as it ever did.

The major difference is that the television broadcasting sector has many more players in the 2000s than it had 20 years earlier and this means that viewers have more choice and that viewing time has become more disaggregated across a greater number of channel offerings. Thus, while BBC1 and ITV1 witnessed a drop in audience share from 62 per cent in 1997 to 43 per cent in 2007, the average amount of time viewers watched television per week (*c.*25 hours) hardly changed at all (Armstrong, 2008).

Although we might readily acknowledge that television in general forms an important part of our lives, this finding by itself does not reveal very much. We need to know what it is about television that we value. For many people, the importance of television is defined by the programmes it provides. Increasingly, however, the way in which programmes are provided is also critical to viewers' evaluation of the medium. The emergence of digital technologies has brought enhancements to conventional television viewing enabling viewers to have greater choice and control over what, when and how they watch.

Research by Ofcom (2006c) found that UK viewers (60%) extensively acknowledged having access to a wide choice of channels as a feature they most valued about television. Other features that were endorsed as having high value by large minorities of viewers were being able to access the BBC (44%), being able to access programmes from other broadcasters (39%), and being able to watch TV content on a normal TV screen (39%). The last finding may seem odd, but was significant in the context of this research that was carried out to assess public opinion towards the BBC iPlayer, a programme catch-up service available over the Internet enabling viewers to watch programmes they may have missed when first broadcast and that they also failed to video-record via their TV sets. Watching of programmes through the iPlayer service therefore requires the user to view them on a computer screen.

The importance of digital

The commitment to going digital with television broadcasting was made at government level and driven by the prospects presented by new communications technology to enhance the information transmission capacity of existing media systems and to introduce new transmission technologies such as the broadband Internet also capable of carrying large amounts of information. Furthermore, these new technologies opened up opportunities for media consumers to become producers and senders of content with 'one-to-one', 'one-to-many', and 'many-to-many' settings. Although one might expect that many members of the public would voluntarily adopt these new media technologies, the fact that digital television was presented as a *fait accompli* without debate as to whether it would or would not happen meant that the public was given no choice in this context.

Research conducted to assess early public reaction to digital television in the UK found that many people expressed anger about being forced to make the switch from analogue transmission to digital transmission. This anger was not expressed only by analogue viewers who had not yet switched. It was also expressed by some viewers who had already voluntarily switched (Klein, Karger and Sinclair, 2003). The adoption of digital television requires a new way of thinking about television. The growth in numbers of channels presents search challenges for viewers and increased interactivity demands a shift in orientation towards the television set that resembles more closely that adopted when using a computer. Faced with forced change, people do not always readily accept innovations. This reaction was registered initially with acceptance of the digital switchover of television broadcasting in the UK (Klein, Karger and Sinclair, 2004a, 2004b).

Clear majorities of respondents said they resented 'the fact that I may need to pick up the cost for switching to DTV' (79%); that it is 'irresponsible of the government to allow people to continue to buy analogue TVs if they are intending to switch to DTV' (75%), and that they were 'angry that the government feels that they can force us to change to DTV' (73%). In addition, two thirds (68%) felt that 'DTV is being pushed through by the government regardless of what people want' (Klein, Karger and Sinclair, 2004a).

Only a minority (25%) acknowledged that the technology switch to digital TV shows that the country is using cutting edge technology (Klein, Karger and Sinclair, 2004a). Thus, regardless of what the digital switchover may say about the UK as a nation, individual viewers harbour serious concerns about its implications for them and their viewing.

Later, more respondents disagreed with the switchover (50%) than agreed with it (38%). This result occurred even after the researchers had taken the trouble to explain the implications of the switchover. One reason for the negative public opinion was that the switchover was presented as inevitable. It was being forced upon people who had not been given a choice. Furthermore, there would be personal costs involved. Viewers would need to get new TV equipment and new video-recording equipment. There was also a widespread belief that all television in the future would need to be paid for, that is, over and above the TV licence fee (Klein, Karger and Sinclair, 2004b).

There was distrust of the government's motives for the switchover and many people were not clear about the rationale underpinning it. Nonetheless, there were many people who recognised that technology was advancing and that the digital switchover could be seen as an inevitable result of progress.

In its *Digital Dividend Review*, Ofcom (2006d) asked viewers across the UK to evaluate a range of new TV services by ranking them according to their perceived importance to society and their personal value to respondents themselves. Looking at the percentages of respondents who placed different options in either first or second place, the most widespread support in terms of both societal and personal importance was given to the idea of 'more digital terrestrial television channels' (65% for societal importance and 63% for personal importance). The next most widely supported TV service was local TV with similar proportions of respondents saying that this was important to society (50%) and personally important (48%). A follow-on question invited respondents to rate the importance of different technologies independently (rather than making a trade-off between them) and clear majorities of UK viewers rated the idea of having more digital terrestrial television channels as important or very important to them personally (67%) and to society as a whole (73%).

Opinions about digital television indicated that most viewers in the UK felt that this new technology could bring important benefits. The real test of how significant these developments might be lies in the extent to which the new technology is voluntarily adopted. Many people objected to having the digital switchover forced upon them, but many others made the switch anyway because of the added value they believed digital services could bring to their viewing choices and experiences. In fact, voluntary digital penetration quickly became widespread in the UK. Digital television first became available to UK viewers in 1999. Within six years, seven in ten (70%) of UK viewers had acquired a digital television set (Ofcom, 2006d). This figure was helped by the introduction of a free-to-air multi-channel digital television package called Freeview in 2005.

As with any new technology, some people took up digital television more readily than others. In the UK, the early digital adopters tended to have a younger and more upmarket profile than non-adopters, regardless of the digital technology platform. There are some in the broadcasting industry who believe that the digital switchover could be successful in pulling young viewers back from their online habits by providing them with more content likely to be of interest to them (Lighting, 2007). This position has been reinforced by research showing that viewer bases for digital terrestrial, digital satellite and digital cable television services each had higher proportions of younger people (and lower proportions of older people) as compared with the analogue viewer base (Ofcom, 2007d). Only one-third of analogue television viewers (33%) were aged under 45 years, while significantly higher proportions of digital terrestrial (46%), digital satellite (57%) and digital cable (64%) fell in this age range.

Turning to the socio-economic status of analogue and digital viewers, users of digital television comprised higher proportions of upmarket viewers and lower proportions of downmarket viewers compared with users of analogue television. More than one in two analogue television viewers (52%) fell in the lower social categories (C2 and DE) compared with much smaller proportions of digital terrestrial (44%), digital satellite (45%) and digital cable (44%) viewers (Ofcom, 2007d).

Psychographic research among television viewers provided further explanations of early adopters and non-adopters of digital television in the UK that in turn yielded insights into the features that define the importance of television in general. In this investigation, four groups were differentiated: 'adopters', 'likelies', 'could be's', and 'won't be's'. At this time (end of 2003) more than four in ten households in the UK (45%) had at least one digital television set and one in five (20%) had gone completely digital (Klein, Karger and Sinclair, 2004a).

The 'adopters' were viewers who had already adopted digital television in some form on at least one television set in their home. 'Likelies' were viewers who had experienced an interest in digital television and were expected to adopt it within the next 12 months. The 'could be's' were people who could be persuaded about digital television but had no plans to adopt it within the next 12 months. Finally, the 'won't be's' were viewers who expressed no interest at all in adopting digital television in the foreseeable future.

In terms of their distribution, two national surveys conducted in the early part and towards the end of 2003 provided data that indicated growth of adoption even during that short time period. Across the two surveys, the proportions of viewers in the digital adopter category increased from 38 per cent to 45 per cent, while those in the 'likely to adopt' category increased from 12 per cent to 17 per cent. The 'could be's' who expressed a disinclination to adopt digital television but might still be persuaded decreased from 29 per cent to 19 per cent, while the 'won't be's' increased from 13 per cent to 19 per cent. These findings indicated a greater polarisation of views about the importance of digital television (Klein, Karger and Sinclair, 2004a).

This research also found that 'adopters' and 'won't be's' could be further subdivided. The 'adopters' could be sub-divided into: 'comfortable adopters', 'marginalised adopters', and 'experimental adopters'. For the 'comfortable adopters' digital television meets their personal needs for more choice from television and to acquire new technologies. For the 'marginalised adopters', digital television is regarded as an acquisition to benefit the whole family, although it might encourage family members to indulge in lone viewing. For 'experimental adopters', digital television offers something new though eventually there was a feeling that they would end up watching largely the same kinds of programmes anyway.

Among the 'won't be's', this research differentiated between 'passive won't be's' and 'active won't be's'. The passives were concerned about declining standards in television and were not inclined to pay for more content, much of which might be offensive. The actives believed that people spend too much time watching television and that increasing the numbers of television channels available to viewers would only make this situation worse.

Further analysis explored a number of factors that were identified as important in terms of driving forward digital adoption:

- platform symbolism
- content attractiveness
- equipment practicality.

With platform symbolism, viewers were asked questions about what digital television really meant for their viewing experiences and whether it could effectively benefit their viewing. In effect, this factor questioned whether 'digital' television represented a step up the evolutionary technology ladder and therefore was intrinsically a good thing. The UK government had presented a positive symbolic representation of digital television. Digital technology would open up communications media and break down old divisions between broadcasting, computing and telecommunications. It would offer consumers more choice and more control. It would take on a technologically advanced form and passive television reception would be enhanced by interactive and transactional capabilities.

The positive spin placed on digital technology by government was, however, roundly rejected by some people who were relatively disinterested in switching voluntarily to digital television. Additional channels, interactivity and transactional facilities held little appeal for these individuals who were satisfied with television as it is (Klein, Karger and Sinclair, 2004a).

In respect of content attractiveness, viewers asked about the kinds of services that would be provided by digital television and the extent to which the digital package offered something that was distinctive from analogue television. It was found that people who had voluntarily switched to digital television enjoyed having the much expanded choice of channels and many also appreciated better picture and sound quality and interactive features. Increased quantity of programme content must not be provided at the cost of reduced quality or diversity. Even in a multi-channel television environment, it is important that digital packages delivered what people said they wanted (Klein, Karger and Sinclair, 2004a).

Having worked through the previous two levels, a further set of drivers were concerned with equipment practicality which addressed questions of technology usability, cost and installation logistics. Numerous practical difficulties can present further barriers to digital television uptake. Viewers needed to know whether installation of new digital television equipment was a straightforward or complicated matter. They also needed to know how much digital television was likely to cost at the point of installation and subsequently. Finally, enhanced technology might also mean that it was more complicated to use. Viewers therefore needed assurances that digital television services were user-friendly. Consumers proceeded through decision-making about digital television at each of these levels and they could reject the new technology at any point.

In a later investigation that surveyed the opinions of viewers across the UK about the development of new television services and communication technologies, respondents were invited to consider the importance of a number of factors in relation to their uptake of digital terrestrial television by their household. Among those people who had already expressed an interest in digital terrestrial television, the factor that they said would most influence their decision to subscribe was the subscription price of the service. Other factors of some importance were whether a set-top box was required to secure reception and the number of new channels that would be acquired. In this research, these factors were given value scores to indicate their importance to respondents relative to other factors that were presented to them (Ofcom, 2006d).

While digital adoption proceeded at a pace faster than predicted by early projections at the turn of the millennium, one pattern that remained constant was that most non-adopters of digital television expressed reluctance *ever* to adopt the new technology. Ofcom (2006b) reported that among viewers who did not currently subscribe to multi-channel television, just under one in seven (13%) said they intended to do so within 12 months. The great majority (73%) indicated this was not likely to happen. By early 2009, however, the proportion of UK homes that had taken up digital television grew to nearly nine in ten (89%), although this was in part reinforced by the start of the forced digital switchover in 2008 (Ofcom, 2009b).

Although the adoption of digital television has taken place anyway, with much occurring voluntarily, it was ultimately driven by technological and accompanying economic imperatives on the part of government. It is also important here to consider the early reasons for non-adoption, not least because they might also have relevance in terms of understanding the likelihood of adoption of further enhancements to television technology in the future. Referring back to the three-level model of adoption decision-making, evidence emerged that people who challenged or rejected digital television tended to identify grounds associated with platform symbolism, content attractiveness and equipment practicality (Klein, Karger and Sinclair, 2004a, 2004b).

There was evidence of decision making at the platform symbolism level with reasons for non-adoption emerging that were connected to the value attached to digital television. Nearly one in two non-adopters (46%) said that while television was important to them, they were happy with what they had and did not seek more (46%). One in four (26%) non-adopters said they did not see the benefit of digital over analogue television. A similar proportion (27%) said they wanted to wait and see how digital television settled down before adopting it themselves. Again, this position suggested uncertainty over the value and utility of digital television as a technology. The value of digital television in terms of its financial cost was also a barrier to adoption. Four in ten non-adopters (40%) said they would get digital television once the cost of doing so had gone down, while over one in four (28%) said they were waiting for other people to get it first so that the cost of adoption would reduce. The list of reasons for non-adoption used here did not explore content attractiveness issues, but did find that equipment practicality made a difference. One in four non-adopters (28%) felt that digital television may be harder to use (Klein, Karger and Sinclair, 2004a, 2004b).

Equipment practicality issues were identified among key reasons for non-adoption of digital television in an earlier report (Klein, Karger and Sinclair, 2003). Drawing upon a national survey of UK viewers, the researchers compared current digital television users with respondents who had not yet adopted digital television but indicated they were likely to do so. The findings here showed that even among individuals who were motivated to acquire digital television there were perceptions of difficulties associated with doing so that were not endorsed to the same extent by people who had already obtained digital television. Fewer digital adopters (40%) than non-adopters (47%) said there were complications in connecting up equipment so that it works. Far few adopters (35%) than non-adopters (53%) said it was necessary to install a new aerial to be able to obtain digital television.

Genuine equipment utility concerns existed not only among non-adopters but also among adopters of digital television. There were significant minorities of digital adopters and non-adopters who said they were likely to adopt within 12 months who identified difficulties associated with the use of digital television. At that time, current digital users and likely future adopters expressed concerns about complications associated with recording digital channels (43% and 33%), use of multiple remote controls (35% and 37%), and use of interactive features (24% and 29%) (Klein, Karger and Sinclair, 2003).

Research conducted reported by Ofcom (2006a) as part of its media literacy audit in 2005 identified four attitudinal segments among those without digital television: those with an intention to acquire digital television (16%); those choosing not to acquire it (37%); those who wanted it but were unable to get it (21%); those who were uncertain (26%). Among those who said they did not intend to get digital television within the next 12 months, the most widely endorsed reason was a platform symbolism reason, namely that they were happy with television as it was and did not wish to see it change (68%). The next most often endorsed reason, mentioned by a lot fewer people, was the perceived cost of digital adoption (27%).

Small minorities admitted to other concerns such as their lack of understanding about the switchover (5%), the perceived quality of content (4%), and difficulty using digital TV (3%). Ofcom regarded these issues as potential barriers to take-up of digital TV. However, much more needs to be known about public beliefs and understanding. Concerns about 'quality' of content, for example, might refer to the quality of programming on newer channels or possibly to quality of picture or reception. If there are public concerns about programme quality, do these refer collectively to new channels (beyond the five main terrestrial channels) or do such concerns attach to specific channels? We do not really know.

Digital television appeals fairly spontaneously to viewers who like to try out new technologies, while others prefer to wait and see what benefits of significance the technology will bring. In the end, though, undecided viewers were confronted with a time limit within which to switch to digital television and faced with the option of conforming to a government decision that had already been taken or be totally excluded from the audience.

The importance of channels

There are now so many channels available on multi-channel platforms that viewers often lack a detailed knowledge about them all. This development has expanded viewers' choices and at the same time posed new challenges for finding out about the programmes they may want to watch. Increased choice may be welcomed by many (though not all) viewers, but does not necessarily result in more time spent watching the box. In behavioural terms, long lists of channels pose search issues even with the availability of electronic programme guides which tend not to offer the level of search sophistication of online search systems.

One premise put forward by this book is that traditional television programme delivery systems and structures will change as new technology developments open up different reception options for viewers. In this context, the growth of on-demand programme delivery systems could render traditional television channels redundant. Viewers' orientations to television will change and they might choose not to be locked in to fixed sequence programme schedules; instead they will expect to choose not just what to watch but also when to watch it – as a norm. If this scenario represents an accurate description of the future, it is relevant to consider the importance of television channels and the value that viewers attach to them.

Conceptually, there appears to be a tendency for viewers to group television channels together in multi-channel environments, especially when two or more small-share channels cover the same thematic content. Hence, when asked to make judgements about television channels, viewers may cluster together sports channels or movie channels or children's channels and discuss them collectively (Towler, 2003).

Newer terrestrial channels such as Channel 4 and Five were felt to be similar in their purpose to provide alternatives to the BBC and ITV channels. It was important therefore that these channels should maintain a distinctive quality about them. They should not simply provide an alternative source of diverse programming, but also provide programmes unlike those that might be found on BBC1, BBC2, or ITV. The image of Five was as a lightweight channel with output that should not be taken seriously. References not surprisingly focused on the high-profile soft-porn movies shown after 11 p.m., especially on Fridays. Even with these channels, concerns were expressed about the transmission of unsuitable content before the watershed. Interestingly, concern centred on controversial themes as much as controversial content such as offensive language. There were scheduling 'tricks' that viewers expressed concern about. One tactic was for a controversial programme to follow immediately after an innocuous one, particularly when the latter was very popular with children and teenagers.

Sky One emerged as perhaps the most salient channel on the multi-channel, satellite and cable packages. Despite this premier position among the newer channels, there was no strong sense of established channel image here in the same way as emerged with the terrestrial channels. Viewers knew about Sky One through specific programmes they had watched. The channel's 'image', if that is the right term to use, was defined, if anything, by programmes such as *The X-Files*, *The Simpsons* and *South Park*, all of which established a cult following.

In further analysis that probed participants' perceptions of other specialist television channels, the expansion of non-public service channels offered viewers an opportunity to make more refined choices about what to watch (Towler, 2003). They did not have the same characteristics as the terrestrial television channels which had more mixed schedules. Specialist channels were more commercialised and viewers seemed to be aware of commercial strategies these channels use to capture and retain audiences.

News channels were valued and interest in such channels was not the preserve of so called 'news junkies'. There was a view that these channels should present news in the raw because they had the airtime to do so. The expectations of viewers tuning in to these channels are not the same as when they tune in to the news on a mainstream BBC or ITV channel. There is an expectation of less filtered news.

Sports channels were seen as a premium and played an important part in attracting viewers to a platform such as Sky. These were also regarded as more commercialised and it was noted by viewers that premium rates were generally charged for access to these channels. There was an expectation that prices would continue to rise for these channels. Indeed, there was a view that these channels served as test-beds for new subscription and pay-per-view strategies on the part of broadcasters that might eventually become extended to other channels. Because channels such as Sky made such a lot of money from sports channels, there was a feeling that some of this money should be ploughed back into the sports

– perhaps at community level. Some people felt that sports channels were 'milking' the audience. Increasingly access to televised sports was becoming controlled by subscription sports channels and viewers were left with no alternative but to become paying customers – or go down the pub to watch.

Entertainment channels on the cable and satellite platforms were treated as light-hearted fun. Such channels were not perceived as having coherent schedules. It was recognised that many of these channels depended on re-runs from the major channels. Even so, they did not have a well-formed image. There was also a tendency for some of these channels to transmit programmes that depict bizarre events.

Shopping channels were grouped with entertainment. They were not compared with commercials on TV. The viewer has to make an active choice to watch them. They tended to present much more information about products than adverts. Adult channels broadcast explicit pornography. Most participants here did not admit to watching these channels themselves, but did not believe it was wrong for others to do so. As long as subscribers knew what they were buying into, there was no problem.

Film channels were seen in a similar vein to going to the cinema. As subscription channels, viewers actively chose to receive these channels and could obtain advance information about movie contents. Hence, they were willing participants and could make their own informed choices about what to watch. Under these circumstances there was less cause for complaint about offensive material.

Children's channels were grouped together as a distinct form of entertainment. Children were frequently mentioned among reasons for subscribing to multi-channel packages. The broad view of parents was that there were lots of these channels available and that they tended to be of poor quality. Their children tended to know much more about these channels than parents did. Although they did not always know what their children were watching, there was more scope for control over children's use of television than over their use of the Internet.

Research published by the Department for Culture, Media and Sport (DCMS) to provide input into the BBC Charter review (DCMS, 2004) probed the public's perceptions of channel image by asking respondents to indicate whether they thought any of a series of 15 descriptions concerning reputation, entertainment and information quality, credibility and originality applied to the BBC, ITV, Channel 4 and Five. These perceptions indicated that viewers can and do distinguish between the major television channels in terms of what they expect them to provide.

All four television brands compared in this survey were widely endorsed for being entertaining. ITV received the widest such endorsement of all among its viewers (54%), with the BBC (44%) and Channel 4 (45%) on more or less level pegging, and Five a little way behind (37%). The particular strengths most often associated with the BBC were its 'good reputation worldwide' (49%), and the perceptions that its services are 'educational' (47%) and 'informative' (45%). On these measures, the BBC outstripped all the other TV services.

Although endorsed by fewer of its viewers on other attributes such as 'high quality' (33%), 'traditional' (33%), 'accurate' (23%), and 'trustworthy' (23%), the BBC again received more widespread endorsement on these characteristics than did the other three TV services.

In terms of having 'something for everyone', the BBC (41%) was matched by ITV (43%). There was less widespread support for Channel 4 and Five on this dimension (22% in each case), perhaps indicating that these services were regarded as providing a narrower or more specialised range of programming. Perhaps reinforcing this interpretation, in part, was the finding that Channel 4 matched the BBC in terms of being seen as multi-cultural (22% in each case). Channel 4 was also perceived far more than any other service as being 'cutting edge'.

A further distinctive perception of the BBC as compared to the other services – and on this occasion the comparison is a less flattering one – was that the Corporation was far less likely than any of the others to be seen as 'modern'. Mirroring this perception, the BBC was far more likely than the others to be seen as 'traditional'.

Summing up, the BBC was seen by viewers as offering a good solid, reliable, high quality service, but also as being perhaps a little staid and old-fashioned. Channel 4 and to a lesser extent ITV were seen as more modern and up-to-date. Despite its relative youth as a channel, Five was rated closer to the BBC than to the other commercial services in terms of being 'modern'. At the same time, Five was certainly regarded as 'traditional'. Hence, its lack of modern feel may refer not so much to an old-fashioned image, but perhaps to one that as yet lacks a distinctive flavour of originality.

The DCMS research then probed viewers further about their perceptions of the BBC. The Corporation was highly regarded as a broadcaster and its reputation was perceived to extend far beyond the national boundaries of the UK. This point was underscored by the significant majority of survey respondents who agreed that 'the BBC has a good reputation around the world'. Within the UK, there was a widely held view (85%) that the BBC has a key role to play in keeping the people informed about what is going on around the country. The BBC was a trusted information source, with over half the respondents in this survey (55%) endorsing the view that its broadcasts were accurate and true. Although important as an information source, there was no majority support for the view that the BBC is too powerful, although one in four respondents (25%) did think that this was true. Nearly one in two (48%) rejected this opinion. What was perhaps a critical comment was that the BBC would be widely missed if it was no longer around (72%).

What we need to ask is whether these public perceptions reveal that specific suppliers of programmes are highly valued or whether through these opinions they are also offering support for the medium of television and its current structural configuration in the form of channels with centrally determined and fixed sequences of programmes. There is widespread support for the services provided by the major television channels that operate under public service broadcasting (PSB) obligations. In addition, there is a strongly favourable disposition towards having access to a multitude of other programmes supplied on commercial channels that have no PSB obligations. What is not clear is whether these opinions signal support for the current structure of television nor whether they will ensure its survival for much longer.

Are we satisfied with television channels?

Given that the primary structure within the television environment is the channel system, it is natural that we should ask how satisfied are viewers with the channels they receive? This question has been asked by a number of major surveys of public opinion towards broadcasting.

Public opinion concerning the quality of television programmes has been tracked over many years in the UK. Annual surveys conducted by the Independent Television Commission and its predecessor the Independent Broadcasting Authority date back to 1970 (Gunter and Svennevig, 1988). Programme standards are not easy to define. The notion of 'quality' is used routinely in common parlance in relation to all kinds of consumer activities, but pinning down exactly what it means in the broadcasting context in a way that will be useful to programme makers and regulators has posed a major intellectual challenge.

In the annual public opinion tracker conducted by the IBA and ITC, viewers were left largely to their own devices in the way they defined programme standards. A core question asked survey respondents each year to say whether they thought programme standards had got better, worse or stayed the same. This question was posed for different television channels as well as for television in general. Those who said that programme standards had changed – whether for better or worse – were then asked to specify their reasons for saying this, in their own words. Over the years, the core questions have been modified in the way they address the issue of standards and quality at the television channel level (Gunter and Svennevig, 1988; Gunter, Sancho-Aldridge and Winstone, 1994).

Over the 1970s and 1980s, perceptions of whether programme standards had got better or worse fluctuated for both BBC1 and ITV. In terms of programmes getting worse, the proportions of UK television viewers holding this opinion varied between 25 and 45 per cent. For BBC1, the range was similar but at a slightly lower level, varying between 20 and 40 per cent. In the case of perceptions that programme standards were getting better, this also varied from year to year over a range of 10 to 20 per cent for both BBC1 and ITV. What was notable throughout this period was that the percentages of viewers saying they thought programme standards had fallen always exceeded the percentages who thought they had got better. Every year, by far and way the largest percentage of viewers thought that standards had not changed (Gunter and Svennevig, 1988).

During the early 1990s, perceptions of programme standards in this annual public opinion tracker were fairly stable, year on year. Each year, though, the perception that standards had got worse was more prevalent than the view that they had got better. Between 1990 and 1993, around one in four UK viewers felt programme standards on ITV had got worse (24–27%) compared with around one in seven (12–14%) saying they had got better. In the case of BBC1, around three in ten (26–32%) felt standards had got worse and one in ten (8–11%) said standards had got better. The gap between proportions saying programmes had got worse or better narrowed markedly in the case of BBC2 and Channel 4. In both cases, similar proportions of their viewers felt they had let their standards slip (16–18%), while slightly more felt standards had improved in the case of Channel 4 (13–16%) than BBC2 (8–12%).

During the early 1990s, satellite and cable television services were just beginning to take off. Their viewers had a rosier glow about these new channels compared with the established channels. In 1993, with both satellite (improved: 34%; got worse: 7%) and cable (improved: 22%; got worse: 14%) services more of their viewers felt they had got better than got worse, a reversal of the traditional pattern for terrestrial channels (Gunter, Sancho-Aldridge and Winstone, 1994).

Throughout the 1980s and early 1990s, the ITC asked respondents to give their reasons for saying programme standards had got worse or improved, separately for each television channel. The main complaint about falling programme standards was that there were too many repeats. This was true of the four terrestrial channels available to viewers at that time. The worst culprit was BBC1. Nearly one in four respondents (20–24%) who said that BBC1 programme standards had fallen mentioned repeats. This was also the most frequently mentioned problem for ITV (17–22%), BBC2 (9–13%) and Channel 4 (8–11%). Among the other most prevalent responses were references to 'not enough quality' (3–7% across channels), 'less interesting for me' (3–7%), less variety (3–7%), and taste and decency matters such as 'more violence' (3–6%) and more bad language (3–6%). There was no indication, however, that any of these factors perceived to underpin falling programme standards had consistently increased in prevalence over time (Gunter and Svennevig, 1988; Gunter, Sancho-Aldridge and Winstone, 1994). The main reason for saying programmes had got better was reference to a 'wider range of programmes' (3–7%) (Gunter, Sancho-Aldridge and Winstone, 1994).

In 2002, the ITC changed its question about programme standards. For the first time, it separated two distinct aspects of programme-related perceptions. One set of questions asked specifically about programme standards linked to issues of 'taste and decency' and a second set asked about programme 'quality'. In asking about taste and decency, the new question prompted respondents to evaluate changing programme standards in relation to the depiction in programmes of swearing, violence and sex. These features had previously arisen without direct prompting in relation to open-ended answers explaining respondents' reasons for saying programme standards had got worse (Towler, 2003).

Initially, respondents were asked whether they thought programme standards, in terms of taste and decency, had got worse, improved or stayed the same. Those who said that standards had either improved or got worse, were then asked to say on which channels such changes had occurred. In 2002, significantly more respondents felt programme standards in terms of taste and decency had got worse (55%) than got better (5%). Such falling programme standards were most likely to be linked to Channel 4 (51%), followed by ITV (45%), Five (44%), BBC1 (31%) and BBC2 (18%). Although similar channel distinctions were made in the case of 'improved' respondents, because the initial base was small, these channel-related results cannot be regarded as very robust.

In response to the question about programme quality, the gap between 'got worse' and 'improved' responses narrowed, but even so, markedly more respondents thought standards had fallen (32%) than improved (19%). On this occasion, falling programme standards were most often associated with ITV (61%) and BBC1 (51%), with Channel 4 (39%), BBC2 (32%) and Five (30%) further behind. Improving programme quality was most often associated with BBC1 (51%) and, interestingly, ITV (40%), with BBC2 (24%), Channel 4 (17%) and Five (8%) further behind (Towler, 2003).

The DCMS research published in 2004 shed further light on this subject. Although the focus of this research was the BBC, comparisons were also made with other major TV channels, most especially ITV, Channel 4, and Five (DCMS, 2004). In what was an encouraging result for the BBC, it attracted a greater volume of satisfied viewers than did the other channels. Three out of four survey respondents (75%) – representing the wider UK viewing population – replied that they were satisfied with the BBC. Smaller majorities were also satisfied with ITV (61%) and Channel 4 (58%), while one in two respondents were satisfied with Five (50%).

Before getting too excited for those channels that fared best here, there are some qualifying remarks that should be made in putting these results into context. The fact that volumes of dissatisfaction ranged between 10 per cent and 15 per cent across all these services meant that there was significant variation between services in numbers of undecided or 'don't know' responses. One in three or more respondents were unclear about their opinions of Five (35%) and Channel 4 (32%) and one in four respondents were uncertain about ITV (26%). A much smaller proportion of respondents (14%) were unsure about their opinions concerning the BBC. The relatively high uncertainty levels for Channel 4 and Five could signal that many respondents had insufficient experience with these two channels to offer a firm opinion one way or the other. Another important point is that opinions were asked about the BBC as a whole, and no attempt was made to split BBC1 and BBC2. Yet, this might have been more meaningful given that these two channels are different from one another in terms of schedule profiles, audience shares and audience profiles.

The same survey also found that satisfaction with TV channels did not reach the same levels across all sections of the audience. It is interesting to note that young adults, aged 16 to 30 years, were more likely than any other demographic group to be satisfied with the BBC (80%) and Channel 4 (71%). This segment of the audience was not significantly more likely than anyone else, however, to exhibit satisfaction with either ITV or Five. In the case of ITV (now technically ITV1), satisfaction with the channel was much less prevalent among social grades AB (53%) and C1 (54%), in other words, the middle classes. With Five, satisfaction with its service was most widespread among the lower, DE social grades (61%).

What we can see here is that television channels provide viewers with a ready-made conceptual structure for classifying and organising the multitude of channels now available through multi-channel packages. The numbers of channels are now so great that it is important to have a system that can enable viewers to produce conceptual groupings of channels into a manageable number of channel 'constructs' defined by content type and expected gratifications. Channels can also develop distinctive brand images and these too can assist viewers in understanding the range and location of programme types available to them. Take away channels and we are left with an even larger universe of undifferentiated content with a lack of order. At present channels provide two kinds of order: (1) an indication of where particular types of programmes might be found, and (2) a linear sequence that signals when specific programmes become available for consumption. While the first attribute will continue to add value, the second attribute could become outmoded as more use of on-demand material conditions new kinds of viewing expectations.

The importance of programme service values

The founding principles of television, when regarded purely or primarily as a public service, were that it should provide information, entertainment and education. It should culturally enrich the society in which it was embedded. Thus, viewers expect television programmes to adhere to certain standards which pertain to production quality and not causing offence. The provision of high standard programming also extends to programme diversity which can be defined in terms of catering to a range of audience tastes and interests via different genres. In the United Kingdom, these basic principles have been more formally framed within the ethos of public service broadcasting. These principles, however, are not simply concepts dreamed up by governments and media regulators, they frequently surface in research in which ordinary people are asked to say what defines television for them as part of their lives.

A BBC survey in 2004 asked people throughout the UK to nominate the kinds of programmes it was most important for public service broadcasters (PSBs) to provide. The top eight were: news, regional news, wildlife, current affairs, soaps, consumer programmes, education and British comedy (Human Capital/Martin Hamblin/GfK, 2004). In this survey, respondents were asked to say how they valued each programme type in terms of its importance to the country as a whole.

Ofcom (2004, April) also conducted a survey which asked about the importance of specific genres of programming. The Ofcom research asked respondents to nominate the programme types they most valued on terrestrial channels. It also asked them to differentiate between what they valued personally and what they thought was important to society. News was rated as important personally and as important to society by nearly 70 per cent in each case. Of greatest societal importance after news were sport, drama, soaps, regional news and serious factual. Of greatest personal importance after news were drama, serious factual, comedy and films.

The BBC's survey noted that ITV1, Channel 4 and Five represented an important part of the UK's public service broadcasting system. ITV and Channel 4 invest significantly in domestic programmes – more so than their counterparts in other European countries (Oliver and Ohlbaum Associates, 2003). Part of the reason for this, claimed the BBC, was the need of these broadcasters to compete directly with the BBC in providing high quality domestic output.

Ofcom's (2004) investigation into PSB identified four headings under which PSB objectives could be outlined: social values, quality, range and balance, and diversity. Questions were framed to probe audience perceptions of each of these aspects of PSB. A clear majority of respondents (71%) saw television primarily as a source of entertainment. Over half (55%) said television was their main source of news. Slightly more (58%) rated television as their main source of knowledge about science, nature and history.

After this, Ofcom explored with respondents the role of television and how important they thought it was for terrestrial PSB television channels to provide each of a number of services, to cater for various needs or to fulfil various objectives. These aspects of television were itemised under the broad headings of social value, quality, range and balance, and diversity.

Under social value, the most widely endorsed aspects of terrestrial PSB television were: news and other programmes that keep the population well informed (87%); a schedule of programmes that protects children from unsuitable content (85%); and a variety of informative factual programmes (82%). Other important features under this heading included educational programmes and programmes that promote learning, promote social action campaigns and preserve the country's national heritage.

Turning to the subject of quality, Ofcom respondents identified the following key attributes most often: high levels of technical and professional skill in programme making (e.g., strong acting, good locations, etc.) (81%); a high proportion of first-run programmes (i.e., not repeats) (80%); and programmes that meet generally accepted standards of taste and decency (79%).

Range and balance were defined by just three widely-endorsed features: a balanced diet of different types of programme (both general entertainment and other types) within the peak viewing hours of 6pm–10.30pm (84%); a choice of different kinds of programme across the main channels at all times of day (82%); and a wide variety of different programme types (e.g., news, sports, documentaries, entertainment, religious, arts, etc.) (82%).

Diversity was related more to the different types of audience sub-groups that are catered for. There was widespread support of the need for programmes that are targeted at a wide range of different audience groups (80%). There was less widespread, but still majority support for programmes that reflect the needs and concerns of different regional communities within the UK (65%). The promotion of awareness and understanding of different communities (59%), representation of a wide range of different political and social viewpoints (58%), and programmes for minority interests (57%) received narrower majorities of endorsement.

Ofcom (2004) conducted an analysis in which it compared different terrestrial PSB channels in relation to specific obligations as perceived by respondents. BBC1 was generally expected to adhere to a variety of public service obligations by more respondents than ITV1, while the same was true of BBC2 as compared with Channel 4. Five was perceived by fewer respondents still as expected to adhere to public service broadcasting obligations.

The five channels came closest in respect of the view that they should each provide a schedule of programmes that protects children from unsuitable content. They were furthest apart in relation to the perceptions that they should provide live coverage of major political/social occasions such as Royal weddings, Golden Jubilees and the budget and in the expected provision of programmes that promote social action campaigns (e.g., 'Crimestoppers'). These latter services were regarded most often as the preserve of BBC1 and ITV1.

The Ofcom (2004) research also revealed that terrestrial analogue television channel viewers differed from multi-channel viewers in some of their attitudes about television. For example, one in six terrestrial channel-only viewers thought sport, arts and religious programmes would be better provided by a specialist channel, but one in four multi-channel viewers subscribed to this opinion. Multi-channel viewers also held more positive views about newer kinds of services such as rolling news formats, though all viewers endorsed the importance of news on the mainstream channels.

In-depth qualitative research revealed that the mainstream television channels were expected to provide (and to continue to provide) a range of content designed to cater to the tastes and interests of many different audience communities (Ofcom, 2004). There was a need to protect the standards of broadcasting in terms of the interests of children and maintenance of taste and decency, but some specific programme-related requirements might be relaxed for certain channels over time. Some of the qualitative research indicated that public service broadcasting is an abstract concept that for many viewers has little or no meaning. Television is primarily regarded as an entertainment medium, but one that is expected to bring benefits to society as a whole. From the perspective of viewers, television has an important part to play in enhancing a sense of national identity through its programmes and this meant that most programmes ought to be produced in Britain. There was a need for television to offer specialist provision to different regional audiences and to minority audiences. Thus, as well as preserving features of traditional national identity, television should also embrace the multi-cultural nature of Britain today.

The Ofcom (2004) public service broadcasting review phase one research also examined indicators of performance derived from the audience. In a survey of viewers across the UK, Ofcom asked respondents to rate a number of public service components in terms of their satisfaction with provision and how important they perceived each component to be.

In respect of news and other programmes that keep the population well informed, 85 per cent rated this as important and 87 per cent were satisfied with provision. In contrast, while the same percentage thought that having a schedule of programmes that protects children from unsuitable content was important, only a minority (28%) were satisfied with the performance of terrestrial channels in this respect. A significant majority rated a balanced diet of different types of programmes as important, while a slim majority (53%) said they were satisfied with provision. A similar result emerged in respect of a choice of different kinds of programmes across the main channels at all times of the day, where 84 per cent thought this was important, and 44 per cent were satisfied with provision.

The problem with these kinds of indicators, however, is that it is difficult to know what can be learned from them that might be of use in terms of recommended changes to schedules and programming. News was compounded with 'other programmes' without any clear definition of what these 'other' programmes might be. The diversity measures, which displayed far lower levels of audience satisfaction than one might hope to find, given how many respondents endorsed these elements as 'important', are again difficult to pin down. What represents 'a balanced diet of programmes'? How many different genres are we talking about? Are some genres more important than others in this context? How should genres be distributed proportionately across a schedule to ensure it is rated as sufficiently balanced in terms of its mix of content types?

Even with an item such as 'a schedule of programmes that protects children from unsuitable content', does the concern rest mostly with the contents of programmes (which programmes?), the way the programmes are scheduled (pre-9 p.m.?), or with the quality of advance warnings given about content that might not be suitable for very young viewers? In future, regulators must move away from these generalised measures to ones that pinpoint more precisely specific features about programmes and schedules that can be changed.

In further questioning, viewers across the UK were asked to evaluate a range of new television services by ranking them according to their perceived importance to society and their personal value to respondents themselves (Ofcom, 2004). Looking at the percentages of respondents who placed different options in either first or second place, the most widespread support in terms of both societal and personal importance was given to the idea of 'more digital terrestrial television channels' (65 per cent for societal importance and 63 per cent for personal importance). The next most widely supported television service was local TV with similar proportions of respondents saying that this was important to society (50%) and personally important (48%). A follow-up question invited respondents to rate the importance of different technologies independently (rather than making a trade-off between them) and clear majorities of UK viewers rated the idea of having more digital terrestrial television channels as important or very important to them personally (67%) and to society as a whole (73%).

The importance of the public service broadcasting purposes and characteristics of television still received widespread acknowledgement in later reviews by Ofcom (2007a, 2007f, 2009d). Key purposes such as informing people's understanding of the world, providing stimulating knowledge and learning, reflecting UK cultural identity and expressing diverse viewpoints were extensively endorsed, and received more widespread support in 2008 than in 2006. In 2008, overwhelming majorities of UK viewers have high importance ratings (a score of at least seven out of ten) to the fact that PSB television provided news that could be trusted (85%, up from 75% two years earlier), news that helps to understand what's going on in the world (84%, up from 75%), and coverage of big national events such as sports, music and major news events (78%, up from 73%).

In terms of their attributes, PSB television services were rated as highly important for their high quality programmes (85% in 2008, up from 68% in 2006), services that could be trusted (85% in 2008 only), and showing programmes that viewers said they wanted to watch (81%, up from 66%) (Ofcom, 2007a, 2009d). Between 2006 and 2008, there was also more widespread satisfaction with the performance of PSB television services in their provision of trusted and high quality programmes that were diverse, informative and challenging (see Ofcom, 2009d). All this evidence confirmed that for UK viewers, despite the growing numbers of television channels offering them much expanded choice, the established public service channels remain not just important in their own right, but also represent important defining aspects of television in general and its place in their lives.

Further evidence of the importance of television has stemmed not just from the opinions that the public espouse about general programme standards, but also about specific programmes they have chosen to watch. Ofcom (2009d) reported findings from a BBC-GFK Pulse survey conducted with viewers from across the UK that asked them about specific programmes they had viewed the previous day. One question asked for each programme endorsed as having been viewed whether the respondent had 'made a special effort to view' it. The data here were obtained in 2008, and were compared with similar data from 2005. This showed that the prevalence of setting out deliberately to watch a programme increased from 44 per cent to 48 per cent over this period. This trend was progressive and increased gradually year-on-year in 2005, 2006, 2007 and 2008. The same trend characterised programmes watched on each of the five public service broadcast channels – BBC1, BBC2, ITV1, Channel 4 and Five. Thus, despite the fact that these channels experienced gradual erosion of their audience shares in the face of competition of other TV channels, a steadily increasing proportion of the programmes that viewers watched on these channels were ones they had made a special effort to see.

Television channels are defined by the programmes they provide and the reputations of the organisations that underpin them. Viewers associated some channels with programmes that observe specific criteria of quality and diversity. Other channels are defined by specific genres or themes of programming. In branding terms, the older PSB channels are associated with certain standards in broadcasting that include adherence to specified principles and values. Even in a rapidly evolving and crowded television broadcasting environment, these standards have retained their importance to viewers.

Increased choice is valued by many viewers, but not at the expense of quality and standards. The importance of television therefore resides not simply in the provision of a convenient source of entertainment or information, but also in the expectation that its outputs will observe minimum standards in terms of content decency, production quality, representation of different interests, and general reliability and trustworthiness. If the Internet is to emerge as a serious competitor to television, it must pose a vigorous challenge in terms of its perceived importance to users. Its importance may stem from the way it caters to similar needs as television (but more effectively) or to different needs to which people do wish to devote a lot of their time.

The importance of programme genres

Television provides a range of different types of content. In this context, the medium is valued by people in relation to the different genres or types of content it transmits. On mainstream broadcast television, programmes are configured sequentially within channels. Channels too have their identity which is defined by the programmes they typically broadcast and also by the principles to which they adhere in respect of their general goals and purposes. In the UK, the older-established public service broadcasting channels are defined in terms of their provision of a diversity of programming. In the rapidly evolving multi-channel television world, however, most channels are defined thematically. Some channels provide only movies, some only news, some only sport, some only comedy, and so on. Other channels can be even more narrowly focused and transmit only programmes concerned with the home, celebrity biographies, nature documentaries, or specific types of sports (e.g., Nigerian football).

The Internet provides access to an even wider diversity of content than multi-channel television. Much of the content on the Internet, however, is displayed in a different format from that of television and the Internet also provides users with access to large and increasing amounts of video content. An important question we could ask here therefore is: Where that video content derives from sources independent of the major broadcasters (that also have a growing online presence), is there any overlap between the genres most widely used online and those most extensively endorsed or viewed on television?

In a public service broadcasting context, television channels are placed under legal or regulatory requirements to provide a diverse mixture of programmes and such terms and conditions can be fixed in terms of specified quotas. Non-PSB channels have no such operational constraints. The survival of thematically specialised channels on multi-channel platforms will depend upon their competitiveness and popularity within the open TV marketplace. If they fail to attract sufficient viewing numbers, advertisers and sponsors will withdraw their patronage, the channels will be unable to maintain their platform rental or running costs, and will eventually go out of business. For PSB channels that are not funded out of the public purse, the critical question is whether they can afford to produce programmes required by their PSB quotas that have limited audience appeal. If these programmes fail to attract advertising revenue, such programmes can place considerable financial strain on commercial PSB channels, especially in multi-channel environments in which their audience shares are already likely to be significantly eroded.

In a 2006 survey, Ofcom asked viewers to choose five programme genres that were important (Ofcom, 2007a). The question was in two parts. Viewers had to choose genres that were of personal importance to them and then genres that they felt were important to society. These two perspectives yielded different 'league tables' of genre importance. In both cases, however, news came out on top and regional programmes – that is other than regional news and current affairs programmes – came bottom in both categories.

Some programme genres finished high up in both league tables of genre importance, most notably comedy, sport, current affairs and serious factual programmes. Even so, marked differences in extent of support were found for quite a few programme types when evaluated for their personal value versus their value to society as a whole. It is clear that while genres such as comedy and sport finished well in both league tables, far fewer people believed they were good for society than personally enjoyable. Genres such as serious factual programmes, children's programmes, and hobbies, leisure and lifestyle were endorsed by similar proportions of people as having personal importance and importance to society. Meanwhile films, drama and soaps were of widespread personal significance to people but much less likely to be seen as important for the good of society.

While programme genres were more likely to be seen as personally important than important to society, this pattern was reversed in the case of educational programmes and to a lesser extent for regional current affairs programmes. These were four times as likely to be viewed as good for society than as personally valuable. Despite debates about the significance for worthwhile television of programme genres such as arts and religion, they received little support. It is also significant to note the relative lack of support for light entertainment, factual entertainment and music (see Table 2.1).

Another indication of the kinds of programmes people really want derives from the extent to which viewers report going out of their way to watch them. Ofcom (2007a) reported findings from a BBC/IPSOS survey

Table 2.1 Perceived importance of television programme genres

Personal importance	%	Importance to society	%
News	56	News	62
Films	51	Education	48
Comedy	50	Current Affairs	40
Sport	41	Comedy	28
Drama	41	Sport	28
Soaps	40	Serious Factual	27
Serious Factual	25	Regional News	25
Current Affairs	21	Drama	19
Regional News	21	Children's	19
Children's	19	Films	18
Light Entertainment	14	Regional Current Affairs	18
Hobbies, Leisure, Lifestyle	14	Hobbies, Leisure, Lifestyle	15
Education	12	Soaps	14
Music	11	Other Factual Programmes	14
Factual Entertainment	10	Religious	13
Regional Current Affairs	8	Arts	12
Arts	7	Factual Entertainment	9
Other Factual Programmes	7	Music	8
Religious	5	Light Entertainment	7
Regional Programmes	2	Regional Programmes	4

Note: The question was: From the following list, please choose the FIVE types of programmes whose presence on the main TV channels you consider to be PERSONALLY valuable to you and your household/you consider to be most important for the GOOD of society as a whole.

Source: Ofcom, (2007a).

carried out in 2004 that asked people in respect of different programme genres whether they 'specially chose to watch' these programme, or 'made some effort to watch' or 'watched because the TV was on'. Programme types that viewers were likely to make a special point of watching were drama series/serials (73%) and soap operas (68%), followed by factual entertainment programmes (61%) and serious factual programmes (60%). News (58%), general factual (57%), hobbies and leisure (55%) and light entertainment (55%) were less often endorsed in this way, though they still commanded the focused interest of a majority of people. Once again, these data are based on the self-reported viewing of survey respondents rather than on any continuous monitoring of their viewing behaviour.

It is clear from the genre preference lists examined earlier that news provision is identified as a key function of television. This is especially true of public service television that is conceived to operate according to sets of ideals that reach beyond the need to make commercial revenue. It has also emerged that even in the Internet era that provides a richness of content of all kinds, media consumers still expect television to provide them with a range of services including plurality in the provision of news. Government sponsored research with the public in the UK found that for a clear majority of people (72%) it was important to have a choice of television channels that provided news for their nation and their region. The more people watched regional news, the more they felt it was very important to have a choice of sources for this information via television (Hamlyn, Mindel and McGinigal, 2009).

Behavioural evidence of what is important to media consumers

Statements of what is or is not 'important' to television viewers or Internet users represent opinions essentially of what they like or dislike. Ultimately, however, the success or failure of a medium depends upon its ability to attract patronage. This is a matter of behaviour, not opinion. Further research based on viewing behaviour analysis has been reported by Ofcom (2009a) that utilised UK television industry viewing statistics produced by the Broadcasters' Audience Research Board (BARB). This analysis examined the audience shares achieved annually by different channel genres in multi-channel television environments. These data excluded audiences for the five public service broadcast channels (BBC1,

BBC2, ITV1, Channel 4 and Five) and focused on the remaining channels on multi-channel platforms that tend to be thematically specialised by programme genre. Data from Ofcom are shown in Table 2.2 for 2003 and 2008. These data show audience shares for each channel genre and the numbers of channels within each genre that were available in each of those years.

Entertainment genre channels attracted the largest audience share both in 2003 and in 2008. This was the only genre that exhibited a marked increase in share over time. The performance share of entertainment genre channels is not surprising, however, given that this was the biggest genre in terms of numbers of channels throughout this period. The number of entertainment genre channels increased by a significant margin across this five-year spell. All the other channel genres exhibited increased numbers of channels as well, but their audience shares either remained unchanged or showed downward shifts. Audience share, of course, does not indicate audience size. Rather it displays the distribution of audiences, whether large or small, between the channels that are available to viewers.

These data indicate that in the open commercial television marketplace, where no 'public service' protection is given the specific genres, the entertainment genre proved to be the most successful in winning audiences. Whatever opinions viewers may articulate about the importance of specific programme genres, therefore, in terms of their remote control choices, entertainment stands out. Increased provision in other genres made little difference to the share of the market they achieved. Ofcom (2009a) also noted, however, that much of the entertainment category's audience share growth had been driven by the

| Table 2.2 | Audience shares of channel genres in UK multi-channel TV homes |

	Audience share (%)		No. of channels	
	2003	2008	2003	2008
Entertainment	15	21	24	39
Children's	6	6	13	20
Sport	4	3	12	18
Movies	4	3	14	24
Documentaries	2	2	10	15
Music	3	2	17	26
Lifestyle-Culture	3	1	10	18

Source: Ofcom, 2009a.

'portfolio' channels produced by the public service broadcasters, such as BBC3, ITV2, E4 and Fiver. By 2008, these channels accounted for half the viewing share of the entertainment channel genre.

The importance of the Internet

Evidence has already been presented that illustrates the rapid expansion of the Internet. Despite initial questions about whether involvement with the Internet would lead people to withdraw from normal life (Kraut et al., 1998), it has become widely established as a source of information and entertainment and a valuable channel of communications that can be utilised to enhance individuals' social networks and to carry out a wide range of transactions.

Not only has Internet penetration expanded rapidly around the world, so too has the amount of time Internet users are willing to commit to online activities (European Interactive Advertising Association, 2007). The value of the Internet to its users has been underscored by the finding that most say they cannot live without at least one of its applications (European Interactive Advertising Association, 2007).

The emergence of broadband has enhanced the capacity of the Internet and also users' experience. The significance of this technology was confirmed in American research by the Pew Institute that found that clear majorities of US broadband users said that this connection was important to them for 'finding out what is going on' (68%), 'to communicate with health care or medical providers' (65%), 'for contributing to economic growth in their community' (62%) and 'for sharing their views with others about key issues' (58%) (Horrigan, 2009).

Among the fastest growing Internet applications is online social networking. For those who engage in this online activity, it has become so interwoven with their daily routines that many cannot imagine life without it. This position was evident in research among American Internet users that found that most social media users (71%) said they could not live without Facebook (Kimberley, 2009). The site attracts 78 million regular users in the USA and more than a quarter of the population of the UK use the site monthly, with half of those returning every day, for an average of 25 minutes.

Research into the impact of being deprived of television has shown that people will seek the next nearest alternatives. Many people who have become dependent on the medium find that even after just a few days with no viewing, they suffer from withdrawal symptoms. Similar reactions have been found to occur in respect of the Internet among those who have become accustomed to going online all the time.

Yahoo! (2004) conducted a large-scale survey of Internet users in which they were asked to give their reactions to Internet deprivation, while a smaller-scale ethnographic study was conducted in 13 households (involving 28 participants) where they were actually deprived of the Internet for 14 days. In the survey, nearly one in two respondents (48%) indicated that they could not go without Internet access for more than two weeks. The median time of five days tolerance of total Internet deprivation indicated that for many Internet users the thought of losing Internet access could be tolerated for much shorter periods of time. Losing Internet access meant that many activities were disrupted, including getting news information, communicating with friends and family, and paying bills.

Turning next to popular genres on the Internet, there is evidence based on users' expressed interests and reported behaviour that entertainment-oriented genres remain the most popular. Although, having said that, it is also clear that demand may exist for a diversity of entertainment formats. Entertainment Media Research (2008) reported among UK Internet users aged 15+ the content types that most interested them in an 'on-demand' setting were top movies only just out on DVD (48% definitely interested), recent movie releases (43%), TV comedy programmes (35%), live music concerts (30%), TV drama programmes (29%), live sporting events (28%), US programmes not yet shown on UK television (27%), stand-up comedy (26%), documentaries (26%), recorded music concerts (23%), music videos (23%) and classic movies (22%). If those saying that they were 'somewhat interested' in these genres are aggregated with those above saying they were 'definitely interested', each category attracted support from at least two-thirds of respondents. More than six out of ten (62%) said they would be definitely or somewhat interested in news and current affairs content.

Ofcom (2009b) reported further data from subsequent research by Entertainment Media Research among UK YouTube users. These data were based on self-report claims of genres viewed on a 'regular' basis. The reportedly most popular YouTube content genres were comedy (67% of users claimed to watch regularly), music (56%), entertainment (50%), sports (33%), film and animation (33%), pets and animals (24%), news and politics (16%), people and blogs (16%), science and technology (15%), how to and style (10%), travel and events (11%), autos and vehicles (10%) and education (10%). It is clear that there is an overlap between television and the Internet in respect of the genres that appeal most to viewers/users.

Concluding remarks

People place much value on television. Furthermore, traditional aspects of television, such as the linear channel structure, the range of genres of entertainment and information it can provide, and the growing amount and choice of content following the emergence of digital transmission technology are all widely respected by the public and underpin the importance that the medium in general has in their lives.

Much of the evidence about the importance of different aspects of traditional forms of television broadcasting derives from public opinion and perception. It is equally relevant to know not only which aspects of television are verbally endorsed, but also which are actually used. Behavioural evidence that derives from audience measurement systems operated by the television industry takes us beyond opinions and perceptions concerning the medium, its channels and its programmes, but does not fully underwrite the proposition that television occupies a central part in the lives of its viewers. Such evidence does reveal some stability in the overall amount of time devoted to television watched via a television set. It also indicates that specific genres – and not necessarily those verbally endorsed as most 'worthy' – dominate viewing. Of particular significance is the use of television purely for entertainment purposes.

As television itself evolves with technology enhancements and the emergence of non-linear content reception systems, are its place and role likely to change? This is the key question being addressed by this book. It is clear from some of the evidence discussed in this chapter that the most popular content genres sought out on the Internet overlap in kind with those most watched on television. To determine whether people are therefore likely to turn to the Internet in place of television or whether the Internet might cultivate an appetite for a different style of television viewing, we need to examine specific aspects of television and Internet usage in a more focused fashion, defined by content types and user motivations to expose more subtle nuances of viewing and online behaviour.

Research evidence emerged long before the Internet entered the wider public domain about the everyday viewing activities of ordinary viewers and how decisions were reached about the use of television. This evidence revealed that simply monitoring macro-level data about television viewing does not provide any explanation of how specific patterns of television usage occur. Television forms part of the living environment of its viewers and its use represents a social behaviour that must often be negotiated with others with whom the viewer resides. The television set is therefore not simply a piece of technology, it is also an aspect of the social fabric of a household that can bring its members together and often in multi-set households pull them apart.

The importance of television is rooted in the significance it has in regulating everyday family routines as well in terms of delivering programmes that viewers want to watch (Lull, 1990). In this context, the distinction between 'activity' and 'passivity' in viewing is rendered redundant because all use of the television is 'active' or dynamic in some way (Silverstone, 1994). The social dependence on television (and increasingly on the use of computer games and the Internet) becomes exposed when these technologies are removed from the household and families are deprived of them even for limited periods of time (Gunter, Hansen and Touri, 2007).

Observations of the use of television in the home have indicated that viewers in the same viewing environment utilise television for different purposes, underlining that it is important to them for different reasons. Television use tends to be functional rather than purely indiscriminate and casual. The same observation holds true for the use of the Internet via a personal computer. If we are to understand more about the way these two technology platforms are used and the mechanisms through which to explain whether and why the newer medium could displace the older medium or cause it to change, we need to examine the reasons underpinning their use. This question will be examined in the next chapter.

3

The functional overlaps of television and the Internet

People turn to communications technologies to access specific applications for specific purposes. In the context of television, this traditionally means switching on the set to watch programmes that cater to a range of interests and needs. Viewers may have favourite programmes or favourite programme categories or genres. Internet users may seek specific types of information or entertainment as well. In so far as television gives its viewers what they want in terms of content, then their continued loyalty may be enhanced. If another medium emerges that offers a better service that fulfils the same needs, however, television may experience audience losses. If two media technologies satisfy functionally distinct need sets via the content they provide, then they could exist in harmony. Thus, if the Internet emerges as a more highly valued source of satisfaction for media consumers than television, it may then become their preferred medium.

This chapter will examine these issues for television and the Internet and consider whether the Internet poses a competitive danger to television or represents a distinctive and different type of service that appeals to different markets. Whereas Chapter 2 focused on the outputs of television and Internet and the importance attached by their users to different classes of content on each medium, this chapter focuses more on the motives of users in respect of the two media and whether the gratifications obtained from each are similar or different.

Displacement effects between media are more likely to occur when two or more media share similar functions. Long before the era of the Internet, media researchers observed that when a new medium provides a better functional alternative than an existing medium, the latter will lose audiences to the newcomer (Himmelweit, Oppenheim and Vince, 1958; Schramm, Lyle and Parker, 1961). As a new medium in the UK in the 1950s, the extent to which people said they watched television was related to reported reductions in listening to radio, going to the cinema and reading comic books. The media most affected by the new medium were the ones with which it shared functional equivalence (Himmelweit, Oppenheim and Vince, 1958). Two decades later in the United States, the emergence of cable television resulted in a fall in viewing of local television services and cinema attendance for similar reasons (Kaplan, 1978). The question now is whether the Internet is having a similar effect on television where functional equivalences can be identified. This chapter and the following two chapters will explore this issue.

Moving away from the simplistic notion of whether the Internet occupies the time of users which is then subtracted from their television viewing, it is important to explore whether displacement is mediated or motivated by other factors. In the past, researchers have identified two broad sets of factors that could be significant here. One set of factors reside within the media and the other set reside within media users. So-called 'media-centric' factors comprise different attributes of the media such as the types of content they present and the formats in which content is presented. 'User-centric' factors are relevant characteristics of media consumers, most especially their motivations or reasons for using specific media. Chapter 2 examined 'media-centric' factors in the context of what features of television and the Internet defined the importance of these two media for their users.

In this chapter, evidence that derives from further studies of media-centric factors and studies of 'user-centric' factors will be examined. Do the Internet and television have features in common that might therefore be expected to bring them into direct competition for media consumers' attention? To what extent do the Internet and television cater to the same needs and interests? In Chapter 4, we will explore the patterns of use of the Internet and television (and other media) specifically in the context of information seeking. In Chapter 5 we will turn to the use of the Internet and television in the context of entertainment seeking.

The importance of media motives

There has been widespread debate over many years about the factors that determine people's use of different media and preferences for different types of content. This debate has paid a great deal of attention to how viewers use television. There are different schools of thought about the inherent nature of television viewing and whether it can be classified as an intrinsically 'active' or 'passive' behaviour (Biocca, 1988). This distinction has become especially significant in relation to analysis of the prospects for more 'interactive' forms of television. The latter include a variety of new (and some not so new) television-related technologies such as 'enhanced' and 'personalised' television facilities. A further type of interaction has been labelled 'cross-media' and refers to interactive arrangements such as when, for instance, a website or SMS text message link is set up in association with a television programme. This allows viewers to engage in interactive behaviour associated with a programme, but not directly with the programme itself (Jensen, 2005).

Enhanced television comprises additional content – graphics, text or additional video material – that may either be presented on top of the live programme or accessed via a link operated through the TV remote control. This additional content can be accessed via the live programme stream or through separate links.

Personalised television is the term used in respect of a digital video recording facility that allows the viewer to capture broadcast programmes on hardware attached to the television set. This facility enables the viewer to time-shift, fast-forward, rewind and pause the recorded content. The most advanced forms of personalised video recording allow the viewer to start watching recorded material before the recording has finished or to watch a live broadcast while simultaneously recording a programme on another channel.

The latter interactive behaviours are all connected to a traditional television scheduling structure involving linearly arranged television channels. In this setting, content flows to the media consumer, but there is no return link from the consumer to the content producer. Increasingly, return path technologies have become established and have formed the basis of new television services that provide content on demand. Such services represent a radical switch from reception of whatever content is available at a time determined by the provider to an on-request service controlled by the consumer (see Bordewijk and van Kaam, 1986). On-demand services offer a wide range of content that can cover all major programme genres and formats and interactive games.

With all these new interactive facilities, television viewers are encouraged to adopt new and different styles of viewing behaviour. Although still linked to television, do they represent the start of a different orientation towards the medium in terms of expectations and gratifications? The emergence of home video recorders in the 1980s was linked to this new technology's ability to cater to a number of specific gratifications, principal among which were the additional control it gave viewers over their television viewing, the social interaction associated with video viewing and the saving of expense of going out to the cinema. Not only did this technology empower viewers for the first time in respect of stepping outside the traditional television schedules with regard to times when they could watch broadcast programmes, it also provided them in effect with an additional television channel over which they had complete control of the scheduling in the form of rented or bought pre-recorded videotapes, usually of movies only shown at the cinema (Levy and Gunter, 1988).

The attraction of the Internet

To begin an analysis of whether the Internet has qualities that television lacks or has appeals that it shares with television that could draw people away from their TV sets and onto their networked home or laptop computers, we need to explore the activities in which Internet users engage and the types of content they seek out. In doing so, it may be possible to identify overlaps in terms of functionalities between the two media. Is the Internet providing a distinctive set of functions and gratifications that are different from any that can be obtained through television? Does the Internet provide similar types of content to television but in a more appealing fashion?

The data concerning the nature of online activities derive from one-off self-reports from survey respondents and from continuous monitoring services that track the behaviour of Internet users while they are online. Self-report surveys have identified a range of activities as prominent in the minds of Internet users when asked to give their reasons for going online. These audits of general Internet use have revealed some areas of overlap with television, but also many areas of distinctiveness between these media. Communications activities such as e-mail, instant messaging and involvement in chat rooms or social networking have been widely endorsed (Gunter et al., 2004; Lenhart et al., 2007).

Of more relevance in the context of determining the displacement potential of the Internet in relation to TV viewing is whether common types of content are sought in each media environment. Searches for news, sports, weather and information about products, travel and holidays are frequently reported (Gunter et al., 2004). In addition, Internet users have often reported seeking out sites linked to TV shows without further qualification (Gunter et al., 2004) or more specifically to websites linked to specific movies, entertainment shows, or sports celebrities (Lenhart et al., 2007).

Even by the end of 2003 in the UK, more than three-quarters of a sample of Internet users in the UK (77%; and well over eight in ten broadband Internet users – 86%) claimed they went online to watch video clips. More than six in ten Internet users in general (62%) and three-quarters of broadband Internet users (75%) were already claiming to download audio-visual content including games and video files while online (Gunter et al., 2004).

According to the Internet behaviour tracking service of Nielsen NetRatings, the most prevalent online activities were use of search engines to find websites (90% of Internet users), use of general interest portals and communities (82%), downloading software from manufacturers' websites (69%), e-mail (61%), and involvement with member communities (59%). At least one in two Internet users also sought out entertainment content (not thematically specified) (52%) and news online (50%). These Nielsen data simply indicated the overall reach of these activities (Changing Media, 2007). We also need to know how much time people spend online with specific activities.

Further Nielsen data reported by Changing Media (2007) indicated that in the UK, the most online time was devoted to acts of communication with other users. Hence, instant messaging (average of 26 minutes per week), social networking (20 minutes per week) and e-mail (15 minutes per week) dominated online behaviour. Although search achieved the greatest reach among Internet users, it occupied much less time on average (eight minutes per week). Turning to the Internet for some form of entertainment occupied 24 minutes per week, divided between online games (11 minutes), multi-category entertainment content (seven minutes) and adult entertainment (six minutes).

Brand popularity online

The Internet represents an open marketplace in which virtually unlimited numbers of content suppliers gain access to large consumer bases. The question being asked in this book is whether the Internet poses a threat to television? There is no simple answer to this question because although the Internet clearly occupies people's time, it is not necessarily true that this time is subtracted from their television viewing. Moreover, broadcasters can and do utilise the Internet as well. Hence, people can now watch television via the Internet. In addition, broadcasters have websites through which they can cross-promote their broadcast output.

One indication of whether the Internet is providing something distinctive from television is whether television broadcasters are the most used online brands. Evidence for the UK has indicated that while broadcasters' websites attract significant volumes of traffic, they by no means dominate the most used sites. Citing Nielsen NetRatings data for October 2007, Changing Media (2007) reported that among the ten most used websites in the UK, only one broadcaster – the BBC – had an entry, in fifth spot. The top four slots were occupied by the major search engine and computer brands, Google (27.8 million users), MSN/Windows Live (21.7 million users), Microsoft (17.0 million users) and Yahoo! (16.4 million users). The BBC had 16.1 million users. Below the broadcaster were eBay (14.5 million users), Amazon (11.8 million users), YouTube (10.0 million users), Apple (9.6 million users) and Wikipedia (9.5 million users).

The above data underline the importance of search as an online activity. The size of the World Wide Web has reached such proportions that online users inevitably use search engines almost routinely when engaged in site exploration. It is therefore not surprising that these sites finish in the top positions in rankings based on consumer reach. What these data do not reveal is how much time search, as distinct from other online behaviour, occupies.

The top-ten league table rankings switched around, however, when different usage measures were applied. Clearly, one of the important issues in relation to the question of television's displacement by the Internet is how much time is devoted to online activities. Two further rankings were reported by Changing Media (2007) based on Nielsen NetRatings data that ranked websites according to the total number of user minutes they attracted in October 2007 and then, more importantly in the current context, the average amount of time spent by individual users on specific websites.

On the total number of user minutes devoted to websites metric, the BBC was again the only broadcaster entry and on this occasion finished in eighth position (with 844,037 minutes of use). The top-ranked websites were MSN/Windows Live (3,581,140 minutes), EBay (1,809,834 minutes), Google (1,571,282 minutes), Yahoo! (1,398,391 minutes), Facebook (1,396,505 minutes), AOL Media Network (1,339,831 minutes) and Microsoft (879,721 minutes). Just below the BBC were Bebo (651,785 minutes) and YouTube (502,434 minutes). This new league table is interesting because when amount of time spent online is used as a metric, a number of social networking sites emerge. Although their consumer reach was a lot smaller than that of search engines, their users had longer-duration visits.

When the average amount of aggregated time per user in October 2007 was adopted as the metric, the top-ten rankings were completely transformed (Changing Media, 2007). None of the sites listed in the other two top-ten rankings appeared in this new league table. The top-ten websites in terms of average amount of time of individual users collectively averaged 18 hours 43 minutes of use across October 2007. Top of the table was the virtual world Second Life (28 hours 43 minutes). The other nine entrants comprised gaming and social networking (or sites that combined both of these elements) including Blizzard Entertainment (24 hours 20 minutes), FullTiltPoker.com (9 hours 39 minutes), PokerStars.com (8 hours 56 minutes), mIRC (8 hours 2 minutes), Playandwin.com (7 hours 53 minutes), Habbo (7 hours 53 minutes), Travian.com (7 hours 27 minutes), Puzzler (6 hours 21 minutes), and paltalk.com (5 hours 47 minutes). These data show averages which mean that some users accumulated smaller and others much greater amounts of time spent with these sites. What we do not know is whether some users visited a number of these types of sites and therefore accumulated even higher individual totals of time spent online. These data do, however, indicate that the websites that command the largest amounts of time from their users appear to be ones that offer something distinctive that cannot be found on television. Primarily, these sites engage their users interactively rather than simply providing content for relatively passive reception.

Research among European Internet users in 2007 indicated that the most prevalent online activities were searching (i.e., using search engines to find content; 87% of all Internet users engaged in this) and then e-mail (81%) (European Interactive Advertising Association, 2007). At some distance behind these two activities were use of social network sites (42%) and text messaging (37%). These activities indicated that the Internet represents a communications medium as much as an information source. In that respect, the Internet appears to be offering users something distinctive from television. Even so, significant minorities of Internet users also said that they downloaded music (31%), watched film, TV and video clips (30%) and downloaded film, TV and video clips (20%). The latter applications indicate some degree of overlap between the way the Internet is used and the sort of content that might be obtained via standard TV viewing.

The same survey attempted to pin down the types of content sought out by Internet users by questioning them about the types of websites they visited (European Interactive Advertising Association, 2007). The results from this question reveal that the Internet is both distinctive from and overlapping with television in terms of genres of content that are used.

The most frequently endorsed websites visited by European Internet users at this time were concerned with news (65%), local information (52%), travel (51%), banking and finance (50%), music (46%), holidays (46%), price comparisons (44%), technology information (41%), films (38%), auctions (36%) and sports (36%). News, films and sports represent clear areas of overlap between the Internet and television. Music represents an area that may be both distinctive and overlapping. Whichever of these two assessments is accepted, the consumption of music is an activity in which users are unlikely to engage at the same time as watching television. The other areas of content all represent genres that might be found on television, but on the Internet combine information content with transactional capabilities and therefore represent online applications that are distinctive from TV viewing. Perhaps the most important result from this survey was a significant (150%) increase in the number of people watching film, TV, or video clips online at least once a month between 2006 and 2007.

Conditional displacement

The idea of functional rather than simple displacement effects between mass media has been written about over many years. Early studies of the impact of the introduction of television broadcasts to different communities in the United Kingdom and United States identified the possibility that television could displace older and longer established media such as the cinema, newspapers and radio if it catered to the same needs of media consumers, but in a more appealing or effective way (Himmelweit, Oppenheim and Vince, 1958; Schramm, Lyle and Parker, 1961).

The observations made above mean that new media need to find a niche for themselves. This means that they must demonstrate an ability to cater to a distinctive set of functions or gratifications that sets them apart from other media. If a new medium can achieve this outcome, it could displace an older medium that would be seen as less satisfactory in its presence.

As explained earlier, media displacement effects have come to be regarded increasingly as linked to specific media attributes or audience attributes. These two forms of displacement have previously been labelled as 'media-centric' and 'user-centric' (see Lee and Leung, 2006). Collectively, they might be termed 'conditional displacement'. What this means is that the mere appearance of a new medium will not invariably be followed by the re-allocation of audience time to existing media in a specific media marketplace. Displacement may be conditional on whether one medium offers something that another medium also offers but in a more appealing way.

If the Internet is to displace television as an activity, therefore, it must be able to provide gratifications of the kind already provided by television. If there is significant overlap between the reasons people have for using the Internet and watching television, then whichever medium is judged to be the better provider of key gratifications will eventually dominate. If the two platforms cater to different sets of needs, however, then there could be room for both of them – with each one occupying its own niche.

Niche theory recognises that it is important that any new medium in a media market establishes for itself a new position that is distinctive from the other media with which it is competing within that marketplace. Hence, if media can be in part defined by the specific audience gratifications they provide, any one medium must establish its distinctiveness by demonstrating that it caters to a gratification not touched by the other media or that it caters to specific gratifications more effectively than other competing media (Dimmick, Kline and Stafford, 2000).

Media richness is another theory that highlights media attributes that can be used to determine the distinctiveness of a specific medium compared to others (see Rice, 1992, 1993). Media are differentiated in terms of the idiosyncratic communication features such as their modality, use of language, and essentially their degree of proximity to direct, face-to-face communication. The latter is often referred to as 'social presence' (see Short, Williams and Christie, 1976). New media developments are becoming more sophisticated in terms of their interactive functionality and this in turn is enhancing the sense of social presence they can create among their users. This is a dimension that has critically defined and distinguished the Internet in comparison with newspapers, radio and television. However, the adoption by the older media of digital technology foundations has opened up new possibilities for content delivery and engagement with their users. The Internet may be differentiated from television in terms of the way it is used, but over time, the distinctive technologies of these two media could merge and media-centric factors may play a lesser part in distinguishing them.

Turning to the user-centric approach, this is characterised by the emphasis placed on the attributes of media users. In particular, it is concerned with the motivations of media consumers and whether they display distinct or overlapping motivational profiles in respect of their reasons for using different media. Research on audience gratifications associated with media consumption has, over a number of years, found that consumption of specific media is associated with particular motives. Given the diversity of content provided by media such as broadcast television and the Internet, however, it is probably over-simplistic to define the use of either of these two media in terms of just one or two dominant motives.

Overlapping functional displacement of television by the Internet

The Internet has grown steadily in terms of how many people, across different age and social groups, go online and in the amount of time people devote to their online activities. Since we all have a finite waking time budget, there are limits to the extent that any new activity in which we engage can be accommodated without reducing the time we spend on other things. In considering the future for television, one school of thought is that the world's most popular medium could be at risk from the Internet. This proposition stems in part from the relentlessly increasing size of the online user population and the growing amounts of time Internet users spend online. In addition, there are more qualified concerns about the threats posed to television by the Internet. These include the observation that the Internet can do much of what television does, but better. In other words, the Internet and television do more than simply occupy the same temporal spaces: they also share the same functions. If this functionality competition is a critical factor, then it needs to be explored in more detail to ascertain whether it does indicate where the threat of displacement lies.

Insights into whether or not there is a potential for functional displacement of television by the Internet have been provided by studies that have compared the reasons for use of different media. In some instances, as reviewed below, these investigations have asked people to indicate the importance they attach to different media (old and new) in respect of the capacity of those media to satisfy different needs they might have. Much of this research has been conducted within the uses and gratifications tradition of media research.

In many of these studies convenience samples of respondents have been recruited and this feature limits the extent to which their findings can be generalised to normative media populations. Nevertheless, this body of research has indicated that media such as television and the Internet are used for different purposes. One study conducted with American university students asked respondents to endorse a range of different reasons for using a number of different media (Metzger and Flanagin, 2002). The list of media included old media such as books, magazines, newspapers, telephone and television and new media or communications forms such as e-mail, web surfing to retrieve information, posting of information online, and online conversations. Media motives were broadly divided into two categories – instrumental and ritualistic. The former represented specific purposive reasons for using a medium, while the latter implied that a medium is used as a matter of habit and for no specific, goal-direct reason. Television use was found to be linked more strongly to ritualistic than to instrumental motives, while use of different Internet applications was generally rated as more instrumental than ritualistic. These findings suggested that television and the Internet could attract people for different reasons and as such these two media displayed limited or no functional overlap. It perhaps should be noted, however, that the Internet-related applications respondents were asked to rate in this study all involved some purposive action such as sending or retrieving information. The comparisons with television were therefore limited and omitted many other types of online activity where functional overlaps (e.g., associated with the search for entertainment) might still have been found.

Evidence of the potential for a limited functional displacement effect of the Internet on television was produced in a study that was referred to earlier in this book by Kayany and Yelsma (2000). Family households were interviewed and completed questionnaires on their own and supplied details about their use and perceptions of different media. This study went beyond measurement of simple displacement effects to ask respondents about the importance they attached to different media (e.g., newspapers, television, Internet) as sources of information and of entertainment. Television was endorsed by more respondents in both cases as their most important source. Heavier users of online media were much more likely to rate the Internet highly than were lighter users in terms of its importance as a source of entertainment and information. In addition, the more highly the Internet was rated as an information source, the less highly television was rated in this regard. Ratings of the importance of the Internet and television as entertainment sources were unrelated, however.

Tsao and Sibley (2004) conducted a survey in the United States among over 2,000 households within a Midwestern state. This investigation was designed to find out whether the Internet had any displacement effects on the use of other media in respect of advertising information. The key measures examined attitudes towards different media as advertising information sources, the use of different media as advertising sources and predicted future use of different media in this context. The researchers gave respondents a list of ten advertising media to evaluate: billboards, daily newspapers, direct mail, free community papers, in-store advertising sheets, Internet, magazines, radio, television and weekly newspapers.

Comparisons were made between respondents who displayed favourable and unfavourable attitudes towards the Internet in terms of their evaluative ratings of other advertising media. These two groups differed significantly in their ratings of all the other advertising media, contrary to the hypothetical predictions of the researchers. Further analysis revealed that attitudes to specific advertising media were especially important predictors of how favourably Internet advertising was perceived to be. Respondents who rated billboards, direct mail, magazines and radio higher as advertising information sources also held Internet advertising in higher regard.

Turning to reported behavioural use of the Internet and attitudes towards other advertising media, this research reported that Internet users compared with Internet non-users exhibited significantly more positive attitudes towards television, direct mail, and billboards as advertising media. Internet users exhibited significantly lower regard for daily newspapers, weekly newspapers, free community papers and in-store advertising sheets. Multi-variate analyses revealed that use of the Internet was predicted by attitudes towards direct mail and television and was negatively related to attitudes towards community papers and weekly newspapers.

Looking at relationships between behavioural use of different advertising media, this research found that Internet users were more likely than non-users to be consumers of advertising information on billboards, radio, television and in magazines. Internet users were less likely to be readers of advertising information in daily newspapers, free community newspapers, in-store advertising sheets, and weekly newspapers. In multi-variate analyses increased used of the Internet was predicted by greater attention to billboards and television advertisements and by lower attention levels to weekly newspaper advertising.

Respondents were finally asked to predict their use of different advertising media over the next five years. Greater perceived use of the Internet for advertising information was predicted by greater perceived use of billboards, direct mail, magazines, and television and by less use of free community papers and weekly newspapers.

That study provided evidence for increase–decrease and increase–increase relationships between the Internet and other media in the context of sources of advertising information. Billboards, direct mail, magazines, radio and television seemed to exhibit synergies with use of the Internet in this context, while free community papers and weekly newspapers exhibited displacement relationships.

Non-overlapping functional displacement of television by the Internet

Functional displacement has been examined as a factor that could underpin the erosion of time people devote to watching conventional television outputs out of preference for spending time with Internet content. The Internet has emerged as a source of many different types of gratification that derives from its diverse range of linked activities. As with television, the Internet can serve as a source of content that people can locate and spend time with. It is also a medium through which users can engage in a variety of more dynamic activities. One remarkable growth phenomenon in the online world during the twenty-first century has been the adoption of online social networking. This type of activity is not currently available to people via their TV sets. To the extent that they occupy people's time and serve important functions for users, such activities could lead to displacement of television viewing. There is not necessarily any functional overlap between the Internet and television here. There are functional decisions being made by Internet users, however, that might lead them to privilege spending time online over watching television.

Online social networking

Social network sites invite users to join online communities with which they can communicate in textual, audio or video modalities. Online community sizes can vary widely and can also be differentiated in terms of whether they are restricted or give preference to specific categories of membership. Many early online networks were founded on specific purposes such as exchanges of information, advice and support among groups that shared problems of a particular nature. Often, these were health-related (Gunter, 2005a). Other sites were established to enable their users to make new social contacts, initially within the context of dating arrangements or catching up with old friends (Gunter, 2008). Further sites were initially established for specific reasons that were confined to a particular community but then expanded to embrace wider communities and purposes far beyond their original purposes. Some social networks developed from online games and others have taken on the form of parallel virtual worlds.

The social networking phenomenon has grown dramatically. A few dominant networks have emerged, however, and created their own competitive marketplace. While some have sustained their growth, others have experienced falls in their user bases in the face of growing competition.

In the context of the theme of this book, at the outset we need to know how many people use social networking sites and how much time they devote to them. We then need to find out whether there is any substantive evidence that use of social networking sites interferes with time spent watching television. In the UK, data for the middle of the first decade of the twenty-first century showed that the most used social network brands were relatively recently established sites. A site developed by the BBC fell significantly short of these other sites in terms of the size of its user base and the amount of time its users devoted to it. Three social networks were dominant on both these metrics. These were Facebook (6.5 million users in October 2007), MySpace (6.4 million users) and Bebo (4.5 million users). BBC communities attracted 1.6 million users. Facebook attracted users' attention for the longest average duration per month (2 hours 32 minutes) followed by Bebo (2 hours 15 minutes) and then MySpace (1 hour 25 minutes). In comparison, BBC communities' users devoted an average of just 14 minutes a month of their time to this site (Nielsen NetRatings data cited by Changing Media, 2007).

In this online world, therefore, television-related brands have a presence, but have not, so far, dominated the marketplace. More generally, online social networking sites occupy the time of their users, but early monthly average time-use figures did not indicate that these sites would remove significant amounts of time from conventional television watching.

Gaming and virtual worlds

As well as social networking sites, Internet users have also been found to use gaming sites and virtual worlds very widely. There is ample evidence in modern societies that playing electronic (computer or video) games, whether online or offline, is an increasingly popular activity. It is especially popular among teenagers who represent the adult media consumers of the future.

Research carried out by the Pew Internet and American Life Project has reported for the United States that virtually all young people aged 12 to 17 years (97%) claim to play games on computers, the web, or a console or other portable devices. Half of all American teenagers (50%) claimed, when interviewed, to have played with such games on the day before the interview (Lenhart et al., 2008a).

There is a diverse range of video game products in the marketplace representing a number of genres. The most popular genres among teenage players in the United States were found to be 'racing games' (played by 74% of all gamers), 'puzzle games' (72%), sports games (68%), 'action games' (67%), 'adventure games' (66%), 'rhythm games' (61%), and 'strategy games' (59%), which at least half of all game players claimed to play (Lenhart et al., 2008a). A range of other genres (simulation, fighting, first-person shooter, role-playing, survival, horror, massively multi-player, and virtual world games) were also endorsed by smaller proportions of American teen game players. Those teens that reportedly played these games every day were especially likely to prefer action, adventure, fighting, first-person shooter, role-playing, horror, massively multi-player, and virtual worlds. Half (50%) of all daily game players claimed to have played with games from between five and eight different genres. A further four in ten (39%) claimed to have played with an even larger number of genres than this.

Well over one in three (37%) of these teen game players claimed to spend up to two hours a day playing 'yesterday', while nearly one in seven (13%) said they played at least three hours. On average, around three in ten (31%) of American teen game players said they played at least once a day, while over four in ten (45%) said they played at least once a week. Thus, video game playing for young Americans can occupy significant amounts of their time. Players tend to seek a variety of forms of interactive entertainment from a number of different themes (Lenhart et al., 2008a). This opens up the possibility that a range of different gratifications may be catered to by this type of entertainment. What we do not know is whether there is any correlation here between video game genre preferences and television programme genre preferences.

Again using Nielsen NetRatings data for the UK, Changing Media (2007) reported that users of the 20 most used of these sites spent an average of 18 hours 43 minutes per month with them. The most popular of these sites was Second Life. Between 2006 and 2007, this site saw its UK user base grow from 79,000 to 211,000 and its users increase the average amount of time spent on the site each month from 9 minutes to 28 hours and 43 minutes.

Average usage levels for online game playing far outstripped times reportedly spent with social networking sites by their average users. Time commitments to online games and virtual worlds seemed to be substantial enough to compete with time devoted to watching television.

User-generated content

User-generated content (UGC) services represent a further strand of online activity that entail Internet users developing original content and posting it onto wesites for others to view. The social networking sites discussed earlier also provide UGC services, but those sites are mainly about establishing interpersonal communications links with others. Services such as Blogger, Flickr, Wikipedia and YouTube invite Internet users to become media producers and to place original text, photographic or video content online for potentially mass audiences.

By October 2007 in the UK, a number of these sites had built up substantial user bases (Nielsen NetRatings data cited by Changing Media, 2007). In the lead was YouTube which attracted over 9.9 million users during that month, followed by Wikipedia (9.5 million users), then Blogger (over 4.9 million) and finally Flickr (over 1.5 million). All of these sites achieved significant year-on-year increases in users. There were wide discrepancies, however, in the average time per month users spent on these sites. YouTube was a long way in the lead on this metric (51 minutes per month) followed by Wikipedia (13 minutes), and then Blogger and Flickr (8 minutes each).

Such findings indicated that this phenomenon was becoming established among Internet users and could grow to become a pre-occupation for many people. If that outcome did occur, it could have serious implications for television if the growing time demands of UGC meant loss of time for television. Later research reported by Ofcom (2009b), however, indicated that while some UGC activities have become widespread, many others have been engaged in by only a minority of Internet users. Between 2007 and 2009 in the UK, for instance, only setting up a personal social networking page or profile exhibited a significant increase in prevalence, increasing from one in five home Internet users in the UK (21%) in 2007 to nearly four in ten (38%) in 2009. For other applications such as uploading photographs to a website, contributing comments to a blog, setting up one's own website or weblog, contributing to a collaborative website such as Wikipedia, and making and uploading a short video to a website, there was hardly any movement between 2007 and 2009.

There were marked age differences in Internet users who engaged in online content creative activities. All of these major activities were far more prevalent among the under-35s than among those aged 35 and over (Ofcom, 2009b). This age difference was especially pronounced in respect of setting up a social networking profile (65% versus 22%), uploading photographs to the Internet (62% versus 32%), contributing to someone else's weblog (43% versus 15%), setting up your own weblog (21% versus 7%) and making and uploading a short video to a website (17% versus 5%).

Concluding remarks

The use of television and the Internet is shaped by their functionality and the motives of their users. If the Internet does pose a threat to television, it is not a matter of simple time displacement. Instead, displacement will flow from the gratifications users of these media are seeking and the level of satisfaction they get in each case in terms of their original reasons for engaging with these media. A distinction can be made between television and Internet catering to the same needs and gratifications, with one performing better than the other and catering to distinctive needs and gratifications, with one medium's provision being rated as more attractive than the other's.

Following up on an observation made in the previous chapter, we also need to know how the use of these media is situated within a broader social context of the environments in which they are used. This point is especially important in relation to the use of television and the Internet at home.

The use of media cannot be understood without examining the social contexts in which this behaviour takes place. Television can be used as a source of entertainment or information, but in so doing, it also serves a social purpose. This purpose is realised in the context of conversations viewers have with other viewers about their television experiences. These conversations can derive from shared information experiences or shared entertainment experiences. In the viewing household social conditions can determine how the television is used, with fixed rules existing or negotiated agreements being reached about the times when viewing should occur and which programmes to watch (Lull, 1990).

The Internet also has a social dimension. Once again, household rules might exist about going online – limiting the amount of time spent online or policing the types of websites visited, especially by child users

(Livingstone and Bober, 2006). The Internet also provides access to social communications systems through which users can maintain contact with their friends or relatives or make new social contacts.

The functionalities of television and the Internet can be quite different, but they can also overlap. In some instances, even where viewing and online activities serve different purposes, the physical use of one medium precludes the use of the other because it may be too difficult for a user effectively to engage with both at the same time.

The varied applications of the Internet include going online to access television programmes and other video material. If specific applications and associated gratifications linked traditionally with the use of television sets migrate to the Internet, the two media will then be brought into direct functional competition. This issue is explored in more detail in the next two chapters, first in the context of information seeking and second with regard to entertainment seeking.

4

The future of television as an information source

Television has long been regarded by the viewing public as their primary source of information about the world (Gunter, 1987; Robinson and Levy, 1986; Towler, 2003). Not only has television been regarded as a valuable source of national and international news, but also for news about regions and local communities (Ofcom, 2007c). In the UK, television news has been ranked as people's primary news source by growing percentages of the viewing population since the 1970s (Towler, 2003). Over the same time period, television has also posed a stronger challenge to newspapers as the primary source of local news (Towler, 2003).

Despite the positive opinions that people hold about television as a news source, there have been reports that the amount of time devoted to watching the news on the major TV channels in the UK has been in decline (Hargreaves and Thomas, 2002). This might reflect the downward trend in audiences for the major public service broadcasting channels in the face of ever growing competition for viewers in multi-channel TV environments (see Chapter 1). It might also indicate that televised news is losing its intrinsic appeal.

There is further evidence that television news often fails to engage effectively with young people. In the UK, up to half of young people aged 16 to 24 years stated that they only follow the news when something important is happening. More critical perhaps was the further finding that between 2006 and 2007 the amount of televised news watched by this age group fell by 50 per cent, from 90 hours to 45 hours a year (Ofcom, 2007c). At the same time the proportion of this age group that perceived televised news to have no relevance to them increased from 44 per cent to 64 per cent during this period (Ofcom, 2007c). What we need to know here is whether these trends represent a generalised alienation from news among young people, a specific concern with the quality of news on television, or the functional displacement of televised news as an information provider by the Internet. These issues will be examined further in this chapter.

The competition that the Internet might pose for television as a news source is considered via a mixture of behavioural and opinion data. How are both platforms perceived by media consumers in respect of their status as news sources? To what extent are these two platforms actively utilised as news sources? Is there any evidence that patterns of news consumption from the major media, and especially from television, have changed as a function of the growing prevalence and prominence of the Internet?

The valued attributes of television news

To set the scene here, it is worth examining evidence that confirms the position that television enjoyed over many decades as a news source. For many years, major surveys of public opinion have indicated that television is regarded by media-consuming publics as their main source for specific types of news. In the United States, for instance, newspapers held sway until the end of the 1950s as the most widely nominated source of world news and in commanding the largest share of the news audience across the major news media. By the early 1960s, television had narrowly overtaken print. Over the next two decades, the gap between the two media grew wider in terms of perceived importance and market share, with newspapers in decline while television grew steadily in prominence (Roper, 1983).

Evidence that was interpreted as an indication of functional displacement effects between successive old and new media derived from the progressive shifts in media rated as people's main news sources. In the United States, a majority of people identified newspapers as this source in 1937. By 1945, majority support had shifted to radio. By the early 1970s, television was the pre-eminent medium at least in terms of public opinion about news sources (Basil, 1990).

Similar findings in respect of the perceived importance of television as a source of world news emerged in the United Kingdom. By the early 1970s, television had forged clearly ahead of newspapers as the most widely nominated source of world news (IBA, 1982). It has retained this dominant position to the present day (see Gunter and Svennevig, 1988; Gunter, Sancho-Aldridge and Winstone, 1994; Ofcom, 2007c; Towler,

2003). At the same time, it is important to note that the Internet has attracted growing nominations as a main news source. In the UK, between 2002 and 2006, television nominations were stable with two-thirds of people (65%) nominating the medium as their main news source. Newspapers (15% to 14%) and more especially radio (16% to 11%) witnessed their support fall, while the Internet (2% to 6%) was nominated more often (Ofcom, 2007c). On the basis of these findings, television remains a long way ahead of the Internet when it comes to people's top-of-the-mind nominations of their main news source.

Such data, however, can be difficult to interpret. What does 'main source' really mean? Does it equate, as a measure, with the 'most used' or 'most liked' or 'most trusted' or something else? We do not know for sure. This measure is simply indicative of the medium that jumps to top of the mind when people are asked to nominate a preferred news source. This perception may, of course, be a function of the level of familiarity people have with television news. It could also be a function of other qualities of television as a news provider. Later in this chapter, we will consider other metrics derived from measures of actual or reported media consumption behaviour.

Another limitation of the basic 'main news source' question is that it fails to differentiate between different types of news. Evidence has already been cited to show that when media consumers are asked to distinguish and think separately about local or regional news versus national or international news, the major news media receive varying levels of endorsement as most preferred sources.

Even at the level of opinion about important sources of news, the significance of television as a news source has been found to vary with the type of news. Although perceived by mass publics as the dominant medium for world news, for many years, television lagged behind newspapers in the public's endorsement as a source of local news. By the end of the 1990s, however, even here television finally caught and then overtook print media (Towler, 2003). This lead was held only temporarily, however, and by the middle of the first decade of the twenty-first century, print media again overtook television in the context of being regarded as the main source of local news. This resurgence of newspapers was led by free local publications (Ofcom, 2007c).

Much of the mainstream news on television concerns political matters. In the UK, the medium was voted the principal source of political news (National Consumer Council, 1999). People do not just turn to television for serious news. In fact, many viewers lack any routine interest in serious issues such as politics. Nonetheless, they do have a taste for news which tends often to be linked to their entertainment and leisure-time interests. So they turn to television for the latest information of culture, entertainment and celebrity issues (see Hargreaves and Thomas, 2002).

Further research into public opinion about public service broadcasting in the UK indicated that a majority of viewers rated news as a genre of personal significance (56%) and of importance to society (62%). Another question asked UK viewers to indicate, by giving marks out of ten, how important it was for the public service broadcasting TV channels (BBC1 and 2, ITV1, Channel 4 and Five) to provide news. Over seven in ten viewers gave marks of at least seven out of ten (indicating high importance) to news programmes that are trustworthy (75%), news and factual programmes that can explain things clearly (74%) and good quality regional news programming (72%). These opinions testified to the perceived importance of news on television as far as UK television viewers are concerned (Ofcom, 2007a).

We should not be too surprised by these data supporting the idea that people attach much significance to televised news. The consumption of news has long been identified as one of the primary motivations for watching television – and not just in the UK (see Rubin, 1983). In fact, information acquisition and learning have been endorsed more highly than entertainment seeking out of the different motives people articulate for watching television (Rubin, 1984). The expectation that insightful learning will take place has also surfaced as a reason for watching specific news and current affairs programmes on television (Levy, 1978). Even if television does not always successfully impart information to viewers, they may still feel that they have learned something useful from tuning in to television news broadcasts (Adoni and Cohen, 1978).

Research in the UK has indicated that the most widely endorsed reason for following the news is somewhat unsurprising 'to know what's going on in the world' which was endorsed by seven out of ten TV viewers (70%). Two out of three people (65%) wanted to know more specifically about 'what's going on in the UK'. More than one in two (57%) followed the news 'for personal interest'. Around one in four people regarded the news as serving more specific functional purposes such as providing topics of conversation with friends (27%) or fulfilling a duty or responsibility to keep informed (26%). Around one in five people (19%) tuned in to news for entertainment (Ofcom, 2007b).

Television has also been greatly trusted as a news source. Many years ago it was rated as the most objective news medium (Youman, 1972). It has been identified as the medium people say they turn to first for their news about the world (Stanley and Niemi, 1990). If the same story appears in newspapers and on television, the television version is the one most likely to be trusted (Lee, 1975; Rubin, 1983). Television is regarded as a factually accurate medium (Towler, 2003).

The changing television marketplace, influenced not only by the growth in television channels but also by competition from the Internet, has found catering to all these information needs increasingly difficult. The production of high quality news is costly. With diminishing advertising budgets, many commercial television companies have found it increasingly difficult to cover all kinds of news. Those that operate under public service broadcasting constraints have found that providing local and regional news is a loss-making activity and have sought to withdraw from such provision (Ofcom, 2009d).

Television versus the Internet

The Internet has emerged as an increasingly important news and information source. In fact, it has been identified as the fastest growing new news source (Ofcom, 2007c). It has the capacity to provide large quantities of information in a variety of different formats. This can also be done relatively cheaply. Major news organisations, including national and regional newspapers, radio stations and television companies, now produce news routinely for online distribution and operate news websites.

The Internet has become established as a primary information source across a wide range of information domains (Gunter et al., 2003). Furthermore, the technology associated with the Internet has empowered citizens and consumers not only through the facilitation of access to an unprecedented quantity of information, but also by allowing them to become information producers and publishers in their own right (Gunter et al., 2009). This has extended the range of sources of information and broken down the divide between producers and audiences. Audiences have become producers and producers have become audiences. Increasingly, those who operate as information producers in the online world occupy different roles at different times as information creators, packaging agents, distributors and recipients.

The Internet has therefore conditioned new styles of engagement with media in the context of information gathering. To what extent does this mean that television – as an information source – must also evolve in the future? Must television emulate the Internet in the way it provides information to its audiences? Already major broadcasters engage with the online world and maintain websites through which they channel large amounts of information. These sites also represent the front-ends to large information archives that visitors can interrogate. News makers are now trained to produce news stories for different platforms. In this rapidly changing news environment, will traditional forms of television news provision survive?

Importance of different information sources

One proposition is that the Internet poses a serious threat to other media news sources. This position was reinforced by observations that young people were not attracted to newspapers but even in its early days regarded the Internet as a more fashionable medium to turn to (Nicholas et al., 1997). In particular, one claim is that as the online news market has matured, it has begun to displace news consumption from other major media such as newspapers, radio and television (Dimmick, Chen and Li, 2004). A different position, in contrast, is that this displacement viewpoint has been overstated and that there is only limited evidence that the Internet is making inroads on the market shares for news consumption of other media suppliers of news (Alexander and Cunningham, 2007).

Earlier in this chapter, the evidence reviewed that showed that people perceive television to be their 'main source' or most 'important' source of news is a somewhat blunt measure. It may not actually indicate which news source is the one from which people get most of their information, regardless of the type of news (see Gunter, 1987; Levy and Robinson, 1986). Ultimately, the most important source is likely to be the one that is used most often. Furthermore, in the rapidly evolving media environment, the traditional divisions between 'media' such as television, radio, and newspapers have been diluted as all three 'media' have migrated onto the Internet where they compete on the same communications platform. On the Internet, the most used news websites in the UK were found to be those associated with major offline news organisations such as the BBC and the *Guardian* newspaper. In addition, new suppliers that have emerged with the online world (e.g., AOL News, Google News, Yahoo! News) have also attained dominant positions (Ofcom, 2007c). News brands associated with search engines do not produce their own news; they merely aggregate it from other news websites.

To continue our analysis of whether the Internet poses serious competition to television in the context of information provision, we need to review relevant evidence on public perceptions of the importance of these two alongside other media sources of information. Much of the attention in the context of perceptions of the value attached to different information sources is focused on news. There are other types of information, of course, that people seek out and in relation to which the use of the Internet has become increasingly prominent. Given the significance of news as a primary function of television, and in particular for television channels in the UK that have public service broadcasting responsibilities, this is the information type that will be examined here.

Findahl (2008) presented findings from a World Internet Institute study that found that the Internet finished in fifth place in terms of its perceived importance as a source of information to people in general, behind friends and family, television, newspapers, and radio. Among 18- to 29-year-olds, however, it was rated ahead of television, newspapers and radio. Such opinions, however, vary from country to country. Despite the diversity of news media now available to them, Canadians still voted TV as their number one news medium ahead of newspapers, radio and the Internet. In response to a question that asked about their primary news source, 48 per cent said TV, 21 per cent newspapers, 15 per cent radio and 14 per cent the Internet (Friends of Canadian Broadcasting, 2009).

Despite the rapidly evolving media landscape, UK media consumers overwhelmingly nominated the main five television channels (90%) as being among their primary news sources (Ofcom, 2007a, 2007b). Newspapers (endorsed by 67%) fell a large distance behind in second position. The Internet finished in sixth place (endorsed by 27%) behind radio (52%), 24-hour news channels in English (36%), and word of mouth/face-to-face conversations with other people (29%). There were marked age differences in the extent to which the Internet was endorsed, with media consumers aged between 16 and 44 years (37%) being far more likely to do so than those aged 45 to 64 years (23%) or aged 65 and over (5%).

The importance of different news sources can vary with the type of news information people seek. It has already been observed that while television has been the dominant medium for international and national news, in the context of local and regional news, newspapers often finish ahead (Gunter et al., 1994; Towler, 2003). When UK media consumers were asked about the sources they used 'regularly' for *local* news, local free newspapers (46%) narrowly edged television (45%) out of top spot, with local paid-for newspapers (41%) not far behind in third position. The Internet (endorsed by 8%) finished in seventh place behind radio (28%), word of mouth (21%) and national newspapers (9%) (Ofcom, 2007b). Here, though, there is conflicting evidence.

In another UK survey that asked adults from across the country to name their most common source of national news and of local or regional news, television was most widely endorsed throughout. While a smaller proportion of respondents named television as their most popular local/regional news source (72%) than as their most common source of national news (85%), newspapers were nominated far less often in relation to both news categories (28% and 26% respectively). The Internet was nominated by much smaller percentages of respondents in the case of national news (22%) and local/regional news (10%). Even so, the Internet received wider endorsement in this survey than in the Ofcom research cited above (Hamlyn, Mindel and McGinigal, 2009).

Another relevant study was conducted in Singapore that involved interviews with 13-year-olds about their use of the Internet and other media (Lee and Kuo, 2002). In this interview, they were specifically invited to say how important they rated different media as information sources. The Internet increased significantly over time in terms of its perceived importance as an information source. TV and radio also improved on this dimension, while newspapers did not change. Increased importance of the Internet also predicted increased importance of TV and of newspapers, but not of radio.

A survey conducted by the Pew Institute in the United States found that television was still being nominated more often than any other medium as the primary source of political information (Moskalyuk, 2004). When asked about their main source of political campaign news, respondents answered TV (78%), newspapers (38%), radio (16%), Internet (15%) and magazines (4%). People in broadband homes were more likely to nominate the Internet as their main source of campaign news (31%). In these homes, the Internet surpassed newspapers (35%) and radio (15%) as a primary source of campaign news. Another interesting phenomenon was noted. Political news sites not aligned or associated with mainstream news organisations had grown in popularity. These sites were used by one in four (24%) broadband Internet users. This equalled the proportion who said they visited websites of major news organisations (24%).

Towards the end of the first decade of the twenty-first century, however, evidence began to emerge that the Internet was being nominated in some parts of the world more often than other media as an important source of news and information. In a survey by We Media/Zogby Interactive with a national US sample of nearly 2,000 respondents, it was reported that more Americans nominated the Internet as their top source of news (48%) than chose television (29%).

In a subsequent simple test of preference, Zogby Interactive asked a sample of more than 3,000 adults in the USA which they would choose if they were allowed only one source of news. More than half of these respondents (51%) chose the Internet and just over one in five (21%) chose television (Reuters, 2009). This finding, however, may give a simplistic view of public opinion about news sources. Other findings nonetheless reinforced this initial forced preference, with more respondents nominating the Internet (40%) than television (17%) as the most reliable source of news.

One further note of caution with these polls is that they were conducted online which means that their samples were drawn from a universe of existing Internet users rather than from people in general (non-users as well as users of the Internet). These samples may therefore have already held an inherent bias towards the Internet as an information medium. Despite this caveat, it is clear that among that ever-expanding number of people who are online, a clear gap has opened up between the Internet and TV in terms of the prevalence with which they are chosen as an important news source.

Although the Internet has emerged as an important news source for rapidly growing numbers of people around the world, even in those national markets where online news has become well-established, television remains a widely endorsed primary news source. One of the factors underpinning the staying power of televised news in public opinion is the degree to which it is trusted. Research from the United States has indicated that while more people said they trusted TV as a news source than the Internet, the prevalence of that trust was not as great as it had been in earlier surveys (Rasmussen, 2004; Rasmussen Reports, 2009). One in five (19%) respondents to a national telephone survey expressed uncertainty about which they trusted more between television and the Internet. The question here asked specifically about network TV news. This narrowing of the gap in perceived trustworthiness between these two media was seen to result not simply from a growth in trust in the Internet but also as a consequence of a decline in public faith in the three main TV networks – ABC, CBS, NBC – as news providers.

Rather than accept such findings at face value, however, we must ask whether such simplistic questioning is comparing 'like' with 'like'. The Internet cannot be regarded as a comparable medium to television in this context. The Internet is a platform that provides multi-modal news coverage from a wide range of sources, including the TV networks. Furthermore, as we have seen, some of the biggest and most popularly used online news sources are associated with the best known offline news brands, including leading broadcasters and newspapers that now maintain a web presence. As such, even if offline new suppliers concede news consumers to online news sources, they may often end up competing with themselves.

Given the complexity of the news media landscape today, it is probably more useful to ask people about their opinions concerning specific, named news sources rather than to attempt to measure their attitudes towards a medium as a whole. The latter type of questions would have had more meaning in the pre-Internet media era with far fewer news suppliers and when TV comprised a relatively small number of channels.

What has also emerged, even at a news supplier type or brand level, is that news source preferences can vary between news topics. This observation extends beyond past findings that have shown that while television is nominated by most people as their main information source for world news, they tend to prefer newspapers for their local news. The Internet has established bigger fan bases than television for some categories of news. A survey by Burst Media of more than 2,200 adults aged 18+ in the USA found that 36 per cent of men and 33 per cent of women named the Internet as their top source of sports news and information. The second most often endorsed sports new source was local TV programming (24% across men and women) with national TV network news broadcasts in third place (15% overall). Almost half the respondents (49%) said they checked sports scores online (51% of men and 47% of women) and over four in ten (41%) said they read sports news stories online (43% of men and 39% of women) (Hahn, 2009).

The rise of the Internet as a dominant news source within specific categories of news has also been mediated by technology advances as the adoption of broadband technology has increased the information delivery capacity of the Internet. Early adopters of this technology have also displayed more diversified online behaviour patterns, including those linked to the search for information (Gunter et al., 2003, 2004). In the USA, people with broadband connections (31%) were found to be proportionately more likely than respondents in general to say that they used the Internet as their main source of political campaign information. Broadband users (35%) were hardly any more likely to say they used newspapers in this context. However, greater use of the Internet for political news did not necessarily mean that other media were used less. In fact, even when online, those seeking out political information used the websites of major news organisations. One in ten Internet users (11%) also used alternative news sites (Moskalyuk, 2004).

Importance of different news sources: Internet users versus non-users

Internet users and non-users have been found to differ not only in terms of their use of the Internet but also in their preferred information sources. The UCLA Internet Project reported the not surprising finding that Internet users were far more likely than non-users to nominate the Internet as an 'important' or 'extremely important' information source (67% versus 26%). The gap between these two groups in their perceptions of television as an important/extremely important information source was much narrower (53% versus 66%). The gap narrowed still further in respect of newspapers (69% versus 66%) (Cole et al., 2003). The same survey also found that Internet users (52%) were far more likely than non-users (29%) to believe that 'most' information on the Internet is reliable.

Canadian research reported that Internet users were far more likely to rate the Internet as an important information source (scoring it four or five on a five-point scale) than were non-users (62% versus 11%). In contrast, non-users of the Internet (60%) were slightly more likely to rate television as an important information source than were users (56%) (Zamaria Caron and Fletcher, 2005). The same study also found that the perceived importance of the Internet as a source of information varied by age group. Adult Internet users aged 18 to 34 years (56%) were far more likely than those aged 55 and over (30%) to rate the Internet as an 'extremely important' source of information.

The future for television news

Rapid changes in communications technologies have posed both threats and opportunities for news providers. These changes include the growth of digital technologies that have transformed the media landscape allowing the numbers of media providers to grow within existing media (e.g., increased TV channels and radio stations) and via new platforms (e.g., the Internet). Such developments have been seen as having particularly acute implications for television as a news source. In the UK, Ofcom (2007c) commented that high quality news provision from public service broadcasting television channels could be placed under threat following the switch from analogue to digital transmissions. While news represents a cornerstone of public service broadcasting, as the television market opens up with continued growth in multi-channel platforms, more and more of which will become universally available, the cost of news provision under these conditions could render it non-viable. As well as expansion facilitated by digital technology with established television transmission systems such as over-the-air, satellite and cable, the Internet has also emerged as a television and video transmission system.

News about international, national, regional and local items will continue to be important to audiences and the supply of news has grown both on television and through the Internet. News is now available 24 hours a day all week long and niche news channels have emerged with rolling news stories throughout the day. Online news is also available and updated continuously. Within this crowded and diverse news environment, there is a need for the limited duration news of public service broadcast channels to stand out. The Internet has created fresh opportunities for broadcasters who can distribute their news online as well. In the online environment, however, news suppliers that have traditionally operated in distinct news markets, such as newspapers, now compete directly with broadcasters and often present news in the same audio-visual formats.

As in any marketplace that is highly competitive, commodities must stand out to be successful in attracting customers (Dimmick and Rothenbuhler, 1984a, 1984b). This is the situation with news. What makes news on television special? Why would people want to continue consuming news from television, when they can find what they need online? What attributes are important to news consumers when choosing a news supplier?

Another important question that applies to the news marketplace in general is what the wider impact of the dramatic growth of news suppliers in the twenty-first century will be. News has become a global business. To be successful on that scale, substantial resources are needed. Few suppliers are likely to be able to operate successfully on an international scale given the costs associated with doing so. There is already evidence that a few major news agencies have evolved that dominate the provision of breaking news stories across the major news media (Ofcom, 2007a, 2007b, 2007c).

Television remains the medium of choice for most news consumers, while newspaper circulation levels have been in decline. Although viewing of broadcast news on television has also fallen away, this has not happened to anything like the same extent as for newspapers. In the UK, the public service broadcasting channels remain the major news suppliers as broadcast news provision has been dominated by the BBC and ITN with Sky News also becoming established as a key supplier. The public believe in the importance of these channels of news supply, with a clear majority (81%) saying that it is important for public service broadcasting channels to keep news and current affairs programmes (Ofcom, 2009a). In fact, most people (80%) endorsed the view that PSB channels should be obliged to provide regular news. Many others also felt that the BBC (61%), ITV1 (56%) and Channel 4 (51%) should not cut down on their provision of news (Ofcom, 2009a). In contrast, one in four people in the UK (25%) felt there was too much news on PSB channels.

As well as the threat from within the television marketplace, the more significant threat comes from without in the shape of the Internet. In the twenty-first century, news consumers have turned increasingly to online sources for their news. It has already been established that young people, aged 16 to 24 years, are the biggest users of the Internet. The biggest users of the Internet for news, however, are men aged 35 to 49 years (Ofcom, 2009a). The key question here then is to what extent online news is displacing televised news. If it is doing so, while both are received via different technologies, what level of broadcast news erosion can be expected once TV sets are fully integrated with the Internet?

Time devoted to television news

The demise of television news, if such an observation is valid, might also be indicated by the extent to which news consumers spent time with it. In the UK, a reduction has been observed of time spent watching news on the major TV channels (Hargeaves and Thomas, 2002). In addition, Ofcom (2007c) reported that the average number of hours per individual viewer devoted to watching national news on the main five terrestrially broadcast TV channels (BBC1, BBC2, ITV1, Channel 4 and Five) fell from 108.5 hours in 1994 to 94 hours in 2000. In 2001, the year of the 11 September terrorist attacks on the USA, annual news viewing on these channels increased to 103.4 hours. The next year it fell away again to 93.6 hours, before showing marked growth in 2003, the year of the war on Iraq. Over the next three years, however, news viewing on the five main TV channels in the UK exhibited steady decline and reached 90.8 hours by 2006.

More than half of this viewing time was devoted to news programmes on BBC1 (53.1 hours in 2006). In fact, between 2001 and 2006, the amount of time devoted to BBC1's news output held up better than on any of the other four major TV channels. Over this time, Channel 4 lost 12 per cent of its 2001 viewing time (while its weekly news output was unchanged over the same time period), Five lost 23 per cent (with a parallel fall of 31% in weekly news output) and ITV1 (fall of 8% in average weekly news output) and BBC2 (100% increase of weekly news output) both lost 25 per cent, while BBC1 (16% fall in average weekly news output) lost just 2 per cent. These findings reveal a general fall in viewing of news on the longest-established TV channels, except for BBC1. This fall in amount of time spent viewing news on these channels was temporarily halted by major news events in 2001 and 2003, and occurred against a backdrop of sometimes falling or sometimes rising or unchanging news provision on specific channels. BBC1 emerged as a powerful news brand that held on to its viewers in a falling market.

Ofcom (2007c) also reported that audiences for the 24-hour television news channels increased dramatically from 2000. Major news events such as the 11 September 2001 terrorist attacks on New York and Washington, DC, the 2003 Iraq war, the London bombings in 2005 and attempted aircraft bombings in 2006 generated extreme spikes in viewing, but despite these, there was an overall upward trend in use of these new news channels.

News consumption patterns vary between different audience sub-groups. Age is a critical factor with young people conventionally exhibiting the least interest in news. In later life, this position changes and news consumption across different media, but notably on television, increases dramatically. There were substantial differences in amount of time devoted to watching national news programmes on the five major TV networks annually in the UK, increasing progressively with age: 16 to 24s – 33 hours; 25 to 34s – 55 hours; 35 to 44s – 73 hours; 45 to 54s – 102 hours; 55 to 64s – 147 hours; 65+ – 195 hours (Ofcom, 2007c).

What is perhaps most significant in the context of the current analysis is evidence that young adults (aged 16 to 24 years) have shown reduced news consumption across major news media platforms such as television, radio and newspapers, but increased use of the Internet. The average consumption of news from television in general among this age group was around 40 hours a year (45 minutes a week) compared to around double that figure for the wider adult viewing population (Ofcom, 2007c).

Self-report data indicated that whereas the traditional news media exhibited declines in the percentages of people who ever consumed news that turned to those specific media between 2002 and 2006, for the Internet the trend was in the reverse direction. Television fared better than either newspapers or radio in this context. Thus, the percentages of news consumers in the UK who ever used newspapers fell from 78 per cent to 61 per cent, while for radio users it fell from 60 per cent to 44 per cent. The fall for television was much smaller, from a much higher base figure – 92 per cent to 86 per cent. For the Internet, in contrast, the proportion of news consumers who used it as a news source increased from five per cent to ten per cent (Ofcom, 2007c).

These data therefore provide mixed evidence of trends in the use of television as a news source. Overall amounts of watching news on the major public service broadcast TV channels (except for BBC1) have been falling in the early part of the twenty-first century. Other televised news services have gained audiences. The medium in general has therefore been holding its own in the face of growing competition in the news marketplace.

Levels of use of online news

The Internet has emerged as a fast-growing platform for news and other information and contains a vast array of information on almost every conceivable topic. The type of information most sought online is related to travel (Gunter et al., 2003; Dutton and Helsper, 2007). Weather information, sports scores, and information about local events have also tended to feature high on lists of most sought-after information online (Gunter et al., 2003; Dutton and Helsper, 2007).

The Internet has become a widely used source of mainstream news information and some major news publishers moved swiftly to establish an online presence even in the early days of the Internet in a number of developed countries. Research in the United States, based on self-reported use of different media, tracked marked growth in regular use of the Internet as a news source over a ten-year period. In 1998, just two per cent of American adults claimed to use online news three or more days a week. This had increased to 37 per cent by 2008. Over the same period, reports of watching the day before interview (i.e., 'yesterday') nightly network news fell from 42 per cent to 29 per cent and local TV news from 64 per cent to 52 per cent (Pew Research Center, 2008). These data do not demonstrate that televised news was being displaced specifically by online news consumption, though falls in consumption of news on radio and of newspapers over the same time period indicated a general adjustment to the distribution of attention to different news media.

Further US research that invited adults aged 18 and over to report the frequencies with which they used different news suppliers provided comparisons both between media and across age groups in respect of patronage of different news sources (Patterson, 2007). In this case, a distinction was made between 'national TV news' and 'local TV news', with 'Internet-based news' not differentiated any further in terms of the type of supplier. In general, television was more likely to be used 'every day' both in respect of national news and local news than was Internet-based news across teenagers, young adults (18–30 years) and older adults. National television news (57% versus 31%) and local television news (62% versus 33%) were both much more likely to be viewed every day by older adults than by those aged 30 and under. In the case of Internet-based news, however, the extent to which it was used every day hardly varied at all across age groups, with around one in five respondents in each age category claiming to consume Internet news on a daily basis.

With Internet news, though, older adults (54%) were far more likely than young adults (45%) and teenagers (32%) to say they hardly ever or never used Internet news. The latter finding is probably as much explained by the greater overall use of the Internet by younger people than by older people as it is by a clear preference difference for Internet news. The different news appetites of older and younger people became clearly manifest when comparing age differences among those who said they made particular use of the Internet as a news medium in terms of whether they sought out the news online. Older Internet users (55%) were far more likely than young adult users (46%) or teenage users (32%) to display this motivation. Most teenage Internet users (65%) said they caught news online by accident as much as by design (Patterson, 2007).

By 2007, nearly seven in ten UK Internet users (69%) said they sought news information from online sources (Dutton and Helsper, 2007). The latter data were based on self-report estimates of survey respondents. Even so, they were largely corroborated by data from continuous monitoring of online behaviour which showed that searching for news online attained a reach of just over seven in ten UK Internet users (72%) in 2007 (Changing Media, 2007).

Indicators of the proportions of Internet users who seek news at all in the online world tell us only about the potential reach of online news and not about how much it is used. In any analysis of functional displacement of television (in this case as an information source) by the Internet, eventually time-based measures are needed.

The top news websites in terms of user traffic volumes comprise a mixture of established news suppliers (or 'brands') from the offline news world and new online news suppliers. What is apparent, whichever news sites are considered, is that the general trend is one of growth of use. Ofcom (2007d) reported data from 2006 that showed BBC News Online as the most used news website with 5.8 million unique visitors during the month of September alone, a year-on-year increase of 17 per cent. In second place, a long way behind, was Guardian Unlimited with two million unique users for the same month, representing a five per cent year on year growth. From the News International news stable, the Times Online (1.3 million users) and the Sun (one million users) achieved lower user bases, but exhibited much higher year-on-year growth (29% and 55% respectively).

One new phenomenon in the online world is the emergence of so-called 'news aggregators' that collate content from other news sites and re-distribute it. The key players in this market were Yahoo! News (1.9 million users), AOL News (1.7 million users) and Google News (1.5 million users). The services supplied by AOL and Google exhibited marked year on year growth (26% and 22% respectively) while Yahoo!'s service reportedly dropped 6 per cent. The longer-term significance of these sources remains to be seen and will depend upon the quality of users' experiences. These search engines have made sweeping claims about the diversity of their news provision, but the reality may be different with some exhibiting strong dependence on a fairly narrow range of major news producers (Ofcom, 2007e).

The amount of audio-visual news content on the Internet has increased not simply because news broadcasters have established an online presence but also because newspapers, traditionally associated with text-based news supported by still photography in the offline world, have introduced audio and video formats to their online sites.

There has also been a dramatic growth of news blogs through which anyone can become a journalist and news publisher. Whether news blogs that are produced by independently-operating 'citizen journalists' are having a significant impact on the use of mainstream news media remains to be seen, but suggestions that they do have been challenged by Gunter and co-workers (2009).

There is no doubt, however, that the online world presents a more complex news marketplace for television news broadcasters to contend with. Online news derives from major news organisations, with broadcasters and newspapers competing together within the same environment, from news agencies with their own online presence and from the news aggregators, a distinctly online phenomenon. Audio-visual reporting of news has been forecast to grow as broadband Internet penetration becomes more prevalent (Ofcom, 2007e). The opening up of the online market in this way may encourage many other, formerly print-only, news publishers to produce news in video formats.

Receptivity of new news sources

Ofcom (2007b) explored the appetites of media consumers not yet users of specified new technology platforms as news sources for these new information suppliers. In general, around one in five current non-users of mobile devices (18%), interactive television (20%) or the Internet (20%) expressed an interest in receiving news supply services via these technologies. Audio and video news services were slightly more widely welcomed than text-based services via mobile devices (9% versus 6%). On the Internet, news websites (14%) and online video news bulletins (12%) had wider appeal than reading blogs (4%).

In every case, young media consumers were more widely enthusiastic about these developments than older media consumers. Those aged 16 to 24 years were far more likely than those 65+ to show an interest in mobile news services (42% versus 4%), interactive TV services (28% versus 7%) and Internet services (26% versus 5%).

It is difficult to predict the longer-term impact of the Internet on the general provision and consumption of news. It has created a level playing field in terms of access to news audiences and has created an environment in which operators with limited resources can still reach mass news consumer markets. As with any other commodity market, the suppliers that succeed the most will be those that give consumers what they are looking for and do so better than anyone else. Quality of provision is likely to remain a crucial attribute, so the major news brands can therefore still expect to enjoy some advantage even in this crowded and competitive market.

News source displacement

It has been argued that the Internet is displacing other major news media, including newspapers, radio and even television, as many people's preferred news source. We have already seen in this chapter that television has retained its top spot as the most often nominated 'main source' of news about national and international issues. The Internet has demonstrated improved performance on this criterion, but still lags some way behind television. Perceived importance data, however, do not demonstrate whether older news media are being displaced by the Internet as growing numbers of news consumers turn online for their news, but some displacement data have emerged to support the substitutability hypothesis. Strong challenges have also been made to the extreme displacement viewpoint.

As with general displacement research, evidence for news and information-related displacement between the Internet and television derives from self-attribution data as well as from correlations between self-reports of amount of use of the Internet and television. We need to observe caution with any self-report data because of their reliance on the ability of respondents to recall accurately their behavioural histories linked to the use of specific media when they may not at that time of consumption have paid much conscious attention to their behaviour.

Even in the fairly early days of the Internet, evidence emerged from among Internet users that they felt it had reduced the amount of time they spent with older media. One online survey in the USA found that nearly one in four American Internet users (23%) reported watching less television since they started using the Internet. Smaller percentages reported reduced magazine reading (20%), newspaper reading (15%) and radio listening (9%). Not everyone agreed with this perception. Some Internet users even reported using other media *more often*: radio (11%), newspapers (9%), magazines (8%) and TV (7%). Others stated that their use of other media remained unchanged: radio (81%), newspapers (75%), magazines (72%) and TV (70%) (Pastore, 2001).

On occasions, the Internet was used to consume other media. Thus, one in six Internet users (17%) said they 'often' or 'sometimes' listened to Internet-based radio stations and more than two out of five (45%) Internet users said they had read an online newspaper in the past 30 days. This represented a significant proportion of Internet users and clearly indicated the emergence of the Internet as a news channel (Pastore, 2001).

Lee and Leung (2006) stated that reported frequency use of the Internet for news and information was negatively related to reported use of newspapers, but unrelated to reported use of magazines and radio. These media were all designated as 'information media' by the researchers. Although designated as an 'entertainment' medium, television also exhibited a negative relationship with reported frequency of using the Internet for news and information.

Robinson and his colleagues examined data from a Pew Centre survey in the USA that explored relationships between time reportedly spent on the Internet and with other media (Robinson et al., 2000). Survey respondents indicated time spent with each medium via time ranges which were then transposed into single average time scores (e.g., 6 to 9 minutes = 7 minutes). Simple time usage scores were then computed for reported use of each medium 'yesterday'. Data were examined for 1994 through to 1998. Internet use first registered in 1995 increased from an average of four minutes per day to 12 minutes in 1998. The use of television for news fell by two minutes per day between 1994 (41 minutes) and 1998 (39 minutes), though it had reached a low point in 1993 (33 minutes), after which it displayed progressive recovery during a period when the Internet was taking off.

The use of television for entertainment purposes also fell between 1994 (126 minutes) and 1998 (116 minutes), but again reached a low point in 1997 (85 minutes).

When statistical controls were introduced for the gender, age, education and income of respondents no significant or clear-cut relationship emerged between reported use of the Internet and time spent watching television news or television entertainment.

In one of its major annual reviews of 'the state of the news media', the Pew Project for Excellence in Journalism (2006) reported further evidence from the United States (originally collected by Nielsen/Net) that nearly half of online news users (47%) said they spent more time online than the previous year and one in five (20%) said they watched less television. In another survey, originally conducted by Big Research, it was reported that young American adults, aged 18 to 24 years, stated that their use of the Internet had caused them to reduce their television viewing. The same report, however, also noted that not all research evidence was consistent on this Internet news-television news displacement phenomenon. Other studies by the Kaiser Family Foundation and the Centre for the Digital Future at the Annenberg School, University of Southern California, found no indications that television news viewing was adversely affected by the use of the Internet as a news source.

Research from Australia indicated that the relationship between the use of the Internet as a news and information source and the use of other mass media in this context can be more than uni-directional. It is important to take into account differences between people in the value they attach to news seeking (Nguyen and Western, 2006). In this case, one in four surveyed Internet users (25%) claimed to be frequent users of online news. Internet users watched less television in general than did non-Internet users. Among Internet users who sought out news and information, however, consumption of public television was greater than that found among non-Internet users. Internet news consumers watched less commercial television than did non-users of the Internet. In fact, the use of the Internet as a news source predicted viewing of public television even in the presence of multiple statistical controls for a variety of demographic variables and reported use of other media such as commercial television, radio, magazines and newspapers. Thus, it is not invariably the case that using the Internet as a news source specifically displaces the use of television in this context (Nguyen and Western, 2006). This study indicated that people who are motivated to seek out news will do so both online and offline.

Not only has contradictory empirical evidence emerged about whether the Internet is displacing other media such as television and newspapers as news sources, there have also been accusations that some evidence has been misrepresented. Cooper (2006) pointed out that despite the claims of some news broadcasters that the Internet is taking news consumers from them, US survey evidence produced by the Pew Institute for the mid-2000s indicated that traditional news sources were still significantly more likely to be endorsed than the Internet as their single source of news.

Even if general populations of news consumers do not necessarily turn away from older news media such as television in favour of the Internet, it is often argued that the young are doing so. The difficulty with this argument is that it is essential first to establish what interest in news the young display at all. It is well-known that children and teenagers have never been great fans of news, regardless of the medium. Television news broadcasts made especially for children such as the BBC's *Newsround* have drawn a loyal following, but these are exceptions. Nevertheless, as they grow older, disinterested teenagers often become highly motivated news consumers in later life. It is therefore perhaps more important to establish whether or not motivated news consumers are rejecting older news suppliers in favour of newer ones.

It has long been known that young people devote far less time to news consumption than do older people, but that interest in news grows as individuals get older. Comparisons of the amount of time devoted to news consumption among different age groups in the United States between the mid-1990s and mid-2000s found little change. That is specific age groups spent no more and no less time on news consumption each day prior to the widespread use of the Internet than after it had become established (Cooper, 2006).

There is a further issue to unravel in any analysis of news displacement effects between new and old media. Much of the news provided on the Internet derives from the major offline news organisations that have now established widely used websites. In the online news world, the most used and most trusted news sources are the big established news brands from the offline world that have now got an online presence.

Canadian research examined the impact of the Internet on political participation (Veenhof et al., 2008). It was recognised that people today have access to a much wider array of political information sources than ever before (Keown, 2007). The Internet has begun to play an important role in people's lives in this context. People go online to obtain political news and to engage with politicians. Whereas they would once have been restricted to ad hoc meetings with political figures giving speeches locally or door knocking or via local and national newspapers and news broadcasts, the Internet has opened up many other channels of communication between politicians and electorates. Despite concerns that traditional news media may be placed under threat by the Internet, many of these media have also established an online presence. This presence not only attracts users online but may also promote use of their offline news outputs.

Although it has been reported in the United States that the proportions of people who report recent use of news on TV, on radio and in newspapers have fallen, while reported use of online news has climbed, assessments of how much time people spend with different news media (based on their estimates of 'yesterday's' news consumption) indicated stability in consumption of televised news. This was judged to average 31 minutes in 1998 and 30 minutes in 2008. By 2008, an average of nine minutes was estimated to be spent with online news. Of further interest was the finding that overall news consumption across the major news media occupied only slightly more time in 2008 (66 minutes) than in 1998 (65 minutes). There was some slight loss over this time period to radio news (down two minutes) and more so to reading newspapers (down five minutes). In 2008, respondents still elected television as their main source of news and well ahead of the Internet in this respect regardless of time of day: in the morning (66% versus 12%), during the day (44% versus 33%), around dinner hour (88% versus 6%) and late at night (89% versus 12%) (Pew Research Centre, 2008).

News preferences, however, were found to vary in the United States with age. In 1998, television finished comfortably ahead of the Internet as the endorsed main source of daytime news (58% versus 5%). Further, this finding did not vary greatly across age groups. By 2008, a different picture emerged. It was only among people aged 50 to 64 (53% versus 23%) and 65+ (76% versus 6%) that television finished ahead of the Internet. For all other age groups, this pattern was reversed (18 to 24s – 30% versus 51%; 25 to 29s – 26% versus 50%; 30 to 34s – 19% versus 56%; 35 to 49s – 36% versus 37%). This could be explained by the relative availability of television and the Internet as news sources during the daytime for those age groups whose members were likely to be out of home, either at places of study or work, during daytime hours on most days (Pew Research Centre, 2008).

Credibility of offline versus online news

For an overwhelming majority of media consumers it is important that news, wherever it comes from, is accurate and impartial. There have been signs, however, that the public has become a little more relaxed in their attitudes in this context over time. This is particularly true of young media consumers. In the UK, Ofcom (2007b) reported a decline in the proportion of adult media consumers (aged 16+) for whom impartiality was an important attribute of news between 2002 (97%) and 2006 (87%). Among respondents aged 16 to 24 years, this requirement reduced in prevalence by a bigger margin (93% to 73%). There is no conclusive evidence available to explain why such opinion change occurred, but it is possible that the wider choice of news sources and therefore of news 'experiences' has broadened the definition of 'news' for many media consumers and changed their expectations about such content.

Historically the major offline news media have commanded widespread and persistent public trust. Television is the most trusted news medium of all. This is not surprising given the political allegiances that are openly adopted by many newspapers and the legislative requirements placed upon broadcasters in the UK to observe strict codes of impartiality in their news reporting. The public might be caused to doubt whether their trust in even the most trusted television news brands is well placed under exceptional circumstances when a news source is found to have misrepresented issues of significance.

This happened in the case of the BBC in the wake of the Hutton enquiry that was launched to investigate an accusation of inaccurate reporting of the British government's case for the Iraq war in 2003. The BBC's editorial procedures were strongly criticised by this enquiry and the Chairman and Director General of the BBC resigned over the affair. Public opinion surveys carried out during this enquiry indicated that ordinary citizens were concerned that the BBC had made errors and that changes to internal editorial procedures and to the way the Corporation was regulated might be called for. These perceptions, however, were focused very much on the specific incident that had taken place and did not colour wider public opinion about the integrity of the BBC as a news provider (Gunter, 2005b).

If the perceived credibility of news sources represents a critical factor determining patronage by news consumers, any gain in credibility of the Internet over television in this respect could create the conditions for the functional displacement of one medium by the other in the context of news provision. As the Internet emerged as a news platform in the 1990s, it attracted news consumers. In medium by medium comparisons during this period, Internet news failed to command the credibility ratings of the other major news media – television, radio and newspapers (Flanagin and Metzger, 2000; Kiousis, 1999, 2001). In later years, some evidence emerged that this position was changing and the Internet, classed as a single news medium, began to challenge the other media in the credibility stakes (Online News Association, 2002). This observation has not been universally supported. In Canada, when asked to name their most trusted source of news, the largest single perception of respondents in a nationwide survey (42%) named TV, with newspapers in second place (23%), radio third (16%), and the Internet (11%) trailing fourth (Friends of Canadian Broadcasting, 2009). However, when asked to indicate the percentage of TV news they would watch on TV versus online, more than one in five respondents (22%) said they would watch news online. The last finding underlines a point made earlier. Simple comparisons between 'television' and the 'Internet' as news media fail to reflect the reality of the contemporary news environment. The same news is available on television and the Internet as broadcasters pump out more and more of their news content online.

Where the quality of Internet news was challenged in terms of accuracy or impartiality, critical observers gave as their reasons for doing so the relative paucity of fact-checking that might be found in journalism operated by mainstream news media (Bucy, 2003; Sundar, 1999). One American study found that Internet users rated the Internet as highly credible to the same extent as television (Bello Interactive, 2004). Such evaluative perceptions have been found to vary, however, with the specific evaluative term being used. UK media consumers in 2006 were only one-third as likely to say that the Internet, as a news platform, was 'impartial' as television (12% versus 36%). Both media also experienced year-on-year falls in the extent to which they were rated as impartial (Ofcom, 2007b)

The perceived credibility of news media can depend upon the specific events being reported. Evidence of this phenomenon emerged during the 2003 Iraq war. Research in the United States found that whether television or the Internet were rated as the most credible medium in terms of reporting about the war depended upon whether those giving the ratings supported or were opposed to the war. War supporters regarded television as also being largely supportive of the war and therefore as credible in its war reporting. Opponents to the war rated the Internet as a more reliable source of war news than television or other major news media (Choi, Watt and Lynch, 2006).

One of the issues that characterise any empirical comparisons of the Internet with other media as quality news sources is the questionable presumption that is invariably made in this research that the Internet represents a single 'medium'. It might be more accurate to consider the Internet as a conduit through which news from a range of sources can flow. Significant quantities of the news content available online are provided by mainstream (offline) news organisations. Virtually every major news broadcaster and newspaper has a presence on the World Wide Web. They maintain online versions of their offline outputs and news story content is shared between these different media.

What may be more significant to news consumers in judging the credibility of news outputs is the particular supplier of that content and their reputation in the news production business. This principle can be expected to apply regardless of the medium in which a particular news supplier is operating. One finding that undermines even this observation, however, is that professional journalists have acknowledged that within specific news organisations less attention and less resource are devoted to online news than to offline news. This inevitably means that online news can lack the quality of offline news produced by the same newsroom (Arant and Anderson, 2000).

A further distinguishing characteristic of the Internet as news supplier is that it is accompanied by the tools that allow ordinary news consumers to become news providers or publishers. Ordinary Internet users without any professional training can become 'citizen journalists'. If the outputs of these amateurs are taken into account alongside other professional news outputs, to what extent do they match in terms of the standards of journalism they both observe? There is some concern that amateur online news producers could undermine the overall standing of the profession (Ruggiero, 2004).

If the Internet is regarded as a repository of news rather than as a single news medium, then its reputation as a news source could depend upon the specific online sources news consumers utilise on a regular basis and the reputations of those sources as credible news suppliers. There is evidence from a number of different samples of Internet users that trust in online news is closely associated with the news 'brand' being used (Center for the Digital Future, 2005). Not surprisingly, the brands that are trusted the most are those with established reputations as news suppliers in the offline world (Rainie, Fox and Fallows, 2003).

Importance of news brands

News brands are probably more central to trust in sources than perceptions of different media. The public's trust in news suppliers can vary both in the offline and online worlds. Thus, not every television news broadcaster commands the same degree of trust even though television has consistently been voted as the most important and trusted news medium (Gunter, 2006a). In the online news world, the most trusted news sources tend to be those with established credibility reputations in the offline world (Gunter, 2006a). The gap between the Internet and television in terms of public trust may be narrowing. By 2005, for instance, research among news consumers in the United States found little difference in the extent to which the Internet and television were voted as news sources people could trust most of the time (Consumer Reports Web Watch, 2005). It is difficult to interpret findings such as this, however, because comparisons between media may depend on experiences with specific news 'brands'. As more prominent news brands have a presence in offline and online worlds, one might expect credibility perceptions of the Internet and other media as news sources to become more similar. There is evidence that important distinctions are made by news consumers between online news supplied by known and reputable sources and by unknown, independent sources. The latter command limited trust, while the former may be widely trusted (Center for the Digital Future, 2005).

Trust in news media is related to which news media are used. There is a tendency for people to trust those media they use most often. Even so, there is accompanying evidence that Internet users exhibit more trust in Internet news than television viewers exhibit in televised news (Abdullah et al., 2005).

The importance of news brands has emerged in comparisons of perceptions of the Internet and television as news platforms. Findings reported earlier for the UK indicated that television (36%) was three times as likely as the Internet (12%) to be rated as an impartial information source by British media consumers (Ofcom, 2007b). When the impartiality of branded news sources on television was rated, the gap between television sources and the Internet grew wider. BBC1 was rated as impartial by nearly five times as many people (54%) as the Internet. ITV finished nearly four times ahead (41%). Other television channels such as Channel 4 (19%) and Five (13%) were rated similarly to the Internet in terms of their perceived impartiality.

The latter television versus Internet comparisons are probably questionable, however, and unfair to the Internet. One reason for this is that the Internet is not a single news source but a platform that conveys news from many branded news sources. A more realistic and certainly fairer comparison would have invited media consumers to evaluate news provided by specific news brands both on television and online.

Pinning down media consumers' perceptions about the impartiality of televised news even further, Ofcom (2007b) reported findings from another survey operated by the BBC in which viewers gave their opinions about specific televised news programmes they had watched. Within this more restricted frame of reference, televised news was rated as very or fairly impartial by overwhelming majorities of viewers on BBC1 (92%), ITV (91%), Channel 4 (94%) and Five (89%). These finding demonstrate the importance of creating common frames of reference for survey respondents when measuring their perceptions of the qualities of different news sources. Viewers' ratings of television channels could be based on a variety of different experiences with those channels. They might also be shaped by prejudices associated with particular news brands. By focusing evaluations on specific news outputs, survey respondents' attention is directed towards their immediate content-related experiences rather than a more generic memory of experiences.

Concluding remarks

Television has held on to top spot as the consistently nominated most important source of news for mass publics from the early years of its lifespan. Although challenged by newspapers in respect of local news, for news that has wider significance on a national or international scale, it is to television that people usually say they first turn for the most up-to-date, accurate and believable information (Gunter et al., 1994; Towler, 2003). As the television marketplace has become more crowded, however, evidence started to emerge that its news broadcasts were losing audiences (Hargreaves and Thomas, 2002). Although viewers were still singing its praises in opinion polls, they tuned in less and less to televised news.

As television news experienced audience losses, the Internet steamed ahead with rapid penetration of populations around the world and emerged as a very useful and convenient news source in its own right. It also started to appear in news source opinion polls among the important news sources being nominated by media consumers (Findahl, 2008; Ofcom, 2007b). Whether it was actually displacing television news, however, was thrown open to doubt (Alexander and Cunningham, 2007).

Although there is as yet little evidence of significant market displacement of televised news by news on the Internet, there can be no denying that it has begun to display 'tipping point' levels of endorsement (10–25%) among large survey samples (Moskalyuk, 2004) and even higher levels of endorsement among Internet users (Reuters, 2009).

All is not lost for televised news. It retains high credibility ratings among the public (Gunter, 2005b) while the Internet, as a medium, has not yet captured the same level of public trust (Ofcom, 2007b). At times when major news events break, television is the medium people switch to first (Ofcom, 2007c). Even so, news websites associated with top news brands have experienced significant user growth (Ofcom, 2007d, 2007e). This is perhaps a key point. It is more helpful to examine the use of news in relation to branded suppliers rather than in simple television versus Internet terms. Major news suppliers operate across technology platforms. The biggest brands in the online world tend to be ones that are also the biggest in the offline world. There are some exceptions, but they by no means dominate the news supply and consumption on the Internet.

Functional distinctiveness will often persist between televised news and Internet news to ensure that there is room for both. This may be defined in terms of the nature of news provision, for instance when mainstream news operations in the offline world ignore or play down stories that deserve more attention, leaving Internet sources such as news bloggers to pick up these stories and run with them instead (Allan, 2006). News consumers may also elect to switch to the Internet where they perceive a supply of news to exist that fits better than that available on television with their own news needs or judgements about news credibility (Choi et al., 2006).

The expanded choice of news on the Internet and its ability to provide access to large quantities of regularly updated information from a wide range of sources will enhance its reputation as a news source. The on-demand facility of online news could also strike another nail in the coffin of television channel structures, with even 24-hour news channels unable to provide the flexibility of coverage and reception of the Internet.

The future of television as an entertainment source

Over the years, television has been used by the public for a range of different forms of entertainment. Television entertains through its drama productions, competitions, game and quiz shows, music and variety shows, and talk shows featuring celebrities and public figures and through its talent contests and reality programming featuring members of the public. The provision of entertainment is regularly endorsed by viewers as one of the most important aspects of the medium (Ofcom, 2004, 2009d). Of course the quality of entertainment programming can vary widely. One factor underpinning 'quality' is cost as some productions are much more expensive to produce than others. For high quality drama, large budgets are virtually unavoidable. In an increasingly competitive and fragmented marketplace, the revenues earned by major television broadcasters diminish and this places them under considerable strain in terms of continued provision of entertainment programming at the high-cost end of the production spectrum (Ofcom, 2004).

In a multi-channel television environment in which significant numbers of television channels routinely achieve very small audiences, revenues earned from advertising or sponsorship are also limited. This, in turn, places severe restrictions on the kinds of programmes that can be purchased. Original productions, for most channels, are beyond their financial capabilities, unless they comprise extremely low-budget programmes (Ofcom, 2004, 2008, 2009a).

The emergence of the Internet has opened up a vast new source of entertainment covering a variety of different genres and formats. In addition, new concepts in entertainment production have been tested through this medium. The greater interactivity of the technology has opened up significant new forms of audience engagement in entertainment. These applications include giving viewers opportunities to choose between different programme endings and to determine the directions of new plot lines in dramas. The empowerment of users observed in connection within online news has its own manifestations in the entertainment sphere. The early popularisation of computers among the general public was founded not in formal educational or business applications, but through entertainment via gaming (Gunter, 1998; Laurel, 1993).

Computer games exploded during the 1980s and their prevalence grew still further in the 1990s (Gunter, 1998) while stand-alone games played via portable devices or hooked up to the TV set migrated online after the public adoption of the Internet in the mid-1990s. Individuals could play games that were streamed online either on their own or in competition with many hundreds and even thousands of other players from all around the world. Electronic games evolved into virtual worlds that enticed users by giving them opportunities to become part of the entertainment rather than simply observers of it. While television programmes could draw in their audiences emotionally through cultivating parasocial links to on-screen actors, computer games allowed users to go one step further by becoming actors on-screen themselves. Not only that, but when played online such games could open up opportunities for users to engage directly with other gamers in real time, creating a dynamic unfolding dramatic narrative that could change unpredictably from moment to moment.

The big question that arises out of such developments is whether they pose a threat to traditional forms of televised entertainment. Can these conventional forms of television entertainment survive? If they are to survive must they evolve? If they must evolve, in the face of the new styles of entertainment being adopted by current generations of viewers, in what ways must this happen? Once again, when considering the evidence for consumer preferences between different media and different types of content, it is important to examine carefully the nature of the supporting data. Some evidence is based on consumers' opinions about what types of entertainment they use and like most. Other evidence is based on self-perceived displacement effects of the emergence of a new entertainment source on an older one. Yet further evidence derives from more sophisticated analyses of relationships between reported levels of use of different media.

Perceived importance of different entertainment sources

Audits of entertainment seeking have shown that people living in developed countries have access to a wide range of leisure activities and sources of entertainment. As one UK study showed, many people engage regularly with traditional forms of entertainment such as listening to radio (51%), reading books (47%), newspapers (41%) and magazines (35%) and going to the cinema (21% regularly; 35% occasionally). At the same time many regularly engage with newer online media for leisure and entertainment purposes, including browsing social network sites (34% regularly; 19% occasionally), visiting newspaper websites (24% regularly; 26% occasionally), playing offline games on a PC (21% regularly; 26% occasionally), playing online games on a PC (20% regularly; 21% occasionally), listening to radio streamed online (18% regularly; 26% occasionally), and playing games on their mobile phone (12% regularly; 20% occasionally) (Entertainment Media Research, 2008). Although the new media activities individually were endorsed by fewer people than the old media activities, given the range of new media activities and the likelihood that it would not always be the same people engaging in each of these activities, the overall reach of new media in aggregate is likely to compare with that for old media.

What was also significant was that the new media offered an enormous range of leisure activities that dwarf the opportunities provided via old media. Moreover, among these online activities were many involving audio-visual entertainment content (Entertainment Media Research, 2008). Internet users, regularly or occasionally went online to watch TV programmes (18%) and movies (16%). Thus, not only might new media time displace television with alternative entertainment activities, but also functionally by providing the same content over a different technology platform.

A number of studies have provided data on the importance that people attach to entertainment on television and on that provided via the Internet. Research among viewers in the UK asked respondents to rate the importance of a range of programme genres on television (Ofcom, 2007a). Respondents rated the personal importance of each genre as well as their perceptions of how important each genre was to society. The findings covered opinions about a number of entertainment-oriented programmes. The previous chapter reported findings from the same survey for information-oriented programmes. With the latter genres, there were more prevalent endorsements of the personal importance than of the societal importance of these programmes. With entertainment-oriented programmes, the reverse pattern emerged. In general, endorsement of the societal importance of entertainment-oriented genres was more widespread than indications of personal importance. This was true for films (51% versus 18%), comedy (50% versus 28%), drama

(41% versus 19%), soap operas (40% versus 14%) and sport (41% versus 28%). These findings are interesting for the reversal of opinions about news and entertainment. The tendency to admit to greater personal importance for news than for entertainment signals an inclination to articulate 'worthy' opinions in regard to the types of programmes rated as most important to self as opposed to important to people in general ('others'). This type of finding is illustrative of the 'third person effect' in its consistency with evidence that people tend to deny personal influence in terms of undesirable effects of the media, but acknowledge them in the case of positive media effects. At the same time, 'others' are perceived to be at greater risk of harmful effects than 'self', but less susceptible to socially desirable influences (Paul, Salwen and Dupagne, 2000; Salwen and Dupagne, 1999). Such responses demonstrate a tendency towards self-image protection (Perloff, 2002)

The perceived importance of the Internet for entertainment can vary with the extent to which it is used. Thus, Canadian research has shown that people who average more than seven hours online per week were much more likely to rate the Internet as 'extremely important' as an entertainment source than were those who went online on average less than two hours per week (43% versus 9%). The same research also showed that there were marked age group differences in the importance attached to the Internet as an entertainment provider. Adult Internet users aged 18 to 34 years (43%) were much more likely to regard the Internet as an 'extremely important' entertainment source than were those aged 55 and over (12%). While these data show that the Internet is defined by some of its users as an important entertainment source, the research did not define what was meant by 'entertainment' here. Perhaps also significant in the context of the theme of this book was that Internet users (62%) differed hardly at all from non-users (60%) in the extent to which they rated television as an important source of entertainment (Zamaria et al., 2005).

In Sweden, Findahl (2008) reported that the Internet was rated behind television (highest), newspapers, friends/family and radio as an important source of entertainment, but finished ahead of radio and on equal pegging with newspapers and family/friends among respondents aged 18 to 29 years. Television still held on to top spot even among young adults.

The importance of entertainment provision on television is underlined not simply by public opinion but also by the behaviour of viewers. Multi-channel television packages have eroded the audiences for the longer-established channels in major media markets such as the UK and USA, but entertainment programming continues to thrive. Data for the

UK even show that entertainment genres are major drivers of the successes enjoyed by new channels in multi-channel television environments. Between 2003 and 2008, there was a 21 per cent increase in the viewer hours devoted to entertainment genres. This increase occurred both for the five terrestrial public service broadcasting channels, BBC1, BBC2, ITV1, Channel 4 and Five, as well as for newer channels in multi-channel packages (Ofcom, 2009a).

The significance of entertainment programming on television was further underlined by data showing that it was the only content category that experienced a growth in audience share (+6.5%) in multi-channel television homes in the UK between 2003 and 2008 (Ofcom, 2009a). While the relative fortunes of different channels varied across this period, as did their relative contribution to the overall share of audience achieved by entertainment programmes, the category itself grew stronger over time. The popularity of entertainment programmes on television has also driven a growth in the number of entertainment-oriented television channels. By 2008, there were 39 entertainment channels on UK television, a two-thirds increase on 2003. Numbers of channels in other programme categories also increased during this period, but their audience shares declined (Ofcom, 2009a). Hence, it is not simply a case that entertainment programming audiences have risen with increased supply. Increased supply elsewhere failed to produce the same impact on audiences, which indicates that entertainment content has intrinsic appeal which has grown stronger even in an increasingly crowded media environment.

The Internet as an entertainment source

Some observed trends in the use of online sources of 'entertainment', if they can be verified, could have significant implications for the future role of television as an entertainment medium. Changing Media (2007) noted three particularly interesting trends in this context: a growing taste for more dynamic forms of entertainment available on demand; increased engagement with user-generated content; and finally a demand for broadcast content to be made available online. Research among Internet users has identified the most prevalent (and presumably popular) forms of online entertainment as music downloading, playing games, listening to radio online, and downloading videos. Men have been found to engage in these online activities more often than women. These interactive online behaviours are more prevalent among younger than older Internet users (Dutton and Helsper, 2007).

Video viewing online

The Internet can provide users with a variety of forms of dynamic audio-visual entertainment. These include online games (including gambling) that sometimes take place in virtual environments, music videos, and online movies and television services. Clearly any online entertainment activity that involves video content must be regarded as a potential competitor to television. How serious a threat this phenomenon might pose to conventional viewing via TV sets depends upon whether the video content is the property of mainstream television broadcasters or derives from a different supplier. The risk to mainstream television consumption also depends upon how attractive the online viewing options are rated alongside regular television viewing.

If Internet video entertainment services cater to different needs and gratifications among media consumers, they may represent a niche that is distinct from conventional television viewing. There could then be space for both types of entertainment platform with displacement occurring only if preferred times of day for consumption for each platform display a significant degree of overlap. If online video entertainment caters to the same needs and gratifications as regular television and does so more effectively or in a more appealing fashion, then media consumers may prefer the online option for their entertainment regardless of time of day when entertainment consumption usually occurs. The latter scenario could pose a greater threat to conventional television.

Research into the use of video entertainment formats on the Internet has indicated that online media consumers seek out both traditional and newer forms of content (Simply/Work, 2008). Traditional television and movie content is available online and is widely utilised. In addition, Internet users seek out video content that derives from a producer base other than mainstream broadcasters or film producers. Popular sites such as YouTube provide access predominantly to user-generated content. Although video material originally made for television or the cinema is available via this site, most of its content derives from the work of independent, amateur producers.

Thus, some online video users seek out short-form video clips which they will watch while doing other things. Others report using online video content in a more precise functional way often connected to information gathering on topics of special interest. Yet others engage in long-form video viewing and go online to catch-up with programmes they missed when initially broadcast on television (Simply/Work, 2008).

In the latter case, the personal computer takes on the role of a TV. Despite the informational utility of online video content, qualitative research has indicated that it frequently has an entertainment function. Moreover, long-form viewing reportedly frequently took place at the same times as regular broadcast TV viewing which meant that watching programmes on a computer had become an alternative behaviour to watching via a TV set (Simply/Work, 2008).

The significance of the Internet as a source of entertainment has been explored in different ways utilising different methodologies. Much of the evidence that derives from the more academic end of the research spectrum has tended to rely upon the self-reported media behaviours of survey respondents. Some industry-derived research has also utilised this type of evidence. In addition, industry research has tracked levels of real-time offline and online media behaviours using more continuous forms of audience measurement.

The self-report evidence has the advantage of yielding data about the use of different media by individual media consumers. Such research can examine directly at the level of the individual how much and in what direction the use of one medium is related to the use of another. The main limitation of this type of research is that it depends upon respondents' self-reports or personal memories of their media behaviour and there is often no way of telling how accurate these reports might be.

Continuous audience measurement is less prone to memory-related errors and in the case of automatic electronic encoding of media consumers' activities, as in the online world, is immune from such errors. At the same time this form of measurement rarely provides an opportunity to determine whether greater use of one medium results directly in reduced use of another.

Self-report measurement of online video viewing

Research conducted by the Pew Internet and American Life Project indicated continued growth in the use of video online, such as YouTube and Google Video, among Internet users in the United States. More than six in ten adult American Internet users (62%) claimed to have watched video on these sites (Madden, 2009). This represented a significant increase on the user level observed at the end of 2006 (33%). Use of these online video sites was especially prevalent among young adults, aged 18 to 29 years (89%). Watching video like YouTube online was more prevalent than use of social networking sites (46% of adult American Internet users).

Jones and Fox (2009) reported further evidence from the Pew Internet and American Life project concerning the prevalence of online video use that indicated that although still most prevalent among young Internet users, it is a phenomenon that is also catching on among older Internet users. The research distinguished between a number of generations: Generation Y (aged 18 to 32), Generation X (aged 33 to 44), Young Boomers (aged 45 to 54), Older Boomers (aged 55 to 63), Silent Generation (aged 64 to 72), and G. I. Generation (aged 73+). In 2007, Generations Y (38%) and X (31%) were more likely to claim ever to download videos when online than were older generations. What was more significant, however, were the rates of increase in this activity among some of the oldest Internet users. In 2007, nearly one in seven (13%) of G. I. Generation Internet users (aged 73+) reported that they downloaded videos, an increase of one per cent on 2005. Silent Generation Internet users (aged 64–72) exhibited a more marked increased in video downloading over the same period (8% to 13%).

In the UK, data derived from Nielsen NetRatings' continuous online behaviour tracker indicated that the video websites attracting the most online traffic comprised a mixture of established broadcasters and new online suppliers (Changing Media, 2007). YouTube, with 9.4 million visitors logged in September 2007 finished in first place ahead of the BBC (6.7 million users). Other major broadcasters, such as Sky (3.0 million users), ITV and Channel 4 (2.1 million users each) occupied fourth, fifth and sixth positions in the top ten. Google Video, already noted as a favourite among Internet users in the USA, was in seventh position in the UK (with 1.8 million users).

These 'reach' figures of course simply indicate the proportions of Internet users who ever sought out video materials online. If this behaviour is to have any significance in terms of how it might challenge more established video-related viewing behaviour via TV sets, we need to have some idea about the frequency with which it occurs. The Pew research reported that around one in five adult American Internet users in 2009 (19% and up from 6% in 2006) claimed to watch video online at least every day. This proportion was much higher among the 18 to 29s (36%).

Online video use is an active behaviour whereby the people who engage in it do not simply spend their time online seeking out content for themselves; they also share what they find with others. Hence there is a social dimension to online video behaviour. This behaviour exhibited a marked increase in prevalence across all age groups. Young adult Internet users became increasingly likely to engage in video sharing everyday (36% in 2009 compared with 30% in 2008). However, even older Internet users including the 30 to 49s (67%, up from 57% in 2008), 50 to 64s (41%, up from 34% in 2008) and 65+ (27%, up from 19% in 2008) exhibited year-on-year increases in ever engaging in such behaviour (Madden, 2009).

The research also indicated that people go online not just to watch short-form videos mostly produced by amateur film-makers, but also increasingly use the Internet as a platform for watching regular television programmes or movies originally made for the cinema. Between 2007 and 2009, the percentage of adult American Internet users saying they had either streamed or downloaded movies or television shows more than doubled from 16 per cent to 36 per cent. Perhaps an even more significant development, although restricted to a small proportion of Internet users overall (8%), was that among those who said they had viewed or downloaded movies and TV shows online, over one in five (23%) said they had connected their computer to their TV screen so they could view video material from the Internet on their television (Madden, 2009). The importance of this finding is that it indicates that some people are already beginning to take video entertainment obtained online and transfer it for viewing to their regular TV set. This brings online video entertainment into direct competition with watching broadcast TV shows on the same technology platform.

There was also a growing interest detected in mobile video viewing. Around one in seven adult American Internet users watched video on their mobile telephones (14%) in 2009 (up from 10% in 2007). Further, one in five mobile phone users (19%) had recorded video material via their cell phones (Madden, 2009).

Further research published by the Pew Internet and American Life Project (Horrigan, 2009) about broadband Internet adoption confirmed the popularity of online video watching. It also found increased movement from short-form to long-form video viewing. More than one in three adult American Internet users in this survey (35%) said they had watched television programmes or movies online. There was a distinctive age variance in this behaviour, with watching of full-length movies or TV shows online being most prevalent among the 18 to 29s (61%), followed by the 30 to 49s (32%), then the 50 to 64s (22%) and finally the 65+ (11%). These findings indicated that this behaviour is now widely established among young adults who may then carry it through into their older years.

Horrigan (2009) also reported that one in five American adults he surveyed (22%) said they had cut back on cable or other TV services in the previous 12 months, while far fewer (9%) said they had cut back on their Internet services. Among those who had cut back on television services, a significant minority (32%) had connected their computer to their TV set to be able to watch downloaded video material on their main television screen. The behavioural prevalence here is well beyond the 'tipping point' range (10–25%).

Rose and Roisin (2001) conducted research to find out about Internet users who engaged in video and audio streaming. The more frequent 'streamies' were most likely to report enjoying this form of entertainment. For many of these online users, however, there was far from unqualified praise for the content received. Among all those who engaged in audio streaming, one in four (26%) said they really liked it, while more than half (58%) thought it was just OK. Among those who engaged in audio streaming monthly, more than one in three (36%) really liked it and the same was true of more than four in ten (44%) of those who engaged in this activity at least once a week. For most of the respondents in this survey, audio streaming (56%) and video streaming (65%) were enjoyed because they were seen as 'new and fresh'.

Although there was still fairly widespread support for standard channels with pre-determined programme schedules (46% of 'streamies') almost as many (44%) preferred even more widespread streaming among young 'streamies' aged 18 to 24 years (52%) and teenagers (59%). These findings indicated that the use of these dynamic online services seemed to condition a preference among media consumers for more personal control over the content received (Rose and Roisin, 2001).

Further confirmation of the growing importance to media consumers of personal choice derived from findings that some video streamers said they were sufficiently interested to be willing to pay a small subscription to watch specific types of content such as music concerts (19% willing to pay for this), major American league football games (11%), programmes too risqué for mainstream television (7%) and various other sports events (6–7%).

Rose and Roisin (2001) also reported opinions among their respondents concerning video streaming and video game playing. The more consumers used streaming media the more likely they were to be frequent video game players. Twenty-one per cent of Americans (aged 12+) in this survey said they played video games at least once a week; 25 per cent of web users played video games weekly, with this percentage growing among those who had ever engaged in audio or video streaming (31%), and those who had audio or video streamed in the past week (38%).

A survey of more than 1,800 American respondents aged 12+ by Magid Media Futures™ in 2007 found that daily use of online video content rose by 56 per cent in one year. At the time of the survey, one in seven Internet users (14%) reported that they watched online video every day, compared with nine per cent making this claim a year earlier. Even more significant, perhaps, was the finding that a much bigger percentage of 18- to 24-year-olds (35%) made this claim which indicated that this type of online behaviour has become widely established among young adult Internet users. Online video viewers consume a variety of types of content, with news, weather, movie previews and comedy material being among the most popular (*www.redorbit.com*, 2007).

Research among American teenagers provided further confirmation of the growing popularity of online video-related activities (Horowitz Associates Inc, 2009). On the evidence provided here these teenagers were widely engaged in creative activities online as well as being passive recipients of video content. A clear majority of those aged 15 to 17 years (71%) listened to music online and one in two (50%) said they viewed videos created by other people on sites such as YouTube on at least a weekly basis. Over one in three (37%) teenage Internet users said they uploaded video content they had made themselves. A similar proportion (35%) said they watched movies online and over one in four (27%) reportedly watched television programmes online at least once a week.

In the context of displacement, industry research from the United States has indicated that standard television viewing and online video viewing can both be accommodated by media consumers for two main reasons. First, they have different peak viewing times during the day and therefore may not physically impede each other. Second, there is evidence that many media consumers can and do carry out both activities simultaneously.

One survey by Interpret LLC that was carried out for a consortium of major media companies obtained data from more than 2,000 broadband Internet users aged 13 to 54 years who had reportedly watched a video online in the previous 24 hours (Marketing Charts, 2009a, 2009b). Most television consumption occurred between 8 p.m. and 11 p.m. The biggest spikes in online video consumption occurred between noon and 3 p.m. and between 9 p.m. and 1 a.m. The lowest level of online video consumption occurred between 6 p.m. and 9 p.m. Although there was some overlap between peak times for television viewing and online video viewing, it was not complete. In the evening, media consumers seemed mostly to turn first to television. Online video viewing then climbed later in the evening when television viewing would normally be expected to tail off (after 11 p.m.).

Another survey sponsored by *blinkx* revealed some additional interesting television online video viewing habits. This online survey collected data in February 2008 from nearly 2,500 respondents aged 18 and over in the United States and found little evidence for a simple displacement effect between use of the Internet and television viewing (*blinkx*, 2008). Many respondents were found to use both the Internet and television and many did so at the same time. These media consumers were labelled as 'double dippers'. The survey, representing the general American Internet-using population, reported that three in four online-active US adults (78%) reportedly went online while watching television. More than one in three online adults reportedly engaged in this simultaneous use of the Internet and television 'often' or 'always'. More than six in ten (62%) 'double dippers' surfed the web for content not related to the programme they were watching at the same time. Others surfed for programme-related content and among these, the content searched tended to be about the actors in the programme they were watching (51%), information about products advertised in the programme, or related upcoming events (39%).

Continuous measurement of online video viewing

The media industries have for many years conducted well-resourced audience research exercises designed to provide continuous flows of data about the behaviour of their audiences. In television audience research, set-meter systems have formed the backbone of such research, coupled with viewers' reports of their physical presence in front of a TV set. The latter are also captured electronically in modern measurement systems. Online behaviour is tracked electronically and the major search engines continuously monitor the online traffic flowing through their systems. Commercial research agencies, often engaged in audience measurement in other media sectors, have also established industry-approved measurement systems for monitoring Internet traffic. Tracking research studies have reported on the comparative sizes of audiences for television, for the Internet and for watching online video content. These studies have also measured the amounts of time devoted to these media by their users.

Research from the United States by Nielsen reported increased use of the Internet and significant audiences for online video content in 2008. At the same time, there was no indication that audiences for television or the average amount of time viewers spent with the medium were falling away (Albrecht, 2009). In the fourth quarter of 2008, more than 285 million people (aged two and over) watched any television per month. This figure compared with 281 million a year earlier. There was a significant upward shift (of 37%) in the numbers of viewers each month that watched time-shifted programming (nearly 74 million). During this period, the monthly reach of the Internet was nearly 162 million people in the US (aged two and over), and a figure of over 123 million specifically in respect of watching video on the Internet (Albrecht, 2009).

If displacement of television by the Internet is occurring, one sign of this might be that less time is being devoted to television viewing, while more time is being commanded by online activities. The same research from the US indicated that the average amount of time spent online by Internet users (aged 2+) per month in the fourth quarter of 2008 was 27 hours and four minutes, an increase of 56 minutes on the year before. Just two hours and 53 minutes, on average, was spent watching online videos. Hence, although the reach figure for online video viewing was a significant proportion (76%) of the total reach of the Internet, the amount of time devoted to online video viewing was, in comparison, a much more modest percentage (11%) of total Internet usage time. What was also important was the finding that the average amount of time spent watching television per month (151 hours and three minutes) represented a year-on-year increase of over five hours. At seven hours and 11 minutes, time spent viewing playback programming viewers had self-recorded also represented a sizeable year-on-year increase (+33%). Hence, although online video viewing, on this evidence, was widespread in the US, it did not appear to be eating into time spent watching television (Albrecht, 2009).

ComScore (2009a) reported data for December 2008 which showed that American Internet users viewed 14.3 billion online videos during that month. This represented a 13 per cent increase on the previous month. This viewing was carried out by 149.5 million unique users. Hence, virtually half the US population had engaged in video viewing that month and watched an average of 96 videos each. This amounted to average viewing of 309 minutes (more than five hours) per online video viewer. In all 98.9 million viewers watched 5.9 billion videos on YouTube (59.2 videos per viewer) and 48.7 million viewers watch 367 million videos on MySpace (7.6 videos per viewer). The duration of the average online video was 3.2 minutes. Hulu.com provided the longest videos that averaged 10.1 minutes each and 24.6 million unique users visited Hulu's site and watched an average of 9.8 videos each (c99 minutes of viewing in one month).

Later, ComScore reported that the total number of online videos viewed in the US for September 2009 was nearly 26 billion

(Marketingprofs.com, 2009). Of these, 10.4 billion were made to Google sites, which mostly meant YouTube; there were 166.2 million unique users of online videos, with each viewer watching an average of 154.4 videos; there were 124.2 million unique users of Google sites, watching an average of 82.7 videos during the month; and Hulu attracted 38.7 million users that month who watched an average of 15.1 videos (one hour and 15 minutes of video per viewer). On average each online video viewer watched 9.8 hours of video per month.

One problem with continuous audience research for online video viewing is that different measurement systems produce dramatically different audience estimates. One online commentator observed, for instance, that Nielsen reported 8.9 million visitors to Hulu in March 2009, while ComScore reported 42 million (Stelter, 2009). Nielsen also reported marked increases in video streams via Hulu across February, March and April 2009, while unique visitors counts dropped over the same period.

NielsenWire (2009) reported data from Nielsen's Three Screen Report that showed that the average American (aged 2+) watched just over 153 hours of live broadcast television every month at home during the first quarter of 2009, an increase of 1.9 per cent on the same period for the year before. The big growth areas here were time-shift viewing and online video viewing. Between the first quarter 2008 and first quarter 2009, there was a 40+ per cent increase in time-shift television viewing (from 5 hours 52 minutes to 8 hours 13 minutes per month). Meanwhile, time spent with the Internet increased by nearly five per cent year on year (to 29 hours 15 minutes per month), and yet time spent by Internet users watching online video jumped dramatically by over 53 per cent, though still at a low base level of three hours per month. Another notable finding was that more time was spent watching video content on a mobile phone than on the Internet by the first quarter 2009 (3 hours 37 minutes per month). Growth data for time spent on this activity were not presented, but usage number data were available and indicated a year-on-year growth in the mobile video user base from 8.8 million per month for the first quarter of 2008 to 13.4 million by the first quarter of 2009.

The average television and Internet usage data reported by NielsenWire (2009) hid a number of significant age differences in consumption of these media. Use of television is linked to age and life stage. Hence, the heaviest use of television was registered among people aged over 65 (210 hours, 52 minutes per month) and then secondly among those aged 45–54 years (175 hours, 42 minutes per month). The latter age group comprises many family households where domestic commitments and financial constraints restrict leisure activities to the home, with television watching being prominent among them. Despite evidence that new media adoption tends to be more widespread among young people (see Gunter, Rowlands and Nicholas, 2009), Nielsen data reported the heaviest Internet use occurred among people aged 35 to 44 (42 hours, 35 minutes per month). In comparison, teenagers aged 12 to 17 (11 hours, 32 minutes per month) and young adults aged 18 to 24 (14 hours, 19 minutes per month) were relatively light users. Young adults aged 18–24 (5 hours, 7 minutes per month) and aged 25 to 34 (4 hours, 32 minutes per month), however, were the heaviest users of online video content. Teens aged 12 to 17 took the lead in respect of watching videos on mobile phones (6 hours, 30 minutes per month).

Further data reported from Nielsen, for October 2009, showed that online video usage in the United States reached 138.6 million unique users who watched 11.2 billion video streams, or an average of 81 per viewer. The average online viewing time achieved was 212.5 minutes per viewer during October 2009, a 23.8 per cent increase on the same period one year earlier. The time spent viewing online video on Facebook jumped by over 1800 per cent year-on-year from 34.9 million minutes in October 2008 to 677 million minutes in October 2009. On average in September 2009, online video viewers spent 195.2 minutes watching video (NielsenWire, 2009).

Crum (2009) reported data for the UK from Comscore Video Metrix showing that between January 2008 and January 2009, the number of unique online video viewers aged 15+ increased from 26.8 million to 29.6 million within one month. This was a jump of 10 per cent. Viewers of YouTube in January 2009 numbered 29.5 million, up 17 per cent from 20 million in January 2008. Audiences for online videos that were shown on BBC websites increased by 18 per cent from 5.7 million to 6.8 million unique viewers. In all, 80.1 per cent of all UK Internet users viewed online video.

In the United Kingdom, a total of 29.6 million online video viewers were logged during one month in January 2009. This represented a 10 per cent year-on-year increase in audience reach (ComScore, 2009b). This viewing figure represented 80 per cent of the total UK Internet audience and, on average, British online video viewers spent 9.5 hours each watching this material. The most widely used sites were those operated by Google (23.7 million users), but virtually all (99%) of this consumption occurred on Google-owned YouTube (25.5 million users). Following some distance behind were sites operated by the BBC (6.8 million users). The biggest year-on-year increase occurred for videos watched on Facebook (+140%).

This dramatic growth in online video watching has been observed elsewhere. Internet audience research in Germany showed an audience reach figure of 28.5 million online video viewers during December 2008, representing a 10 per cent year-on-year increase. German Internet users watched 3.4 billion videos online during this one month, an average of 119 videos per viewer or four videos per day. Given that the average duration of an online video was just over four minutes, however, this did not amount to a significant amount of time per day (Robertson, 2009). Nevertheless, the data indicated a widespread phenomenon. At present it is based largely on viewing of short-form videos. If online viewing behaviour changes, with increased supply of relevant content, to more long-form video watching, then the time occupied by online video could mean that it will become a much bigger competitor to ordinary television viewing.

Online video viewing versus television

There is mounting evidence from a number of different parts of the world that online video viewing has been a key driver of Internet use in the second generation (i.e. Web 2.0) Internet era. As we will see below, much of the evidence derives from commercial research, although some relevant studies have also been published by academic writers. The key question is not just how much do Internet users watch online videos, but whether it displaces their watching of television. Much of the industry-sector research has relied upon self-report evidence of self-attributed changes in viewing habits as a function of using online video.

American research agency Magid Associates published research showing that many consumers reported spending less time with television as they preferred to devote more of their time to web-based activities including social networking and using online video. An overwhelming majority of Internet users (92%) claimed to use their personal computers for entertainment purposes on a weekly basis. Over one in three (35%) said they were watching less television because of this. Among online video viewers, more especially, one in four (25%) said they watched less television since they started using online television replay and repository services such as Hulu. Internet users aged between 12 and 64 years endorsed the Internet (21%) marginally more than television (18%) as their preferred source of entertainment (Emigh, 2008).

Further evidence from the United States indicated that not only is the use of online video widespread among Internet users, it has begun to rival the use of television as a source of entertainment in terms of how much time consumers spend with each medium (The Bridge, 2008). Data reported from ComScore Video Metrix indicated that 77 per cent of American Internet users watched over 10 billion videos online during December 2007. The most widely visited online supplier of video content was Google, whose sites, including YouTube, were used during this one month by 43 per cent of US Internet users.

In the context of how the Internet might compete with television as a source of entertainment were further data reported by The Bridge (2008) from an IBM survey of US consumer digital media and entertainment habits, again from 2007. This survey asked respondents about the amount of time spent each day with the Internet and watching television. Fewer respondents reported less than two hours per day of Internet use (25%) than reported the same amount of television viewing (37%). The percentage of respondents that claimed to use the Internet for between two and six hours a day (59%) outnumbered by a small margin the proportion claiming to watch television (57%) for that amount of time. The most substantial margin of difference, however, occurred at over six hours a day of usage, which was more prevalent in the case of Internet use (26%) than for television viewing (16%). These data do not demonstrate evidence of Internet displacement of television viewing, but they reinforce the idea that the Internet is growing in popularity and in the extent to which it occupies significant portions of people's time each day.

A further finding from the IBM survey that also has important implications for the potential impact of Internet use on television viewing concerned the types of online sources of video content that were used most often. A number of online video sources were mentioned in this context but the ones most widely identified were sites providing user-generated content (39% of online video users) followed by sites operated by television networks (33%), search engines (32%), and social networks (28%). Pay-TV operators were mentioned by a much smaller proportion of online video users (8%). Thus, television companies had some presence in this market as preferred sources, but they were certainly not dominant (The Bridge, 2008).

One year later, IBM conducted another Digital Consumer Survey. This was conducted online in the third quarter of 2008 and covered six countries: Australia, Germany, India, Japan, the UK, and the USA. It achieved 2,800 responses. Three out of four respondents (76%) said they had watched an online video on their personal computer and one in three (32%) said they had done so over a mobile device. A large minority

(45%) claimed to watch online videos on a regular basis. Over half the online video viewers said that they watched less television as a result, with some (15%) saying they watched 'slightly less' and many more (36%) saying they watched 'significantly less' (Around the Net in Online Media, 2008).

Self-reported reductions in television viewing attributed by respondents to their use of online videos were found in research conducted in the UK by the BBC. Online video watching was a minority activity at the time of this survey in 2006, with just over one in five (22%) of the population claiming to do it either regularly or occasionally. Online video viewing was more prevalent among young people aged 16 to 24 years and over one in four (28%) claimed to watch videos online at least once a week. Among this age group, more than four in ten (43%) claimed to watch less television because of their online video viewing (BizAsia, 2006; Slocombe, 2006).

The research commissioned by the BBC also explored what media consumers in the UK thought about how online video viewing might affect their usual television viewing (Nesbitt, 2006). The data here were self-reports of own behaviour or probable future behaviour. One in five respondents (20%) claimed that they watched a lot less normal television as a result of watching video online or via a mobile phone. Twenty-three per cent said they watched a bit less normal TV for this reason. For more than one in two (54%) online video viewing seemed to make no difference to their normal television viewing. A few respondents (3%) claimed that they watched more television because of their online video viewing.

In Hong Kong, Lee and Leung (2006) surveyed Internet users and found that a self-reported proportion of daily media time devoted to using the Internet for entertainment purposes (i.e., web surfing, playing games) was negatively related to the reported proportion of media time each day spent on using television for the same reason. Using the Internet for entertainment was also significantly associated with smaller proportions of media consumption time each day devoted to reading of newspapers and listening to radio.

Not all self-report survey studies have produced evidence of displacement of television viewing by online video viewing. A survey of American Internet users by LRG in 2008 found that reported use of online videos was increasing, but this did not mean for most online video viewers that they also reduced their television viewing (see Albrecht, 2009). One in three respondents to this survey (34%) said they watched online videos on at least a weekly basis. This represented an increase on one year earlier (31%). Only eight per cent of those surveyed who watched online videos strongly agreed that they watched less television; many more (75%) strongly disagreed with this perception. Even among teenagers who were surveyed, far fewer reported strong agreement with a statement that they had reduced their use of television than expressed strong disagreement with this statement (18% versus 61%).

In the UK again, a survey conducted by Deloitte with YouGov questioned more than 2,100 television viewers, who were also Internet users, about video on demand. In the reporting of this research, the findings that were headlined focused on the apparently limited appeal of video on demand (Laughlin, 2009). Although most respondents (83%) were aware of on-demand programme reply sites supplied by the major public service broadcasters (more than were aware of YouTube – 76%), most viewers (69%) claimed to watch television online for less than one hour a day. Nearly three in ten (29%) reportedly also felt there was little importance in having the option to watch television online. Further, over half the respondents (53%) could not apparently be persuaded to watch more television online even with faster broadband speeds. There were other findings, however, that did signal that online video material could represent a significant alternative to ordinary television watching. Among those who did access television over the Internet, a clear majority (71%) did so to watch catch-up programmes they missed on main television. Thus, although online television is a supplement to conventional television viewing, it does represent a type of long-form online video viewing and a type of television viewing that takes place in 'on-demand' mode. As such it can be seen as representing an activity that could condition an alternative orientation towards television viewing and a movement from short-form to long-form video consumption online.

Research evidence has emerged elsewhere to indicate that although media consumers are turning increasingly to the Internet and report that going online occupies as much of their time as watching television, the Internet is used by many as an alternative television viewing platform. Marketing Charts (2007) reported on an IBM Institute for Business Value survey of 2,400+ households in the United States, United Kingdom, Germany, Japan and Australia. One in five respondents (20%) reported spending 6+ hours a day on personal Internet usage versus just under one in ten (9%) saying they spent this much time watching television. In all, two-thirds (66%) reported viewing 1–4 hours of television per day with six in ten (60%) reporting the same levels of personal Internet usage.

In the USA, a far larger percentage of respondents to this survey said they devoted six or more hours per day to the Internet (26%) than said the same of television (16%). Most respondents said they spent between one and four hours a day with each medium (54% for the Internet and 58% for television). The most popular websites visited by those who went online tended to have video content. Most frequently mentioned of all were YouTube (39%) and sites operated by the major television networks (33%).

Video game playing

We have already seen that video game playing is a widely popular activity and represents a form of video-based entertainment. Research conducted in the United States by the Pew Institute has found that over one in two Americans aged 18 years and over (53%) reportedly played video games, and one in five (21%) reportedly played these games every day or almost every day (Lenhart, Jones, and Macgill, 2008b). We saw earlier that virtually all American teenagers were found to play these games (Lenhart et al., 2008a). Video game playing was found to be far more prevalent among the 18 to 29s (81%) and 30 to 49s (60%) than among the 50 to 64s (40%) and 65+ (23%).

Video game playing also occupies time, though the Pew research did not report on how much time average adult players devote to this pastime. However, nearly one in two gamers (49%) reported playing games at least a few times a week (Lenhart et al., 2008b). This distribution held for nearly all age groups. The surprising finding was that it was the oldest game players (aged 65+) who were proportionately the most likely to play at least a few times a week (64%).

Pew researchers have also reported that for American teenagers online game playing is a major attraction (Jones and Fox, 2009). For teenage Internet users game playing is their favourite online activity with wider reported use (78%) than e-mail (71%).

Noting the prevalence of computer or video game playing alone does not provide direct evidence that television viewing is being displaced by it, whether it takes place online or offline. One study that did examine inter-relationships between the use of these media and time devoted to a range of other physical and activities among Canadian teenagers found that use of computer/video games was negatively related to watching television (Mannell, Zuzanek and Aronson, 2005). This study used an experience sampling method in which teenage respondents kept a time-use diary which they completed each time they were beeped via a radio pager that they carried around with them all the time. Overall, across the sample of more than 2,100 12 to 19 year-olds, more time was spent watching television or videos (29% of time accounted for) than with computer or video gaming (6% of time) or surfing the Internet (5% of time). However, the greater the amount of time that was devoted to computer/video gaming, the less time was spent watching television or videos.

Concluding remarks

Television remains an important source of entertainment for its users and they regard entertainment programmes as a cornerstone of the medium's content provision. Entertainment in this context covers a number of programme genres ranging from various forms of drama made for television, televised movies, comedy, game and quiz shows, music, talent contests, talk and variety. In addition, the popularity of the Internet has also been driven by the entertainment-related gratifications its users derive from its content and online services.

In direct comparisons, television continues to be rated ahead of the Internet as an entertainment source among samples drawn from general national populations, but opinions on this point can vary between different sub-groups in societies where the Internet is now widely established.

One key factor that has opened up the media entertainment market is that the overall amount of entertainment content has grown significantly over time during the Internet era. This growth has occurred on television as well as online. The portfolio of entertainment programming transmitted via television has expanded both with the growth in numbers of television channels and with bigger provision via older-established channels (Ofcom, 2009a). The amount and consumption of video entertainment available via the Internet has also grown exponentially in the twenty-first century (Changing Media, 2007; Horrigan, 2009; Madden, 2007). Online entertainment content is especially popular among teenagers and young adults (Horowitz Associates Inc., 2009; Rose and Roisin, 2001).

The diversity of entertainment forms has also expanded during this period as there have been substantial increases in the total amount of interactive forms of entertainment available to media consumers both online and offline. The latter include more entertainment programmes on television with which viewers can get involved and take part at home via telephone and Internet links and a wide variety of video games played live online or offline via stand-alone consoles or television sets.

Online tracking research has indicated that more people are spending more time consuming more video content via the Internet (ComScore, 2009a, 2009b; NielsenWire, 2009). In general, however, there are no signs that the dramatic acceleration of online entertainment consumption has resulted in any decline in time devoted to conventional television viewing (Albrecht, 2009; Armstrong, 2008). One reason for this, however, could be that most online video watching has involved short-form video content with the average video duration lasting no more than a few minutes (ComScore, 2009a, 2009b). Thus, in spite of the impressive numbers of downloads (Crum, 2009), on aggregate they occupy fairly limited amounts of time out of media consumers' monthly media-related time budgets (Marketingprofs.com, 2009). As media consumers move towards watching long-form video content online, this position could change dramatically.

It is important, therefore, to continue to monitor online and offline media developments. The fact that Internet use has followed an upward track while television viewing has remained largely unchanged at the macro levels measured by industry audience trackers is not in itself evidence on non-displacement of television by the Internet. The reason for this conclusion is that such macro-level data do not differentiate between heavy and light users of the Internet to determine whether the former exhibit greater reductions in their television viewing that can be directly attributed to their time spent online. To know this, measurement of media habits at the level of the individual is necessary.

At the same time, it is also advisable to treat with caution self-report data from surveys in which their respondents have been invited to provide personal impressions about the influence of their use of the Internet on their television viewing. Such evidence of television's displacement by the Internet could be based on problematic estimates. Although these surveys satisfy the condition of providing individual media consumer level accounts of media habits, they tend to obtain simplistic data from respondents about their allocation of time to different media that may not represent accurate indicators of that behaviour. Research that has compared self-report television viewing frequency data with direct observations of viewing behaviour over the specified time periods has confirmed that self-reports of television-related behaviour are often wrong (Allen, 1965; Anderson et al., 1985; Bechtel, Achelpohl and Akers, 1972).

Despite these caveats evidence has started to emerge that when continuous and direct measures of media behaviour are applied at the level of individuals, those who report more time spent with video games also reveal less time spent with television (Mannell et al., 2005). Whether this finding signals a warning to conventional television broadcasters, however, depends upon how they respond to change. More video content is appearing on the Internet, but as we will see in the next chapter, mainstream broadcasters are among the perpetrators rather than simply being victims of this development. Moreover, broadcasters in the offline world are contributing long-form video content that occupies more of a media consumer's time. Further, well-known broadcasters have the advantage of brand strength that could help them to stand out in a crowded online media marketplace.

It is possible, however, that the widespread adoption of online video entertainment formats will bring about changes that signal the demise of conventional styles of television viewing. The key changes we might envisage here include the preference for on-demand services for standard viewing and for greater levels of direct involvement with content on screen. The final chapter explores these issues by presenting an overview of the key technological changes to television and the Internet and the functional and behavioural implications they have for television in the future.

6

Future audiences, future services

As communications technologies continue to evolve, so will the ways that users engage with them. If online technologies are conditioning new mindsets in relation to content access and utility, will television have to evolve to engage with fresh public expectations that arise out of new cognitive models of dealing with entertainment and information content? Already, television services have migrated onto the wired and wireless Internet. In addition, television sets are becoming more computerised allowing for the more advanced interactive functionality of the kind more closely associated with Internet access. In essence these distinctive technologies will eventually merge in terms of their functionality so that they all – television sets, personal computers, games consoles, mobile phones – perform the same functions and permit access to similar ranges of applications and content. In a world in which users can switch seamlessly via their television sets between programmes, movies, websites, virtual reality environments, and social networks, for instance, what future might there then be for traditional television broadcast services? This chapter will consider these issues and examine relevant data on consumer behaviour in multi-application technology environments.

Television is moving through a period of unprecedented change Government, media regulators, media organisations and media commentators have engaged in vigorous debate about the future of television. Between 2008 and 2012 in a rolling programme around the UK, the analogue television signal will gradually be switched off and replaced by digital television broadcasting. The public will have no choice here.

In this setting, questions have been asked in particular about the future of traditional television services. Much public debate has centred on the future of public service broadcasting (PSB) services. Arguments have been made for ensuring that public service oriented television channels, such as BBC1, BBC2, ITV1, Channel 4 and Five, should continue to enjoy protected status. Protection of the BBC channels tends to be regarded as paramount because these are non-commercial programme providers funded out of the public purse. There are questions being asked about whether the BBC should be granted such privileged status unilaterally or whether a future public service broadcasting model should have an in-built competitive element whereby any protected funded channel should be open to competition to programme makers from outside the BBC as well (DCMS, 2006).

For the commercial PSB channels (ITV1, Channel 4 and Five) there are questions about whether they represent feasible business models in an increasingly competitive television environment given the PSB constraints placed upon them (Ofcom, 2008). Can these channels continue to meet their PSB obligations while remaining competitive? We have already seen that PSB channels have experienced significant erosion of their market shares in the face of competition from the multitude of channels now available on multi-channel platforms. It is not simply the increasingly crowded television marketplace – with the progressive penetration of multi-channel TV packages – that is causing these channels problems, however, but the threat of the Internet as well.

The role played by the Internet as an alternative supplier of television services is being promoted by government and by the broadcasters themselves. Within the PSB context, one area that has been identified for the relaxation of PSB obligations is the provision of regional news. While provision of this service will continue on the BBC, the Internet has been perceived as providing a viable alternative platform of provision (Ofcom, 2009d).

The evidence on displacement or substitutability effects between the Internet and television reviewed in this book so far has indicated that such effects can easily be overstated and often are. Even so, there is evidence that the Internet is used increasingly as a technology platform for television viewing, but the television set itself is increasingly taking on the characteristics of a computer with increased interactive functionality and content archiving capacity. As technology mergers continue to evolve, eventually the distinctions between the personal computer and television set will disappear completely.

Television versus the Internet: continuing distinctions

Television viewing via the Internet is largely non-linear in format which means that channels are largely irrelevant. Although programmes are provided in channel formats via Internet protocol television (IPTV) services, there is a significant and growing amount of programme content stored in non-linear repositories from which downloads can be made on demand. With the emergence of interactive and non-linear reception properties within the standard TV set environment, viewers are gradually becoming accustomed to not just the concept but also the practice of on-demand viewing. One implication of these developments is that the traditional channel structure of television could eventually disappear. The big question here is how long will this take? If this does happen, it will render debates about the future of public service broadcasting channels largely redundant. Instead, it will be more relevant to talk about the production of public service broadcasting programmes and the construction of repositories from which users will be able to extract whatever they want to watch on demand. It is worthwhile at this point taking a closer look at some of the technology changes that have been taking place and the new viewing practices that have evolved from them.

The traditional configuration of television comprises sequences of programmes organised within 'channels'. Channels provide fixed sequences of programmes with pre-determined start times over which viewers customarily have had little control. In the online environment, users can access content according to their own schedules of consumption as their content consumption choices are not constrained by content producers and distributors in the same way that TV viewers are. We saw earlier in Chapter 2 that television channels are still valued in that they provide recognisable brands in which the public feel they can place their trust. As multi-channel environments have grown, however, so too has the problem of finding the programmes you want to watch. While it contains even more content than multi-channel television packages, the Internet provides its users with more advanced search tools. Although media consumers welcome more content and more choice, they also need convenient ways of finding the content they seek.

Television in the digital era has evolved to deliver greater flexibility in modes of consumptions. Multiple TV channels can be used to broadcast the same programmes with different, staggered start-times giving viewers more choices about when they can watch specific programmes. Computerised personal video recorders now permit viewers to record large quantities of programming that can be stored on a hard drive and viewed at the user's convenience. They also allow viewers to control their own viewing start times by permitting them to start viewing a programme that is being recorded, while that recording process is ongoing. Some services also offer viewers choices of multiple camera views at specific broadcast events, usually sports events.

Television companies themselves, however, are now taking advantage of Internet technology to provide online TV catch-up viewing services and broadcast content repositories from which viewers can make selections at their own discretion. There are important questions about whether these new services are conditioning new forms of viewing behaviour and viewer expectations and represent the beginnings of a new structure for television in which traditional channel formats will become redundant.

The promise of digital

Digital television has been sold principally on the basis that it will provide consumers with more choice. The digital switchover could, however, signal much more than an increased range of services. It introduces a technological basis for a transformation of television and the way it is used.

The big question is whether viewers really want the digital switchover or would welcome the changes to their television landscape that it will bring. There is the technological argument that emphasises the additional choice that will be provided to consumers through digital transmission because it can convey significantly greater amounts of televised content. Also, technologically it is asserted that picture quality will improve. If these features are to be real drivers of uptake and acceptance, however, we need to know how important they are to viewers – and not just to politicians or broadcast technocrats.

One possibility is that the digitisation of television will not simply drive changes in the form of increased numbers of channels, which might simply mean more of the same. Rather it will usher in radical changes to the way television viewing, as an activity, is conducted. Technology developments that are already taking place will fundamentally alter the nature of television viewing and herald sweeping changes to the way people engage with television and the way television as a medium operates.

Ease of making choices

It is also important to recognise that not all people welcome change anyway. This point may be especially pertinent when change affects a familiar household appliance such as the television set. Technological changes may bring an enriched viewing experience in terms of quantity of content, but do all viewers crave the new channels being offered? An 'enriched' viewing experience might also mean a more complex experience. For many (and possibly most) viewers, television watching must be a comfortable and easy experience (Klein, Karger and Sinclair, 2003; Klein et al., 2004a, 2004b). Being made to work harder to gain access to the content you seek is not a change that is likely to go down favourably in many television households. Even when television adopts interactive facilities that require viewers to engage with content repositories as they would via PC-Internet link, users of online services via television sets were discouraged from content searching when the navigation system required them to make three clicks of the remote control rather than one or two (Gunter, 2005a; Nicholas et al., 2002). Greater choice of what to watch and when to watch could be welcome developments – but there is a trade-off between benefit and cost in this context. 'More' does not invariably mean 'better'. This last point may be especially acute if the amount of effort viewers must make to get to the content they desire is more than they would normally tolerate.

In an analysis of channel selection in a multi-channel Internet protocol television setting, research from Germany has found most (60%) of a user's channel switching in a 150-channel system occurred within 10 seconds. This search and selection time varied between genres with news selection (four seconds) taking less time than children's music or sports programmes (seven to eight seconds), and documentaries and movies (10–13 seconds) taking longest. While one in ten viewers (10%) settled on their first channel selection, the same proportion searched anything from six to 100 channels before deciding what to watch. In the latter instance, a significant amount of viewing time could be taken up simply finding something to watch (Cha, Gummadi & Rodriguez, 2008).

Enhanced content archiving at home

Technological change that pre-dates the digital era provided viewers with the capacity to re-schedule programmes to suit themselves. The introduction of the home video-recorder in the 1980s led to rapid and widespread adoption by media consumers who did not wish to be tied to the original television schedules (see Levy, 1983; Levy and Gunter, 1988). Further technological advances have meant that viewers can now pre-programme recording devices over longer periods and can record larger quantities of material. The emergence of personal video recorders in which content is captured on a hard drive means that viewers can store even larger volumes of content, but can also freeze or rewind 'live' programmes at any point. Personal recording systems such as Sky⁺ allow viewers to record two programmes simultaneously and have much simplified the advance recording process as compared with the 'programming' required with a standard videotape recorder. Viewers can accumulate large content archives for playback when convenient for them.

Online content archives

The Internet not only represents a further platform over which television programmes can be transmitted to viewers' homes, it also contains a huge repository of old and new programme content. With the development of broadband connections that have spread rapidly across TV homes in the country, media consumers can now watch and download films, television programmes and other content online at any time of the day. Some specialist online suppliers can now provide consumers with access to huge multi-modality and varied content archives. Blinkx.com, for example, has compiled over 35,000,000 hours of audio and video content that web surfers can browse and then access (see *www.blinkx.com*). These archives contain large quantities of back episodes of television shows and their customer bases are growing rapidly.

The Internet has an advantage for producers of content in that it allows them to reach consumers directly without the need to pass through the intermediary stage of gaining access to a broadcast network. The consumers are out there and, provided the price is right, they will purchase content in this way. Some television broadcasters have already got wise to this new development and have begun to establish their own websites through which they sell off old television content they own. Such online content selling can occur over more than one platform, with mobile telephones (as well as Internet-connected, desk-top computers) offering an access route to consumers for certain types of content.

A different view

A different line of argument is that going digital will accelerate radical shifts in the way consumers use television and television itself will change in its intrinsic nature. Further merging of technologies will occur with television sets becoming more computerised. This will expand the functionality of television and, as a technology, it will become more interactive and as such it will adopt functions which consumers currently turn to personal computers to satisfy. The television set will become a communications medium as well as a receptacle of entertainment and information content. Viewers will be able to communicate out through their television sets and will therefore be able to engage in transactions as they can at present via PCs linked to the Internet. Experiments in online public services, including health and local government, have already been carried out through digital interactive television technology as early demonstrators of this new form of television usage (Gunter, 2006b; Hancer, 2006; Nicholas et al., 2002).

Increasingly, the Internet will become accessible via television sets and not just through personal computers. This will mean that many of the expectations of the Internet will transfer to television. In this evolved environment, even the way viewers expect to receive content will change. The channel configuration of video streams on television may become a thing of the past as viewers expect a more personalised service tailored to their individual tastes and needs. Content databases will become the order of the day in this evolved television environment and electronic programme guides will need to evolve as search engines to enable users to find the content they need when they choose to consume it.

If these changes occur, they will obviously go far beyond the short-term view of the digital switchover that is conceived primarily to bring increased numbers of television channels to more people. The challenge to public service broadcasting will also become more acute. If television channels disappear, what kind of future exists for PSB operators? Television content producers will need to seek prominence through skilful use of search engines. In considering, the pace of these developments, we also need to examine the degree of welcome for change on the part of TV viewers and the extent to which new developments are occurring anyway with a natural market demand already in motion.

Future audiences

Television as a technology is evolving rapidly. The migration to digital from analogue technology is one manifestation of this evolution, but is really only the tip of the iceberg. The rapid establishment and roll-out of video-on-demand services and other forms of online television are creating a television viewing environment that will expand content choice exponentially. At the same time, these developments will create a highly diverse universe of media content with which media consumers will need a lot of assistance and support. The initial task, in any viewing experience, of finding out what's on will become more complex and therefore more challenging in this expanded media universe. The roll-out of Internet protocol television, video-on-demand services, and online catch-up programme archives not only represent radical changes to the structure of television services, they also demand a different orientation on the part of viewers.

What kinds of television viewing will emerge in the future?

With the adoption of digital technology, television as a medium will become far more complex. The growth in numbers of television channels represents the first stage of development that will eventually see television transform into a fully interactive technology through which a wide range of communications functions can be conducted. Viewers will no longer simply be 'viewers'. Instead, television will evolve into a fixed and mobile technology that will seamlessly allow users to move between consumption of audio-visual or textual content and more dynamic transactions and interpersonal communications. The model of content consumption that has emerged with the Internet and World Wide Web will migrate to television and these changes are already starting to emerge. Television services are being made available on the Internet, television sets can be used to engage with the Internet, and television programmes can be streamed over mobile phones.

Television is not the only technology that can transmit television programmes and other audio-visual content. These developments are associated with wired and wireless telecommunications networks and the evolution of broadband telephone systems has meant that the Internet has evolved into a medium that can distribute television programmes. Broadband telephone systems have already been utilised in the UK to provide localised television distribution networks available on a subscriber basis. Further experiments have been carried out with mobile television whereby television programmes and other video materials have been distributed to consumers via their mobile phones.

Research evidence that derives from both the self-reports of viewers and continuous audience measurement systems has confirmed a growing preference for and utility of on-demand television and video services, regardless of whether these operate over the Internet or via standard television sets. Furthermore, once viewers begin to use these facilities, they do it on a regular basis. In the UK in 2008, more than eight in ten users of digital video recorders (83%), more than six in ten users of on-demand services from television broadcasters (65%) and more than one in two users of online on-demand services (55%) reportedly used them at least once a week. Furthermore, significant proportions said they used online on-demand (57%), digital recorders (47%) or televised on-demand services (44%) more at the time of interview than they had done one year earlier (Ofcom, 2009d). The same survey also found that clear majorities of people said they were able to watch more programmes that they enjoyed because of their digital personal recorder (80%), on-demand services via the television (75%) and on-demand services available online (65%) (Ofcom, 2009d).

These new developments are in their early stages, but could they spell the end of television viewing as we know it? Both web-based television and mobile television could bring on board fresh competition for PSB television operators from new suppliers outside the traditional television marketplace. Both technologies have also been identified as avenues for future development by existing television broadcasters, including the PSB channels. The key changes that might turn viewers away from conventional channels, despite favourable opinions voiced about some channels in recent surveys, include the following developments:

1. Near-video-on-demand systems on multi-channel television platforms.
2. Online television catch-up services via the Internet.
3. The use of personal video recorders with large storage capacity and versatile playback functions.
4. Enhanced television applications.
5. Watching television via the Internet.
6. Online content reported through television sets.
7. Mobile television viewing.

1. Near-video-on-demand systems on multi-channel television platforms

Some conventional television channels are adding '+1' channels into their stable in multi-channel environments. These new channels show the same schedule of programmes as the core channel, but with a one hour delay on that channel, thus allowing viewers alternative start-times for all the channel's programmes. These options are widely used. In fact, +1 channels can add significantly, in some cases, to the total audiences for a channel's programmes.

Ofcom figures showed that for Channel 4, its +1 channel added 0.8 per cent to its 6.7 per cent share in multi-channel homes. For E4, 0.6 per cent was added by its +1 to a 1.6 per cent share for the core channel. For ITV2, 0.4 per cent was added to a core channel share of 1.9 per cent. With G.O.L.D, its +1 added half as many again (0.3%) to the core channel's 0.6 per cent share (Ofcom, 2009d). These are all small channels with small audience bases, but the rates of growth of their audiences, not just individually but collectively, indicates a new shift in style of television viewing within a structured, linear channel environment that partially mimics a non-linear, on-demand video setting.

2. Online television catch-up services via the Internet

There is plenty of evidence for a demand among media consumers for these services. Prior to the launch of the iPlayer, the idea of a seven-day television catch-up service over the Internet was endorsed by half a sample of UK viewers, particularly if it also allowed them to use a television series link to program the system automatically to record all the episodes of a TV series for up to 13 weeks (Ofcom, 2006b).

In the UK, the BBC iPlayer – while a long time in gestation – has proved highly popular with viewers and triggered other versions among commercial television operators. This seven-day TV catch-up service was launched on Christmas Day 2007 and during its fourth full month of operation (April 2008), around 21 million BBC programmes were downloaded and daily users averaged 700,000. Taking one of the BBC's consistently most watched programmes, *EastEnders*, by April 2008 the serial attracted 460,000 'plays' on iPlayer, which was 2.3 per cent of its total audience reach, including live TV broadcasts and on-air omnibus repeats. For other less-watched programmes, iPlayer replays added up to 20 per cent to regular television audiences (Bulkley, 2008). While iPlayer and other such catch-up services were initially launched for reception via personal computers, these services will eventually migrate onto other technology platforms and become receivable through mobile phones and games consoles.

Fletcher (2009) reported that the VoD market was growing apace and although the major broadcasters are contributors to this growth, they are in no way the dominant force. The VoD catch-up services offered by the

BBC, ITV, Channel 4, Five and Sky have quickly captured significant user bases: in 2008, the BBC's iPlayer received 271 million programme requests. Yet, taking all the VoD services offered by the major broadcasters together, they accounted for only 2.5 per cent of online video viewing. If the early rate of adoption of services such as iPlayer continues, however, we can expect the share of online media consumption time (and of online plus offline media consumption) occupied by on-demand video viewing to grow to a point where it could become the dominant mode of reception. This bold view of the future is reinforced by a range of other online service developments that will further contribute to the wider re-conditioning of conventional television viewing.

The online television environment has become further complicated via new operators who provide online streams of programmes from the mainstream public service television channels in the UK. Leading names in this emergent sector are Livestation, Inuk and Zattoo. A loophole in UK copyright law allows these companies to provide streams from public service broadcast channels without needing special contracts to do so. In some instances, these companies have also included streams from commercial non-public service broadcasters, though generally under contractual agreement. These services can also track the numbers of people who watched specified programmes which means they can give precise figures, rather than the more generalised calculations of metered audience measurement services, about the numbers of viewers who watched at particular times (Kiss, 2008).

The complexity of the online television environment has opened up opportunities for online search engines to enter the market to provide a one-stop shop for viewers who wish to know what's on where. Online video search tools, such as Blinkx, have launched a package of themed channels that can be readily searched for the types of content they offer each day. Other Internet-protocol television (IPTV) services that offer walled garden packages have aimed to develop multi-platform services that offer search facilities and on-screen content identification features (including animated characters) to help viewers know what's available and how to get to it (Hargrave, 2008).

All the major PSB broadcasters, BBC, ITV, Channel 4, Five and Sky have distribution deals to ensure that their content is offered on demand via a range of platforms and a growing number of viewers are using VoD via TV. Virgin media's VoD service is available in nearly 3.5 million homes and registered 516 million views in 2008. This represented a 60 per cent improvement on 2007. More than half of Virgin Media's digital TV homes regularly used VoD in 2008 and averaged total VoD views per month was 53 million compared with 33 million in 2007. Average VoD views per month per user increased from 23 to 30 from 2007 to 2008, while average VoD reach also improved from 47 per cent to 52 per cent across these two years. Data here were from Virgin Media/Ofcom. Virgin Media also launched a TV version of the BBC's iPlayer catch-up service in May 2008 and by December, this iPlayer accounted for 95 million views on Virgin Media's TV platform (Ofcom, 2009c).

Channel 4 registered 80 million+ views of its programmes on the VoD platforms of Virgin Media, BT Vision and Tiscali TV in 2008. BT Vision, a hybrid platform that offers Freeview (DTT) channels and on-demand content via IPTV had 398,000 subscribers in February 2009; this represented a significant increase on its subscriber base 12 months earlier (120,000). Tiscali TV – the former HomeChoice IPTV platform – had around 60,000 subscribers at the end of 2008 (Ofcom, 2009c).

In the United Kingdom, there is a range of online TV services available, including BBC iPlayer, ITV Player, 4oD and Demand Five. BBC's iPlayer reported 277 million requests to stream and download in 2008, with 41 million made in December 2008 alone. The BBC introduced new developments for iPlayer throughout 2008, including a version for children, downloading for MAC and Linux users, high definition content and versions available for Apple's iPhone, the Nokia N96 mobile phone and the Nintendo Wii games console.

ITV's online catch-up TV service was re-branded as ITV Player in December 2008 and reported 15.7 million video views in November 2008, an increase of 598 per cent on November 2007. Five re-branded its online video service as Demand Five in summer 2008. Channel 4 then announced plans in February 2009 to launch a new catch-up TV player to be closely integrated with the broadcaster's website. Sky offered a range of its programming and content from third parties on its Sky Player service and also launched Sky Player TV, an online-only subscription TV service. This service was aimed at consumers without a satellite dish.

The BBC, Independent Television and British Telecommunications then revealed proposals for Project Canvas, a joint venture for an 'open standard' to create Internet-connected on-demand television services at no additional content charge to consumers. The project, which received initial BBC Trust approval in 2009, was designed to offer an open technical standards platform to deliver a range of on-demand content to television sets for broadband subscribers.

In research for the Association of Television on Demand (2009), conducted by YouGov, it was reported that 50 per cent of the population have used on-demand services and 20 per cent use them every week. The survey also found that 76 per cent of the population were aware of VoD. Nearly half of those using on-demand services (48%) watch them via TV sets and over four in ten (41%) watch via PCs, with 30 per cent using laptops.

Ofcom (2009b) reported growing use of the Internet to watch catch-up TV services and that nearly one in four people in the UK (23%) claimed that catch-up TV is watched in their household. Catch-up TV users tended to have a more youthful profile (33% of 15 to 24s made this claim) than the general TV audience, although even one in ten people aged over 65 (10%) claimed to use these services. The BBC's iPlayer was perhaps the major driver of this viewing phenomenon. According to Ofcom, by May 2009, nearly 15 per cent of Internet users in the UK had used the iPlayer. While other catch-up services were available to viewers provided by other leading broadcasters, the BBC's service was the clear market leader. All catch-up services exhibited a young audience profile with adults aged under-35 disproportionately represented among their users. In the case of virtually all these services, however, the age profile closely matched that of the general online universe. The exception was 4oD, the catch-up service offered by Channel 4, which attracted a disproportionately high number of users aged 18 to 34 and a much lower than average percentage of users aged 35 to 64.

Catch-up TV services can be viewed over personal computers, laptops, hand-held devices and TV sets. Most users were found to watch these services via an Internet link. During its first year, the BBC iPlayer service received around 372 million requests of which around 275 million (74%) were delivered over the Internet (Ofcom, 2009b). With the much less widely used 4oD service, most views took place through a TV service rather than over the Internet.

Catch-up TV services provide viewers with an alternative route for watching mainstream TV broadcasts. Although most offer only temporarily archived programmes (usually for up to 30 days after original on-air transmission), they nevertheless allow viewers who missed the live transmission and did not record it another opportunity to see a programme. Because catch-up services represent a form of on-demand TV, however, they could play an important role in conditioning a style of viewing behaviour that departs from that associated with traditionally organised linear TV channels. Perhaps one of the most significant indicators of the potency of this new viewing experience is the degree to which it is adopted by viewers when it is readily available via their TV sets. By the end of 2008, Virgin Media data indicated that more than half of digital cable subscribers (52%) who could receive on-demand video services via their TV sets took advantage of this service. Virgin Media subscribers recorded up to 30 video on-demand views per month (Ofcom 2009b). Depending upon the average length of the programmes watched, this could accumulate to a significant amount of viewing time. If the average length of these catch-up programmes was 30 minutes (and it is unlikely to be less than this), aggregated video on demand viewing would reach 15 hours per month. If many of these programmes were full-length dramas, documentaries, or movies, the total aggregated time could reach two to four times this amount. If so, that might comprise half or more of an individual's *weekly* viewing diet.

3. The use of personal video recorders with large storage capacity and versatile playback functions

Personal or digital video recorders (PVRs/DVRs) are devices that allow viewers to record television programmes for later playback on a hard drive built into the decoder box of a multi-channel television package attached to a television set. Viewers had previously been able to record broadcast programmes on video-recorders (VCRs) for later playback. The PVR, however, offers a number of significant advances over the VCR. It provides a far greater recording capacity allowing viewers to capture 50+ hours of programming and often allows viewers to record two programmes simultaneously. It also provides a facility for what is known as 'offset viewing' whereby a viewer can begin to watch a recording of a programme before the programme's live transmission (when the recording is taking place) has finished. Using a 'series link' it is also possible in a single click to program the PVR to record every episode in a TV series for its entire duration or until available space on the hard drive is exhausted.

In effect, the PVR allows viewers to re-schedule programmes in a number of ways. PVRs also provide a more user-friendly technology for recording through which viewers can simply click on a programme's name listed on their electronic programme guide (EPG) on screen using the record button on their TV remote control handset. There is no need for intricate programming of recording times and durations in advance of transmission.

Ofcom (2009a) reported that personal digital video recording devices attached to TV sets were becoming more and more prevalent. In the first quarter of 2009, 27 per cent of the UK population reported having a DVR (a four per cent increase on 12 months earlier), and this position had been reached over seven years. Sky Anytime – a 'push' VoD service available on Sky⁺ set-top boxes – was regularly used by one million plus viewers. Programmes can be downloaded instantly onto the hard drive of the set-top box and it is in effect a VoD service. BSkyB reported that Anytime programmes represented 2.3 per cent of all viewing, and this was a higher share than either Five or ITV2 achieved in a multi-channel environment. Pop-Up TV, a pay digital terrestrial TV operator, offers a 'push' VoD service for those who subscriber to its 'TV Favourites' package, which gives access to up to 700 shows per month. Once again, programmes are stored in the hard drive of the set top box.

Not only have PVRs rapidly expanded in prevalence, but for many people now they define the way they watch television. One survey found that only a small minority of people in the UK claimed that they *only* watched live programmes (4%) with a larger minority saying that they *mostly* watched live programmes. More than one in five 'only' (5%) or 'mostly' (18%) watched programmes they recorded and more than one in three (35%) said they watched live and recorded programmes equally (Entertainment Media Research, 2008).

Data for the five public service broadcast (PSB) channels (BBC1, BBC2, ITV1, Channel 4 and Five) indicated that the great majority of their viewers (81% to 87%) watched initial broadcasts as they were transmitted. The remainder engaged in time-shifting of programmes. On average less than one in ten (7% to 10% across the five channels) time-shifted and watched the same day as the original broadcast. Similar proportions (5% to 11%) time-shifted and viewed between two and six days after broadcast (Ofcom, 2009a).

Ofcom (2009a) reported that 16- to 34-year-olds time-shifted a higher proportion of their viewing on the five main PSB channels than did other age groups. In general across all age groups, 15 per cent of PSB programme viewing was time-shifted. Among 16 to 34s, it was 19 per cent. Among the over 55s it was 11 per cent. Those aged 35–54 and 4–15 at 15 per cent and 16 per cent respectively were on par with the overall viewing population average. Sky⁺ owners time shifted more of their viewing from the five main PSB channels (19%) than did Virgin V+ users (11%) or Freeview users (9%).

Data on the extent to which media consumers use tools such as personal video recorders can indicate the prevalence of PVR-related behaviour. What we also need to know, however, is whether using PVRs represents one aspect of a different type of cognitive orientation towards watching television. What do people think about PVR-based viewing? Is it perceived as an adjunct to ordinary television viewing? Or does it represent a shift in the nature of the use of television and in the expectations that people increasingly have about the control they should have over their viewing choices? There is evidence that people report feeling empowered by PVRs and that the availability of this technology can enhance the enjoyment they derive from their viewing experiences. Certainly, PVRs bring specific benefits such as allowing viewers to fast-forward through advertisements on television and to capture programmes on broadcast television that were scheduled at inconvenient times, but there also emerged a more holistic shift of attitude towards viewing that derives from use of this technology. Furthermore, the time-shifting facility of personal video recorders was associated with generally more positive evaluative ratings of the overall television viewing experience (Ferguson and Perse, 2004).

Other research from the United States (Bernoff, 2004) and United Kingdom (Wood, 2004) confirmed that PVR users reported getting a great deal of satisfaction from these devices. The key perceived benefits included ease of recording, fast-forwarding through TV commercials and being able to pause live television programmes (Bernoff, 2004). PVR users also report time-shifting substantial proportions (up to 40%) of their viewing, although such data were derived from respondents' self-reports rather than direct, real-time measurement of viewing (Wood, 2004).

Brown and Barkhuus (2006) reported an investigation of television watching practices among early adopters of personal hard-disc video-recorders (PVRs such as TiVo™ or Sky⁺) and Internet downloading of shows. The study used in-depth interviews with early adopters of these new technologies. For PVR users and downloaders, watching television has become a less passive process and a more dynamic interactive experience. PVRs allow for recording and playback of an archive of programmes recorded from live broadcast television onto a hard disc. The downloading of television programmes from the network represents an alternative to standard television viewing, it breaks the traditional relationship between viewer and broadcaster. The viewer proactively seeks out content for consumption at a time of their own choosing.

Brown and Barkhuus used a small sample of 21 early adopters of PVRs and downloaders and a small number of individuals who used standard video-recorders to capture live televised content. The participants were not representative of the viewing population but were drawn from a range of age and occupational groups. All participants were interviewed about their television viewing habits, which shared PVRs had a major impact on the use of television. Eight of nine Sky⁺ households had moved entirely to watching pre-recorded shows from the PVR and viewers would queue up programmes to watch, and use series links to record entire series.

As multi-channel packages become the norm in all TV households with the switch-over from analogue to digital transmission systems, those services that provide PVR facilities, according to some observers, can be expected to take a market lead. As VCR manufacture ceases, PVRs will become the standard recording device and will be expected on the part of viewers (Looms, 2005). Its storage capacity and features that allow a range of flexible playback choices to users could not only enhance ordinary TV viewing, but change it in nature quite fundamentally.

4. Enhanced television applications

Do people want television to become more interactive? The answer to this question is 'yes' for some viewers. Younger viewers, perhaps not surprisingly, have shown some enthusiasm for interactive engagement with television through a variety of applications. Enhanced television applications refer to interactive functions that accompany programmes and enable viewers to engage with programmes in a more dynamic way. These applications include access routes to supplementary content linked to specific programmes that may be available in text, image or video formats. They also include access to alternative versions of mainstream content, such as different perspectives on news stories, camera angles at live sports events, or additional choices (e.g. ability to choose between a number of live tennis matches being played simultaneously in a tennis tournament). These facilities are believed by some to add value to standard broadcasts enabling them to differentiate their programme services from their competitors and potentially expanding their viewing markets (Swedlow, 2000; Maad, 2003).

One innovative enhancement that has been trialled is the use of an avatar newscaster that serves as a mediator between the viewer and news stories between which the viewer can choose. This facility, with the acronym MARILYN (Multimodal Avatar Response Live Newscaster), allows viewers to select news content on demand. The avatar, in female form, could respond to viewers' requests vocally and with hand gestures and facial expressions (Maad, 2005).

Children become more interactive with television as they grow older and enter their teens. Research reported by Ofcom (2005) showed that significant minorities of 8–11s, however, also used some interactive applications. The most popular forms of interactive engagement with television programmes are visiting a programme's website (28% of 8–11s; 44% of 12–15s) and pressing the red button on the remote control to engage directly with interactive features available via the TV set (32%

of 8–11s; 39% of 12–15s). Girls were more likely than boys to interact with programmes. This was especially true among 12–15s where girls (58%) were much more likely than boys (29%) to say they had visited a programme's website. Even among 8–11s, girls (18%) were more likely than boys (12%) to have telephoned a programme and were much more likely to have sent in an e-mail to a programme (18% versus 3%).

The next question is why do viewers use interactive facilities associated with television programmes? Ofcom (2005) pursued this question with children aged eight to 15 years. The reasons given for engaging with interactive features were to enter a competition (33%), to play a game (32%), to vote on something (28%), to find out more about something featured in the programme (24%), to respond to a feature on the programme (12%), to take part in a quiz (8%), to change the viewing angle/use playercam (7%) or to donate to charity (3%). Eight to 11 year olds (41%) were far more likely than 12–15s (26%) to say they interacted with TV to play a game. Among 12–15s, girls (38%) were more likely than boys (15%) to have voted on or nominated someone or something through TV interaction.

Research in the United States explored the reasons people give for using interactive features on television using a uses and gratifications approach in which study participants endorsed a range of reasons for the use of this technology (Livaditi et al., 2002). The ability to draw broader implications from this study is limited by its use of a small, convenience sample that appeared to be comprised mostly of staff and students from a single university. Participants responded to a list of items designed verbally to measure their motives for using digital television (which was distinguished from ordinary television by having interactive applications). The results indicated that participants who used digital television did so for reasons associated with seeking entertainment, companionship and escape. News and information-seeking motives did not emerge as significant predictors of digital television consumption.

5. Watching television via the Internet

Existing TV channels as well as new entrants into the TV marketplace have begun to utilise broadband telephone lines as a platform for delivery of TV services into people's homes. The emergence of IPTV – Internet Protocol Television – means that television pictures can now be received via computer/telecommunications networks without serious degradation of quality. The rapid expansion of broadband across the UK has made this approach to television transmission increasingly attractive, the increased capacity afforded by broadband means that download speeds are sufficient for normal reception of video material. The migration of television onto the Internet will render it more interactive and personalised, demonstrating consistency with the Internet in general. In due course, this merger of technologies could play a significant part in driving the evolution of television as we know it towards a wholly different configuration and pattern of use.

The use of online sources to access audio-visual content is not a completely new phenomenon. There has been evidence for a number of years that Internet users go online to retrieve live 'streamed' video content or to download such content onto their computers for later consumption. Rose and Roisin (2001) reported data from a twice-yearly tracker survey of use of the Internet conducted by Arbitron and Edison Media Research in the United States that examined use of streamed audio and video content. They identified 'streamies' – Internet users who watch or listen to webcasts online. In July 2001 they surveyed 2,507 people via telephone across the USA. By this time one in three (34%) of all Americans aged 12+ had reportedly experienced Internet audio or video content. Although more than one in two (52%) Internet users had 'ever' tried streaming media, one in four (25%) said they had listened to or watched audio or audio-visual online in the past month.

Most 'streamies' had experienced webcasting within the last year. Among audio streamers, 19 per cent had done this first more than two years earlier, 20 per cent had done it first between one and two years before and 56 per cent had first done this within the previous 12 months. The equivalent percentages for video streaming were 28 per cent, 22 per cent, and 49 per cent. Streamers in the last week said they had spent approximately 2.5 hours with streaming video and 3.5 hours with streaming audio each week. Only half (48%) of streamers could name an Internet audio provider (Rose and Roisin, 2001).

Movie trailers and music videos were the most popular types of streamed video content. Nearly 60 per cent mentioned these, while 57 per cent mentioned music videos, 36 per cent online weather forecasts, 32 per cent short or full-length movies, 31 per cent video highlights of sporting events, and 31 per cent video newscasts. The use of streamed content was also linked to increased use of websites associated with newspapers, radio and television stations. The latter finding underlines the significance of branding in a crowded on-demand marketplace. Media consumers seek greater choice and control over their viewing of video content, but also seek out the badges of quality associated with well-known media brands.

In an attempt to understand media consumers' orientations towards content even further, one small-sample qualitative study (Barkhuus, 2009), conducted largely among students in California, found that television was watched over the Internet via computer as well as over a conventional television set and comprised viewing of re-runs of broadcast programmes and edited extracts from programmes, for example, replayed on YouTube. While ordinary TV viewing was often carried out with other people, viewing over the Internet tended to be a solo activity. This study was conducted on such a small scale that it is difficult to generalise from it to wider populations with any confidence.

In the UK, there is evidence of growing awareness of on-demand video-based services via the Internet. By 2008, more than one in three people aged 15+ said they used YouTube regularly or occasionally (37%). Smaller, though not insignificant minorities said they occasionally or regularly used other on-demand video services supplied by Virgin Media (20%), Channel 4's 4OD (15%), BBC iPlayer (13%) and Google Video (13%). Reported use of YouTube and Google Video were especially prevalent among teenagers (65% and 38%) and those in their early 20s (65% and 32%). Although some on-demand services associated with well-known offline broadcast brands were also reported, it was clear that the on-demand marketplace had already become highly crowded and competitive and that these brands did not command market dominance in this media environment (Entertainment Media Research, 2008).

Broadcasters, according to Ofcom (2009b), are placing a growing emphasis on distributing content on the Internet. They are also developing technologies to bring Internet video to the TV set. Much of the video content associated with the dominant, new online suppliers such as YouTube has only a short duration, thus even large numbers of visits by large amounts of online traffic can aggregate to relatively modest viewing times. This could change as consumers demonstrate a growing orientation towards watching long-form programming on personal computers. The Ofcom research found that one in three (32%) media consumers said they had watched online video clips or 'webcasts', while nearly one in five (19%) said they had watched TV programmes on the Internet facilitated by higher broadband speeds and greater availability of content online.

New broadband television initiatives have been established that offer fully developed packages of television content organised largely on the old 'channel' model. Thus, viewers can subscribe to online television packages that consist of television channels that are also available on other digital platforms (cable, satellite and terrestrial) plus other content that is unique to the broadband package. In addition, some television channels have established web-based platforms for the re-distribution of their broadcast programmes.

Broadband television developments have been introduced by a number of new players – both old and new to broadcasting. In December 2006, British Telecommunications (BT) announced its new BT Vision service available to broadband subscribers. The BT Vision service also promised to include 40+ television channels and access to a library of 1,000 films. The service was offered through a set-top box and made available to customers of BT's broadband service at a standard monthly subscription tariff, an initial outlay for the decoder, and additional premium services, such as films and football for which subscribers were charged additional pay-per-view fees.

Another model is to use the web to distribute programme content originally made for transmission over other digital platforms, A number of the PSB television operators in the UK – most notably BBC, ITV and Channel 4 – have entered this market with services offering media consumers simultaneous transmission of content over digital television and Internet platforms. The BBC offered a non-subscription service over the Internet consisting of time-limited access to programme clips and complete shows from BBC1 and BBC2; Channel 4 launched a service in which selected programme content from the channel was made available over the Internet; while Five launched a web-based pay-per-view service offering downloadable episodes of its motoring series *Fifth Gear.*

Other services were launched by non-PSB operators. MTV made music video clips available for free via the Internet and AOL, in a deal with Warner Studios, made films available for downloading over the Internet. Then BT introduced a pay-per-view video content downloading service via the Internet that includes a range of cinema films, archived television programmes and near-live Premier League football matches. IPTV is still at an embryonic stage of development. Nevertheless, over one in four Internet users in Britain (27%) said they knew what it was in October 2006 and the same percentage said they had heard of it, though did not know what it was (Nielsen Media Research, 2006).

The Internet is therefore being used by established and new television operators alike to distribute programme content originally made for standard TV transmission. These developments are accelerating the engagement by media consumers in a new style of television viewing. The traditional technological and functional distinctiveness of television and the Internet are being eroded. In this vein, Findahl (2008) reported that the Internet cannot be regarded as a standalone medium separate from other major mass media. The reason for this is simple. Many television and radio services, newspapers and magazines are available online. In Sweden, Findahl reported that 16 per cent of the population claimed to go online to watch television at least weekly. This percentage was higher for those going online to watch video material (21%) or to listen to or download music (34%).

Ofcom (2009b) conducted research into non-linear TV viewing and viewers of on-demand services claimed it enhanced their viewing experience. In all, nearly eight in ten (78%) agreed they 'watch more programmes that I enjoy because of on-demand services through the TV'. In addition, eight out of ten DVR users (80%) said they 'watch more programmes that I enjoy because of my DVR'. Then, two-thirds (65%) of online content users made a similar claim about that service.

One of the most dramatic online developments that occurred largely from 2005 was the rise of online social networking. The penetration of these networks and time devoted to them by their users has set them up as potential competitors of television for people's leisure time. More than this, however, research has indicated that users of online social networking recognise that it also has the capability to stream video content. Nearly three in ten online social networkers in the UK (29%) were found to have already streamed video through a social networking site. More than one in four (27%) agreed that, provided the quality is good enough, social networks could become a primary way to access this type of content in the future (Entertainment Media Research, 2008).

The use of social networks varies significantly with age. Given that more than half of male teens (55%) and male adults in their early-20s (59%) and around two-thirds of female teens (64%) and female adults in their early-20s (68%) in the UK said they used social networks, and that they will mature into future older generations of media consumers, the scene is being set for this channel of video entertainment consumption to become more prominent in the years ahead (Entertainment Media Research, 2008). When questioned further, among those who claimed to watch streamed video content online, nearly one in five (18%) said it made them watch less scheduled television. This reaction was most widespread among teenage males (31%). It was also acknowledged by one in four young adult males aged 20 to 34 years (25%). Around one in five female teens and young adults also reported a shift from scheduled television watched to consumption of online video streaming (Entertainment Media Research, 2008).

Another major new initiative in IPTV in the UK, that was introduced earlier in this chapter, is Project Canvas that will combine on-demand television services with Internet access via television sets linked to a set-top decoder. Research into public opinion about this proposed new service found that most UK viewers (61%) expressed some degree of interest in it, especially for its catch-up viewing facility operating via the BBC's iPlayer system and also for its personal digital recording facility (Opinion Leader, 2009). Interest was greater among young people from the better off socioeconomic classes who already possessed television equipment with some of the functionality proposed by Canvas.

Probing for the perceived attractiveness of individual features offered by this new system, being able to catch up on programmes missed when first broadcast (78%) interested) and high definition channels (77% interested) finished well ahead of being able to access the Internet via your television set (54% interested). Yet most of all, the most widespread interest was expressed for simply being able to continue to access standard television channels (83%) and being able to record your own programmes from those channels (81%). Hence, despite the interest in on-demand being widespread, there was still overwhelming support for continuance of regular television reception and recording facilities.

Another issue that was explored by this research considered whether viewers would use Canvas only on their main television set or whether they would consider using it on a second set. The key finding here was that pay television subscribers were far more likely to say they would use Canvas on a second television set than were non-pay television users (56% versus 25%). Those who already paid for multi-channel television packages were therefore more likely than other viewers to envisage using a service such as Canvas as a substitute for their existing television system. The significance of this finding could be that among this rapidly growing sector of the viewing public were many people who would consider a new television system that comprised on-demand television services and Internet access as core components as an alternative for their existing channel-based system.

6. Online content reported through television sets

A number of consumer electronics manufacturers have introduced television sets incorporating broadband connections that enable Internet content to be displayed on the television. Thus, activities that would normally be performed on a personal computer can be carried out via a television set. The range of activities includes sending and receiving e-mail, instant messaging and searching the World Wide Web. The significance of this development lies in the fact that Internet use is brought into direct competition with television viewing on the same technology platform (Digital Lifestyles, 2006).

In 2009, Yahoo! and Intel announced plans to bring a selection of Internet video and other applications to television sets through a venture called Widgets. They have signed deals with manufacturers including Samsung, LG and Toshiba who will integrate the Widget chip set into broadband enabled television sets (Ofcom, 2009b).

The implications of this development for standard television watching are not yet fully understood. While, Internet access content could displace viewing programmes on traditional television channels, the closer proximity of the online world and broadcast environment could open up new opportunities for broadcasters to utilise the web to support their programmes and to entice viewers into new forms of interactive viewing behaviours. Research with interactive digital television in the context of supplying media consumers as citizens with transactional access to public services via television sets has indicated that the user-friendliness of screen interfaces and content navigation systems are crucial to their adoption (Gunter, 2005a; Nicholas et al., 2006).

7. Mobile television viewing

As with the Internet, delivering content over mobile phones may enable broadcasters to reach audiences in a different way. Indeed, because mobile television could provide opportunities for some viewers to watch at times when they normally would not, it could capture essentially 'new audiences'. If the content producers and distributors could attract advertising and sponsorship alongside this re-purposed broadcast content, command subscription charges from users or generate phone call income, it could yield a significant new revenue stream for old material. For transmissions of new 'live' material, such as news or sport, premium telephone or pay-per-view rates could be levied. Another potential advantage could be audience retention if users could switch seamlessly from watching programmes on their television sets to watching them on their mobile phones. In this case, viewers would be given an opportunity to continue watching something they started watching at home even after departing from home, for example, on their way to work.

A number of major mobile telephone companies have provided third generation services capable of delivering video clips and web services, particularly ones carrying news and sports content. Deals have been struck between mobile phone operators and broadcasters so that programme extracts can be streamed to consumers via their cell phones. These services have attracted users, though not yet on a truly mass scale

(Waller, 2008). The mobile phone is not the only portable technology through which television programmes can be distributed. On-demand television services are now being made available for download onto iPods, where users can capture material permanently.

Across the viewing population as a whole, it remains unclear how popular mobile television is likely to be. It is clear, however, that mobile phones have evolved into devices that are defined by diverse functionality with voice telephony representing only a small part of its appeal and utility. The range of uses of mobile phones signals that it will become a key digital entertainment platform in the future. Mobile owners surveyed in the UK regarded as 'important' or 'very important' having functions such as being able to store music and video content (49%), sending and receiving e-mails (48%), being able to access the Internet (47%), ability to play video (40%), playing high quality games (28%), and ability to stream video (27%) (Entertainment Media Research, 2008).

So far, however, despite their perceived importance, many of the video-related functions of mobile phones are not extensively utilised and consumers' appetites for them remain muted. The most widespread mobile entertainment activity indicated by UK mobile phone users was streaming or downloading music. Fewer than one in five (19%), however, did this regularly or occasionally. Using mobile phones as a platform for video-based entertainment was much less widespread: regularly or occasionally streaming/downloading of music videos (11%); clips from television programmes (9%); full-length television programmes (9%); full-length movies (9%); movie trailers (8%); and clips from sporting events (8%). Similar percentages among those not already doing each of these activities said that they would be (somewhat or very) keen to do so in the future (Entertainment Media Research, 2008). If these anticipated future users were aggregated with actual user percentages, video-based mobile entertainment activities would start to show a more serious level of penetration. What we also need to know, however, is how much time mobile entertainment users devote to video forms of entertainment and at what times of day. This information would then indicate the threat that such viewing might pose to standard television set viewing.

One indication came from the same study when all respondents (whether mobile phone users or not) were asked to indicate the activities in which they would like to engage when commuting between home and work or college. One in two (50%) named listening to music. Other popularly mentioned activities included listening to radio (38%), sending text messages (37%), and reading a book (36%). Video-related activities were far less widely endorsed in this context: watching music videos

(10%), watching news clips (9%), watching television programmes on mobile (8%), watching movie trailers (7%), watching clips from television programmes (6%) and watching sports clips (6%). The limited support for video activities, of course, might be explained by the lack of familiarity with doing them while on the move (Entertainment Media Research, 2008).

Earlier research with UK consumers in the middle of the 'noughties' decade had indicated that while most had heard about third generation (3G) mobile phones and their capacity to enable users to watch television or video clips (96%), far fewer attached value to being able to watch television programmes as they were broadcast (16%) or to watch pre-recorded clips from programmes (13%) (Ofcom, 2006b).

Small-scale tests of pilot television services have indicated some public appetite for this kind of television, larger scale surveys of viewers across the UK have yielded only minority support for it. Ofcom (2006d) reported that less than one in five UK television viewers regarded mobile television in 2006 as being important to society (17%) or personally significant to them (19%). When the nature of the question was changed such that respondents did not have to make a trade off between one technology and another, but were permitted instead to give independent ratings of the importance of specific new technologies becoming available, mobile television received somewhat more widespread support, with over four in ten rating it as important or very important both to society (44%) and to them personally (43%).

A number of test projects with mobile television have been run involving broadcasters, mobile operators, telecommunications operators and transmission infrastructure providers, Trials have used the DAB spectrum in London and the DVB-H standard in Oxford. Early indications were that people would be prepared to pay for these kinds of services, according to Ofcom (2006d). In fact, price was regarded as the most influential factor in relation to any decision to take up mobile television among those people who expressed any interest in this medium (Ofcom, 2006d). Mobile TV would be used at times when normal television viewing did not take place, such as when commuting to work. When UK viewers were asked to think about the occasions when people might use a mobile television service, the most popular replies were on long journeys (55%), when commuting or travelling (51%), while on public transport (40%) or while waiting for public transport (29%).

A number of mobile television partnerships have become established using 3G mobile networks to transmit television programmes and other video material. *Sky by Mobile* was launched by Vodaphone in October

2005 with 19 television channels bundled into Factual and Entertainment packages, with subscribers being charged £5 per month for either package. One trial, run by VirginMobile/BT and DAB broadcasting in June 2005, indicated that this service generated usage levels of one hour per week. Another trial, run in September 2005 by Arquiva, O2, and Nokia, used the DVB-H mobile television standard. It offered access to 16 live television channels including Discovery, MTV, cartoon network and the five main networks. Initial audience research indicated viewing levels at around three hours per week.

Research conducted by Telephia and published online on 25 October 2006 reported that 33 per cent of all mobile television and video viewers in the UK watched BBC1 and 29 per cent watched Sky Sports. The BBC came top among mobile Internet sites, with 28 per cent of all mobile web users using the BBC's site. Sky Sports scored a 23 per cent reach among mobile Internet users. Other most popularly used TV services on a mobile television platform were the Discovery Channel (23%), and BBC2, BBC3, BBC4, and ITV1 (all 22%).

Among all UK mobile subscribers there was an even 50/50 gender split. However, both mobile television and Internet users were more likely to be men and there were some differences between genders in the types of activities carried out over the mobile phone. Males were more likely than females to have accessed the wireless Internet (64% of those who did this were male) and to have played or downloaded audio/music (59% were male) and most dramatically to have downloaded, watched and paid for mobile television shows (70% were male). The use of mobile phones to watch television, however, was found to occur at a very low level (only 3% of subscribers).

Final thoughts

This book has examined changes and developments to television and the Internet to consider their implications for the future of television and the way it is used. Its author cannot claim to have a crystal ball with all the answers. Nonetheless, the evidence that has been collated in this volume from a wide range of academic and commercial sources does provide clear indications that traditional forms of television are evolving into new forms of programme delivery that will encourage more and more people to conduct their viewing differently in the future from the conventions of the past. In addition, parallel technological developments linked to the Internet and computer/video games are conditioning new forms of engagement with media content by media consumers (Holden Pearmain, 2006).

Television broadcasting had begun to expand dramatically even before the Internet went 'public' and the switch from analogue to digital transmissions systems has created opportunities for further growth in terms of content volumes. In addition, digital technology will enable television to offer a range of more sophisticated applications that invite viewers to become more active in terms of content choice and content manipulation. The latter developments are consistent with applications that have been rolled out to media consumers independently via the Internet. The Internet through its close association with computer technology was always a dynamic, interactive communications system that required a different kind of cognitive orientation from conventional television viewing.

Accompanying changes to television set and PC-Internet technologies will be the continuing evolution of mobile technologies that will provide 'on-the-move' facilities for engaging with video based content for entertainment and information purposes. This development will have more significance in terms of the enhancing opportunities to watch video-based entertainment and information at different times of the day. It will also mean that television viewing will no longer be tied to specific viewing locations. Its significance in terms of styles of viewing and therefore in relation to conditioning video content consumption patterns that render traditional linear television schedules redundant is probably to be found in enabling viewers to cope with watching extended video content in shorter chunks, picking up seamlessly where they left off at the end of the previous viewing occasion, regardless of the location of that viewing episode.

The migration of television programmes and other video content onto the Internet has already encouraged viewers to undertake viewing behaviour in a more dynamic environment than that associated with regular television broadcasting. At the same time, the television set is increasingly used in a more dynamic fashion as a video game console that involves an interactive mode of engagement on the part of players. It has been proposed in this book, that these varied activities are gradually conditioning a different kind of video content-using mentality and accompanying behavioural scripts that will eventually lead to the demise of traditional linear television schedules.

It is not envisaged that this change will result in the total demise of television channels within the next ten years. Despite the widespread adoption of personal video recorders, for example, research in the UK has shown that nearly nine in ten PVR users (88%) 'always' or 'almost always' checked the live television schedules for what was on before turning to recorded programming (Ipsos MediaCT, 2009).

Beyond the next few years, however, current growth trends in new media entertainment and information applications and services indicate that many will have reached levels of penetration that takes them beyond critical mass or 'tipping point' stages after which they can be expected very quickly to reach a point where they dominate media consumers' preferences. Nearly one in five (18%) of UK adults stated in 2008 that they had 'ever' watched television programme over the Internet, but just eight per cent had done so in the past week. Hence, viewers are experimenting with these new technologies. Among younger viewers, aged 18 to 34 years, however, the respective percentages were notably higher (28% and 12%), within the 'tipping point range' for more regular use (Ipsos MediaCT, 2009).

The critical shift will come when television sets evolve in terms of their level of computerised sophistication and are web-enabled. Whether they watch programmes on the telly or over their PC, most viewers (62%) said they prefer to watch on-demand content over a television set (TalkTalk, 2008). When this technological shift happens, traditional linear broadcast content formats and structures could quickly cease to be viable.

References

Abdulla, R. A., Garrison, B., Salwen, M. B., Driscoll, P. D. and Casey, D. (2005) online news credibility. In M. B. Salwen and P. D. Driscoll (eds) *Online News and the Public*, Mahwah, NJ: Lawrence Erlbaum Associates, pp. 147–63.

Adoni, H. and Cohen, A. (1978) Television economic news and the social construction of economic reality. *Journal of Communication*, 28, 61–70.

Adoni, H. and Nossek, H. (2001) The new media consumers, media convergence and the displacement effect. *Communications*, 26(11), 59–83.

Albrecht, C. (2009, 23 February) Online video viewing up, impact on TV 'negligible'. Available at: *http://www.newteevee.com/2009/02/23* (accessed on 28 August 2009).

Alexander, P. and Cunningham, B. M. (2007) Public and private decision making: The value of diversity. In P. M. Napoli (ed.) *Media Diversity and Localism: Meaning and Metrics*, Mahwah, NJ: Lawrence Erlbaum Associates.

Allan, S. (2006) *Online News: Journalism and the Internet*, Maidenhead: Open University Press.

Allen, C. (1965) Photographing the audience. *Journal of Advertising Research*, 5, 2–8.

Alps, T. (2008) The myth of the missing viewers. *Television Magazine*, 44(11). Available at: *http://www.rts.org.uk/Info_page_two_pic_2_det.asp?art_id=6807&sec_id=3274* (accessed 30 July 2009).

Alps, T. (2010) Online TV is no threat to the industry. *The Guardian: MediaGuardian*, 22 February, p. 4.

Anderson, D. R., Field, D. E., Collins, P. A., Lorch, E. P. and Nathan, J. G. (1985) Estimates of young children's time with television: A methodological comparison of parent reports with time-lapse video home observation. *Child Development*, 56, 1345–57.

Arant, M. D. and Anderson, J. Q. (2000) 'Online media ethics: A survey of US daily newspaper editors'. Paper presented to the Newspaper Division, Association for Education in Journalism and Mass Communication, August, 2000, Phoenix, AZ.

Armstrong, S. (2008) Everyone's a winner. *The Guardian, TV Today* supplement, 3 March, p. 1.

Around the Net in Online Media (2008, 18 November) Report: Online video cannibalizing TV consumption. Available at: *http://www.mediapost.com/publications??a=articles.showarticle&art_aid=94989* (accessed 28 August 2009).

Association for Television on Demand (2009, 18 March) ATVOD survey shows that half of Britons are now choosing video on demand. Available online at: *http://www.atvod.co.uk/news-and-events-article/2009/15.*

Barkhuus, L. (2009) Television on the Internet: new practices, new viewers. *CHI*, 4–9 April, Boston, MA, USA. ACM 978-1-60558-247/09/04.

Basil, M. D. (1990) Primary news source changes: Question-wording, availability and cohort effects. *Journalism Quarterly*, 67, 708–22.

Bechtel, R. B., Achelpohl, C. and Akers, R. (1972) Correlates between observed behaviour and questionnaire responses on television viewing. In E. A. Rubinstein, G. A. Comstock and J. P. Murray (eds) *Television and Social Behaviour*, Volume 4. Washington, DC: U.S. Government Printing Office.

Bello Interactive (2004) *Online Credibility Survey: How Credible are Online News Sources?* Available at: *www.dallasnews.com/sharecontent/dws/spe/credibility.*

Belson, W. A. (1961) Effects of television on the reading and buying of newspapers and magazines. *Public Opinion Quarterly*, 25, 366–81.

Berman, S. (2004) Media and entertainment 2010 scenario: the open media company of the future. *Strategy and Leadership*, 32(4), 33–44.

Bernoff, J. (2004) The mind of the DVR user: Acquisition and features DVR user survey reveals infectious enthusiasm. Forrester Research, USA, 31 August, pp. 1–16.

Biocca, F. (1988) Opposing conceptions of the audience: The active and passive hemispheres of mass communication theory. In J. A. Anderson (ed.) *Communication Yearbook 11*. Newbury Park, CA: Sage, pp. 57–80.

BIS/DCMS (2009, June) *Digital Britain: Building Britain's Future. Final report.* London: Department for Business, Innovation and Skills and department for Culture, Media and Sport.

BizAsia (2006, 29 November) Online videos eating into TV viewing times. *http://www.bizasia.com/Internet-it/zemfv/online_videos_eating_TV.*

blinkx (2008, 28 February) Blinkx survey of TV and online video habits reveals surprising user behaviour. Available at: *http://www.blinkx.com/article/* (accessed 28 August 2009).

Bolter, J. D. and Grusin, R. (1999) *Remediation: Understanding New Media*. Cambridge, MA: MIT Press.

Bordewijk, L. and van Kaam, B. (1986) Towards a new classification of tele-information services, *Intermedia*, 14, 16–21.

Briggs, A. (1961) *The History of Broadcasting in the United Kingdom*: Vol. I. *The Birth of Broadcasting*. Oxford: Oxford University Press.

Briggs, A. (1979) *The History of Broadcasting in the United Kingdom*: Vol. IV. *Sound and Vision*. Oxford: Oxford University Press.

Brown, B. and Barkhuus, L.K. (2006) The television will be revolutionised: Effects of PVRs and filesharing on television watching. *Proceedings of CHI 2006*, Montreal, Canada: ACM Press, pp. 1–4.

Buckingham, D. (2006) Is there a digital generation? In D. Buckingham and R. Willett (eds) *Digital Generations: Children, Young People and New Media*. Mahwah, NJ: Lawrence Erlbaum Associates, pp. 1–13.

Bucy, E. P. (2003) Media credibility reconsidered: Synergy effects between on air and online news. *Journalism and Mass Communication Quarterly*, 80(2), 247–64.

Bulkley, K. (2008) iPlayer came, we watched, it conquered. *The Guardian*, 30 June, Online TV the BBC Supplement, p. 1.

Bulkley, K. (2010) Magic of the moving image. *The Guardian: MediaGuardian – Commercial Break*, Supplement, 22 February, p. 1.

Center for the Digital Future (2005) *Fifth Study by the Digital Future Project Finds Major News Trends in Online use for Political Campaigns*, Annenberg School, University of Southern California. Available at: *www.digitalcenter.org/pdf/Center-for-the-Digital-Future-2005-highlights.pdf.*

Cha, M., Gummadi, K. P. and Rodriguez, P. (2008) Channel selection problem in live IPTV systems. *SIGCOMM'08.* 17–22 August, Seattle, Washington.

Changing Media (December, 2007) *UK Internet Usage 2007.* London: Changing Media Ltd. Available online at: *bbctrust@changingmedia.co.uk.*

Choi, J. H., Watt, J. H. and Lynch, M. (2006) Perceptions of news credibility about the war in Iraq: Why war opponents perceived the Internet as the most credible medium? *Journal of Computer-Mediated Communication,* 12(1), Article 11. Available at: *www.jcmc.indiana.edu/vol12/issue1.choi.html.*

Cole, J. and Robinson, J. P. (2002) Internet use, mass media and other activity in the UCLA survey. *IT and Society,* 1(2), 121–33.

Cole, J., Suman, M., Schramm, P., Bel, D. V., Lunn, B., Maguire, P., Hanson, K., Singh, R. and Aquino, J. S. (2000) *The UCLA Internet Report: Surveying the Digital Future Year One.* Available at: *http://www.ccp.ucla.edu.*

Cole, J., Suman, M., Schramm, I., Lunn, R. and Aquino, J. S. (2003) *Surveying the Digital Future: Year 3.* Los Angeles, CA: UCLA Center for Communication Policy.

Cole, J. I., Suman, M., Schramm, P., Lunn, R. and Aquino, J. S. (2004, September) *Ten Years, Ten Trends: Surveying the Digital Future, Year 4.* Los Angeles, CA: USC Annenberg School, Centre for the Digital Future. Available at: *www.digitalcenter.org* (accessed 2 November 2009).

ComScore (2009a, 4 February) U.S. online video viewing surges 13 percent in record-setting December. Available at: *http://www.comscore.com/press_events/press_releases/2009/2/* (accessed 27 November 2009).

ComScore (2009b, 17 March) UK online video viewing audience grows 10 per cent during past year to nearly 30 million viewers. Available at: *http://www.mediametrics.com/Press_Releases/2009/3/* (accessed on 28 August 2009).

Conformity e-News Breaks (2006, 12 January) Congress sets deadline for digital TV switchover. Available at: *http://www.confirmity.com/enews011206/Article2* (accessed 11 March 2010).

Consumer Reports Web Watch (2005) *Leap of Faith: Using the Internet Despite the Dangers.* Available at: *www.consumerwebwatch.org/pdfs/princeton.pdf.*

Cooper, M. (2006) Internet media usage and substitutability. Available at: *http://www.freepress.net/files/study_2_media_usage_and_substitutability.pdf* (accessed on 25 February 2010).

Cooper, W. (2010) Towards a connect future. *The Guardian: MediaGuardian – Commercial Break,* Supplement, 22 February, p. 4.

Crum, C. (2009, 17 March) Online video viewing grows by 10% in the UK. Available at: *www.webpronews.com/topnews/2009.03.17* (accessed 27 November 2009).

Cummings, J. N. and Kraut, R. (2002) Domesticating computers and the Internet. *The Information Society,* 18(3), 1–18.

Curran, J. and Seaton, J. (1997) *Power without Responsibility: The Press and Broadcasting in Britain* (5th edn), London, UK: Routledge.

DCMS (2004, June) *Quantitative Research to Inform the Preparation of the BBC Charter Review 2004.* Report prepared by MORI for the COI

Communications Research Unit on behalf of the Department for Culture, Media and Sport, London.

DCMS (2006) *A Public Service for All: the BBC in the Digital Age*. London: Department for Culture, Media and Sport.

DCMS/BIS (2010, 11 March) Digital Television. TV is changing. It's going completely digital. Department for Culture, Media and Sport and Department for Business, Innovation and Skills, available at: *http://www.digitaltelevision. gov.uk* (accessed 12 March 2010).

Digital Lifestyles (2006, 27 November) UK online video viewing bites into TV viewing. Available at: *http://www.digital-lifestyles.info/206/11/27*.

Dimmick, J., Chen, Y. and Li, Z. (2004) Competition between the Internet and traditional news media: the gratification opportunities niche dimension. *Journal of Media Economics*, 17(1), 19–33.

Dimmick, J., Kline, S. and Stafford, L. (2000) The gratification niches of personal e-mail and telephone: Competition, displacement and complementarity. *Communication Research*, 27, 227–48.

Dimmick, J. and Rothenbuhler, E. (1984a) The theory of the niche: Quantifying competition among media industries. *Journal of Communication*, 34, 103–19.

Dimmick, J. and Rothenbuhler, E. (1984b) Competitive displacement in the communication industries: new media in old environments. In R. Rice and Associates (eds) *The New Media: Communication Research and Technology*, Beverly Hills, CA: Sage, pp. 297–304.

Dryburgh, H. (2001) Changing our ways: Why and how Canadians use the Internet. Statistics Canada Cat. No. 56F0006XIE, 26 March. Available online at: *http://www.stat-can.ca*.

Dutton, W. and Helsper, E. J. (2007) *The Internet in Britain: 2007*. University of Oxford: Oxford Internet Institute.

Emigh, J. (2008, 25 November). Analysts: Consumers drop TV, turn to Internet for entertainment. Available at: *www.betanews.com/article*.

Entertainment Media Research (2008) *Digital Entertainment Survey*. Available at: *www.entertainmentmediaresearch.com* (accessed 30 March 2008).

European Interactive Advertising Association (2007, September) EIAA Mediascope Europe 2007: Media Consumption Study. Available at: *www.eiaa.net*.

Ferguson, D. A. and Perse, E. M. (2004) Audience satisfaction among TiVo and ReplayTV users. *Journal of Interactive Advertising*, 4(2), available at: *www. jiad.org/article44*.

Findahl, O. (2008) The role of Internet in a changing mediascape: Competitor or complement *Observatoria Journal*, 6, 209–22.

Finholt, T. and Sproull, L. (1990) Electronic groups at work. *Organization Science*, 1(1), 41–64.

Flanagin, A. and Metzger, M. (2000) Perceptions of Internet information credibility. *Journalism and Mass Communication Quarterly*, 77(3), 515–40.

Fletcher, M. (2009, July/August) Battle of the brands. *Revolution*, pp. 47–49.

Franzen, A. (2000) Does the Internet make us lonely? *European Sociological Review*, 16, 427–38.

Frechette, J. (2006) Cyber-censorship or cyber-literacy? Envisioning cyber-learning through media education. In D. Buckingham and R. Willett (eds)

Digital Generations: Children, Young People and New Media, pp. 149–71. Mahwah, NJ: Lawrence Erlbaum Associates.

Friends of Canadian Broadcasting (2009, 5 June) TV still number one, most trusted, news source; newspapers second, Internet last. Available at: *www. friends.ca/news-item/8380* (accessed 24 November 2009).

George, M. and Lennard, L. (2007) *Ease of use issues with domestic electronic communications equipment.* Report for Ofcom. London: Office of Communications.

Gershuny, J. (2002) 'Web-use and net-nerds: A neo-functionalist analysis of the impact of information technology in the home'. Working Papers of the Institute for Social and Economic Research, paper 2002–1. Colchester: University of Essex.

Gershuny, J. (2003) Web use and net nerds: A new functionalist analysis of the impact of information technology in the home. *Social Forces*, 82(1), September.

Gladwell, M. (2000) *The Tipping Point: How Little Things can Make a Big Difference.* London: Little, Brown.

Grotta, G. L. and Newsom, D. (1982) How does cable television in the home relate to other media use patterns? *Journalism Quarterly*, 59, 588–91, 609.

Gunter, B. (1987) *Poor Reception: Misunderstanding and Forgetting Broadcast News.* Hillsdale, NJ: Lawrence Erlbaum Associates.

Gunter, B. (1998) *The Effects of Video Games on Children: The Myth Unmasked.* Sheffield: Sheffield Academic Press.

Gunter, B. (2005a) *Digital Health: Meeting Patient and Professional Needs Online*, Mahwah, NJ: Lawrence Erlbaum Associates.

Gunter, B. (2005b) Trust in the news on television. *Aslib Proceedings*, 57(5), 384–97.

Gunter, B. (2006a) Who do online news consumers trust? *Library and Information Update*, 5(9), 40–1.

Gunter, B. (2006b) Advances in e-democracy: Overview. *Aslib Proceedings*, 58(5), 361–70.

Gunter, B. (2008) Internet dating: A British survey. *Aslib Proceedings*, 60(2), 88–97.

Gunter, B., Hansen, A. and Touri, M. (2007) Screen Deprivation and Family Life: A Research Project for BBC Panorama. Leicester: Department of Media and Communication. Available at: *www.le.ac.uk/mc/research/documents/*.

Gunter, B., Campbell, V., Touri, M. and Gibson, R. (2009) Blogs, news and credibility. *Aslib Proceedings*, Special Issue: Blogging and the Erosion of Public and Private Life Spheres, 61(2), 185–204.

Gunter, B., Sancho-Aldridge, J. and Winstone, P. (1994) *Television: The Public's View – 1993.* London: John Libbey.

Gunter, B. and Svennevig, M. (1988) *Attitudes to Broadcasting Over the Years.* London: John Libbey.

Gunter, B., Rowlands, I. and Nicholas, D. (2009) *The Google Generation: Are ICT innovations changing information-seeking behaviour?* Oxford: Chandos Publishing.

Gunter, B., Russell, C., Withey, R. and Nicholas, D. (2003) The British Life and Internet Project: Inaugural survey findings. *Aslib Proceedings*, 55(4), 203–16.

Gunter, B., Russell, C., Withey, R. and Nicholas, D. (2004) Broadband in Britain: how does it compare with narrowband? *Aslib Proceedings*, 56(2), 98.

Gunter, B. and Svennevig, M. (1988) *Attitudes to Broadcasting Over the Years.* London: John Libbey.

Gunter, B., Sancho-Aldridge, J. and Winstone, P. (1994) *Television: The Public's View – 1993.* London: John Libbey.

Hahn, J. (2009, 11 September) Internet is top source for sports news and information. Available at: *www.dmconfidential.com/blogs/column/Marketing/2461* (accessed 24 November 2009).

Hamlyn, R., Mindel, A. and McGinigal, S. (2009) *Digital Britain: Attitudes to supporting non-BBC regional news from the TV licence fee.* London, UK: Department for Culture, Media and Sport.

Hammersley, B. (2006) Get with the programme. *The Guardian: MediaGuardian,* Supplement 'Changing Media,' 20 March, p. 1.

Hancer, J. (2006) Digital TV is coming of age and local government is starting to take note. *Aslib Proceedings,* 58(5), 429–35.

Hargrave, S., 2008, Confounded by choice, *The Guardian,* Online TV Supplement (30 June) p. 5.

Hargreaves, I. and Thomas, J. (2002) *New news, old news.* London, UK: Broadcasting Standards Commission and Independent Television Commission.

Harvey, M. and Rothe, J. (1985–6) Video-cassette recorders: Their impact on viewers and advertisers. *Journal of Advertising Research,* 26(1), 19–27.

Henke, L. and Donohue, T. R. (1989) Functional displacement of traditional TV viewing by VCR owners. *Journal of Advertising Research,* 29, 18–23.

Himmelweit, H. T., Oppenheim, A. N. and Vince, P. (1958) *Television and the Child.* London: Oxford University Press.

Holden Pearmain/ORC International (2006, December) *Digital Dividend Review: A report of consumer research conducted for Ofcom by Holden Pearmain and ORC International.* London, UK: Office of Communications. Available at: *www.ofcom.org.uk.*

Holmewood, L. and Hughes, S. (2009, 6 July) With all this online, why watch TV? *The Guardian: MediaGuardian,* p. 1.

Horowitz Associates Inc (2009, 29 January) Communication, entertainment drives internet use among teens. *http://www.cy-gb.facebook.com/note.php?note_id.*

Horrigan, J. (2009, June) Home Broadband Adoption 2009. Pew Internet and American Life Project, Washington, D.C. Available online at: *http://www.pewinternet.org.*

Human Capital/Martin Hamblin GfK (2004) *A study measuring the value of the BBC,* London: British Broadcasting Corporation.

IBA (1982) *Attitudes to Broadcasting.* London: Independent Broadcasting Authority, Research Report.

Internet World Stats (2009) Usage and population statistics. Available at: *www.Internetworldstats.com/stats. Accessed 15th February 2010.*

Ipsos MediaCT (2009, December) The On-Demand Market: Handing over Control. Bite-sized Thought Piece. Available at: *http://www.ipsos-mori.com/DownloadPublication/1173_MediaCT_thoughtpiece_the%20on_demand%20market_Dec09_web* (accessed 12 March 2010).

Ipsos MORI (2007, September) Technology Tracker September 2007: Two-thirds use Internet at home or work. Available at: *www.ipsos-mori.com.*

James, M. L., Wotring, C. E. and Forrest, E. J. (1995) An exploratory study of the perceived benefit of electronic bulletin board use and their impact on other communication activities. *Journal of Broadcasting and Electronic Media*, 39, 30–50.

Jensen, J. F. (2005) Interactive television: New genres, new format, new content. *Proceedings of the Second Australasian Conference on Interactive Entertainment*, Sydney, Australia.

Jones, S. and Fox, S. (2009) Generations Online in 2009. Pew Internet Project Data Memo, 28 January. Available at: *http://www.pewinternet.org/trends.asp*.

Kaplan, S. (1978) The impact of cable television services on the use of competing media. *Journal of Broadcasting*, 22, 155–65.

Kayany, J. and Yelsma, P. (2000) Displacement effects of online media in the socio-economical contexts of households. *Journal of Broadcasting and Electronic Media*, 44, 215–30.

Keown, L. A. (2007) Keeping up with the news: Canadians and their news media diet. *Canadian Social Trends*, No.83, Catalogue No.11-008-XIE, pp.12–18.

Kestnbaum, M., Robinson, J. P., Neustadtl, A. and Alvarez, A. (2002) Information technology and social time displacement. *IT and Society*, 1(1), 21–37.

Kimberley, S. (2009, 21 July) Facebook takes the social world by storm, *Media Week*, pp. 10–11.

Kiousis, S. (1999) *Public trust or mistrust? Perceptions of media credibility in the information age.* Paper presented to the Mass Communication and society Division, Association for education in Journalism and mass Communication, New Orleans, LA.

Kiousis, S. (2001) Public trust or mistrust? Perceptions of media credibility in the information age. *Mass Communication and Society*, 4(4), 381–403.

Kiss, J., 2008, Throw away your TV, it's all on the laptop, *The Guardian*, Online TV Supplement, 30 June, p. 7.

Klein, J. A., Karger, S. A. and Sinclair, K. A. (2003) *Digital Television for All: A report on usability and accessible design.* Prepared for the Digital Television Project. Cambridge: The Generics Group with the Department of Trade and Industry. Available at: *www.genericsgroup.com*.

Klein, J. A., Karger, S. A. and Sinclair, K. A. (2004a) *Attitudes to Digital Television: Preliminary findings on consumer adoption of Digital Television.* Prepared for the Digital Television Project. Cambridge: The Generics Group with the Department of Trade and Industry. Available at: *www.genericsgroup.com*.

Klein, J. A., Karger, S. A. and Sinclair, K. A. (2004b) *Attitudes to Digital Switchover: The impact of digital switchover on consumer adoption of digital television.* Prepared for the Digital Television Project. Cambridge: The Generics Group with the Department of Trade and Industry. Available at: *www.genericsgroup.com*.

Kraut, R., Patterson, M., Lundmark, V., Kiesler, S., Mukhopadhyay, T. and Scherlis, W. (1998) Internet paradox: a social technology that reduces social involvement and psychological well-being. *American Psychologist*, 53(9), 1017–31.

Kraut, R., Scherlis, W., Mukhopadhyay, T., Manning, J. and Keisler, S. (1996) The HomeNet field trial of residential Internet services. *Communications of the ACM*, 39, 55–65.

Kraut, R., Olson, J., Banaji, M., Bruckman, A., Cohen, J. and Couper, M. (2004) Psychological research online: Report on Board of scientific Affairs' Advisory group on the Conduct of Research on the Internet. *American Psychologist*, 59, 105–77.

Kraut, R., Kiesler, S., Boneva, B. and Shlovski, I. (2005) Examining the impact of Internet use on TV viewing: Details make a difference. In R. Kraut et al. (eds) *Computers, Phones and the Internet: Domesticating Information Technology*, Series in Human-Technology Interaction, Oxford University Press.

Laughlin, A. (2009, 10 August) Fast broadband 'will not boost online TV' Available at: *http://www.digitalspy.co.uk/digitaltv/al70409/* (accessed 1 September 2009).

Laurel, B. (1993) *Computers as Theatre*. New York: Addison-Wesley.

Lazarsfeld, P. F. (1940) *Radio and the Printed Page*. New York: Dell, Sloan and Pearce.

Lee, P. S. N. and Leung, L. (2006) Assessing the displacement effects of the Internet. *Telematics and Informatics*, 23(1), 22–37.

Lee, R. (1975) Credibility of newspaper and TV news. *Journalism Quarterly*, 55(3), 282–87.

Lee, W. and Kuo, E. C. Y. (2002) Internet and displacement effect: Children's media use and activities in Singapore. *Journal of Computer-Mediated Communication*, 9, 2. Available online at: *http://www.ascuse.org*.

Lenhart, A., Maden, M., Macgill, A. R. and Smith, A. (2007, December) *Teens and Social Media*. Pew Internet and American Life Project, Washington, D.C. Available at: *http://www.pewinternet.org*.

Lenhart, A., Kahne, J., Middaugh, E. Sr., Macgill, A. R., Evans, C., Sr. and Vitak, J. (2008a, September) *Teens, Video Games and Civics*. Pew Internet and American Life Project and John D. and Catherine T. MacArthur Foundation. Available at: *http://www.pewinternet.org*.

Lenhart, A., Jones, S. and Macgill, A. R. (2008b, December) *Adults and video games*. Pew Internet Project Data memo. Pew Internet and American Life Project, Washington, D.C. Available at: *http://www.pewinternet.org*.

Lesnard, L. (2005) Social Change, Daily Life and the Internet. *Chimera Working Paper Number 2005–07*. Colchester: University of Essex. Available at: *www.essex.ac.uk/chimera*.

Levy, M. (1978) The audience experience with television news. *Journalism Monographs*, No. 55.

Levy, M. (1983) The time-shifting use of home video recorders. *Journal of Broadcasting and Electronic Media*, 27, 263–68.

Levy, M. and Gunter, B. (1988) *Home Video and the Changing Nature of the Television Audience*. London: John Libbey.

Levy, M. and Robinson, J. (1986) *The Main Source*. Beverly Hills, CA: Sage.

Lighting, J. (2007) We need younger eyeballs. *The Guardian; MediaGuardian*, 15 October, p. 8.

Livaditi, J., Vassilopoulou, K., Lougos, C. and Chorianoouplos, K. (2002) Needs and gratifications for interactive TV applications: implications for designers. *Proceedings of the 36th Hawaii International Conference on System Sciences*. Available at: *http://www2.computer.org/portal/web/csdl/doi/10.1109/HICSS.2003.1174237* (accessed 1 September 2009).

Livingstone, S. (2003) Children's use of the Internet: reflections on the emerging research agenda. *New Media and Society*, 5(2), 147–66.

Livingstone, S. and Bovill, M. (2001) 'Families and the Internet: An observational study of children and young people's Internet use'. Final Report to BT. London: Department of Social Psychology and Media, London School of Economics.

Livingstone, S. and Bober, M. (2006) Regulating the Internet at home: Contrasting the perspectives of children and parents. In D. Buckingham and R. Willett (eds) *Digital Generations: Children, Young People and New Media*. Mahwah, NJ: Lawrence Erlbaum Associates, pp. 93–113.

Looms, P. O. (2005) Recent developments with PVRs and the free-to-air television market in Europe. Available at: *http://www.itu.dk/courses/PDI/E2005/Looms_PVR_Aalborg-290805* (accessed 1 September 2009).

Lull, J. (1990) *Inside Family Viewing*. London: Routledge.

Maad, S. (2003) MARILYN: A Novel Platform for Intelligent Interactive TV (IITV), In Proceedings of Human Computer Interaction International HCII2003 Conference, Crete, Greece, July.

Maad, S. (2005) The potential and pitfall of interactive TV technology: An empirical study. Fraunhofer: Institute for Media Communication (IMK), Germany. Available at: *www.mit.edu/cms/mit3/papers/maad* (accessed 5 February 2010).

Madden, M. (2007) YouTubers meet lens to lens. Pew Internet and American Life Project. Available at: *www.pewinternet.com* (accessed 13 August 2009).

Madden, M. (2009, July) The audience for online video-sharing sites shoots up. Pew Internet and American Life Project, Washington, D.C. Available online at: *http://www.pewInternet.org/Reports/2009/13-The-Audience-for-Online-Videosharing-Sites-Shoots-Up.aspx*.

Mannell, R. C., Zuzanek, J. and Aronson, R. (2005) 'Internet/computer use and adolescent leisure behaviour, flow experiences and psychological well-being: The displacement hypothesis'. Paper presented at the Eleventh Canadian Congress on Leisure Research, 20 May, Nanaimo, BC, Canada.

Marketing Charts (2007, 22nd August) IBM Consumer Survey: Internet rivals declining TV as primary media source. Available at: *www.marketingcharts.com/television/ibm* (accessed 24 November 2009).

Marketing Charts (2009a, 10 August) Online video: prime time rules don't apply. Available at: *http://www.marketingcharts.com/television/* (accessed on 28 August 2009).

Marketing Charts (2009b, 31 October) October video streams up 26%; Facebook viewing jumps 1.840%. Available at: *www.marketingcharts.com/october-video-streams-up* (accessed 27 November 2009).

Marketingprofs.com (2009, 3 November) Fall TV drives record online video viewing. Available at: *www.marketingprofs.com/charts/2009/3139* (accessed on 24 November 2009).

Mendelsohn, H. (ed.) (1964) *Listening to Radio*. New York: Free Press.

Metzger, M. J. and Flanagin, A. J. (2002) Audience orientations toward new media. *Communication Research Reports*, 19(4), 338–51.

Moskalyuk, A. (2004, 28 October) Major news sources for political information: TV (78%), newspapers (38%), radio (16%), Internet (15%), magazines (4%). Available at: *http://www.zdnet.com/ITFacts/?p=6385* (accessed on 24 November 2009).

National Consumer Council (1999, December) *Tuning in to Consumers: Public Service Broadcasting in the Digital Age*, London: National Consumer Council.

Negroponte, N. (1995) *Being Digital: The Roadmap for Survival on the Information Superhighway*. London: Hodder & Stoughton.

Nesbitt, A. (2006, 27 November) Online video versus TV – is it eroding or growing? Available at: *www.digitalpodcast.com/podcastnews/2006/11/27/* (accessed 27 November 2009).

Nguyen, A. and Western, M. (2006) The complementary relationship between the Internet and traditional mass media: The case of online news and information. *Information Research*, 11(3), paper 259. Available at: *http://www.InformationR.net/ir/11-3/paper259*.

Nicholas, D., Frossling, I., Martin, H. and Buesing, P. (1997) (Really) getting to grips with the Internet: What it has to offer in the way of newspapers. *Vine*, 52(3), 98–114.

Nicholas, D., Huntington, P., Williams, P. and Gunter, B. (2002) Digital visibility: Menu prominence and its impact on use. Case study: The NHS Direct Digital channel on Kingston Interactive Television. *Aslib Proceedings*, 54(4), 213–21.

Nicholas, D., Huntington, P., Williams, P. and Gunter, B. (2006) First steps towards providing the UK with health care information and advice via their television sets: An evaluation of four Department of Health sponsored pilot services. *Aslib Proceedings*, 55(3), 138–54.

Nie, N. H. and Erbring, L. (2000) *Internet and Society – A Preliminary Report*. Stanford, CA: Stanford Institute for the Quantitative Study of Society. Available online at: *http://www.stanford.edu/group/siqss/Press_Release/Preliniary_report.pdf*.

Nie, N. H. and Ebring, L. (2002) Internet and society: A preliminary report. *IT and Society*, 1(1), 225–83.

Nie, N. H. and Hillygus, D. S. (2002) The impact of Internet use on sociability: Time-diary findings. *IT and Society*, 1(1).

Nielsen Media Research (2006) User-generated content drives half of US top 10 fastest growing web brands, according to Nielsen NEtRatings. Source: Nielsen/Netratings. Available at: *www.nielsen-online.com/pr/PR_060810* (accessed 10 October 2009).

NielsenWire (2009, 20 May) Americans watching more TV than ever: Web and mobile video up too. Available at: *http://www.blog.nielsenwire* (accessed 27 November 2009).

Norris, P. (2001) *Digital Divide: Civic Engagement, Information Poverty and the Internet Worldwide*. Cambridge: Cambridge University Press.

OECD (2008) 'Enhancing Competition in telecommunications: protecting and empowering consumers'. Ministerial background report. OECD Ministerial meeting on the Future of the Internet Economy, Seoul, Korea, 17–18 June. Available at: *http://www.oecde.org/dataoecd/25/2/40679279* (accessed 12 March 2010).

Ofcom (2004, April) *Ofcom Review of Public Service Television Broadcasting: Phase 1 – is television special?* London: Office of Communications. Available at: *www.ofcom.org.uk*.

Ofcom (2005) The Communications Market Report 2005. London: Office of Communications. Available at: *www.ofcom.org.uk/research* (accessed 10 March 2008).

Ofcom (2006a, May) *Media Literacy Audit – Report on Media Literacy Amongst Children*. London: Office of Communications. Available at: *www.ofcom. org.uk*.

Ofcom (2006b, July) *Communications Market: Special Report. Consumer Engagement with Digital Communications Services*. London: Office of Communications.

Ofcom (2006c, August) *BBC iPlayer Market Impact Assessment: Consumer Survey: Evaluating the Impact of BBC iPlayer*. London: Office of Communications. Available at: *www.ofcom.org.uk*.

Ofcom (2006d, December) *Digital Dividend Review: A report of consumer research for Ofcom conducted by Holden Pearmain and ORC International*. London: Office of Communications. Available at: *www.ofcom.org.uk*.

Ofcom (2007a, March) *Public Service Broadcasting Annual Report 2007*. London: Office of Communications. Available at: *www.ofcom.org.uk*.

Ofcom (2007b, June) *Annexes to New News, Future News: Research and Evidence Base*. London: Office of Communications. Available at: *www.ofcom. org.uk*.

Ofcom (2007c, July) *New News, Future News: The challenges for television news after Digital Switch-over*. London: Office of Communications. Available at: *www.ofcom.org.uk*.

Ofcom (2007d, August) *The Communications Market Report 2007: 2. Television*, London: Office of Communications. Available at: *www.ofcom.org.uk*.

Ofcom (2007e, August) *The Communications Market Report 2007: 4. Telecommunications*. London: Office of Communications. Available at: *www. ofcom.org.uk*.

Ofcom (2007f, December) *Summary of focus group research: Annex 15 to pay TV market investigation consultation*. Research Document (December 2007). London: Office of Communications. Available at: *www.ofcom.org.uk*.

Ofcom (2008) *Ofcom's Second Public Service Broadcasting Review: Phase 2. Preparing for the digital future*. London: Office of Communications. Available at: *www.ofcom.org.uk*.

Ofcom (2009a) *The Communications Market 2009: 2. Television*. London: Office of Communications. Available at: *www.ofcom.org.uk*.

Ofcom (2009b) *The Communications Market 2009: 5. Converging Markets*. London: Office of Communications. Available at: *www.ofcom.org.uk*.

Ofcom (2009c) *The Consumer Experience 2009*. London: Office of Communications. Available at: *www.ofcom.org.uk*.

Ofcom (2009d) *Public Service Broadcasting Report 2009*. London: Office of Communications. Available at: *www.ofcom.org.uk*.

Oliver and Ohlbaum Associates, 2003, *UK Television Content in the Digital Age: Opportunities and Challenges*. Report for PACT. London: PACT.

Online News Association (2002) *Digital Journalism Credibility Study*, available at: *www.banners.nictissdot.com/termetro/boletines/docs/marcom/prensa.ona/2002*

Opinion Leader (2009, November) *BBC Trust Project Canvas*. Available at: *www.bbc.co.uk/bbctrust/assets/files* (accessed on 5 February 2010).

Parliamentary Office of Science and Technology (2006) *Analogue to Digital TV Switchover.* Postnote, June, Number 264. Available at: *www.parliament.uk/ documents/upload/postpn264* (accessed 8 February 2010).

Pastore, M. (2001, 10 May) *Internet becoming preferred information source.* Available at: *www.clickz.com/762881* (accessed 24 November 2009).

Patterson, T. E. (2007, July) *Young People and News.* Report from the Joan Shorenstein Centre on the Press, Politics and Public Policy, John F. Kennedy School of Government, Harvard University. Available at: *www.hks.harvard. edu/presspool/publications/reports* (accessed 20 January 2010).

Paul, B., Salwen, M. B. and Dupagne, M. (2000) Third-person effect: A meta-analysis of the perceptual hypothesis. *Mass Communication and Society*, 3, 57–85.

Perloff, R. M. (2002) The third-person effect. In J. Bryant and D. Zillmann (eds) *Media Effects: Advances in Theory and Research* (2nd edn) Mahwah, NJ: Lawrence Erlbaum Associates, pp. 489–506.

Pew Project for Excellence in Journalism (2006) The State of the News Media: An Annual report on American Journalism. Available at: *www.stateofthenewsmedia. org/2006/narrative-online-audience.asp?cat=2&media=5.*

Pew Research Centre (2000, January). The Internet news audience goes ordinary. Available at: *http://www.people-press.org/tech98sum.htm.*

Pew Research Centre (2008, August) *Audience Segments in a Changing News Environment: Key News Audiences Now Blend Online and Traditional Sources.* Washington, DC: The Pew Research Centre for the People and the Press. Available at: *http://www.people-press.org.*

Provonost, G. (2002) The Internet and time displacement: A Canadian perspective. *IT and Society*, 1(1), 44–53.

Rainie, L. K., Fox, S. and Fallows, D. (2003) *The Internet and the Iraq War: How Online Americans have used the Internet to Learn War News, Understand Events and Promote their Views.* Pew Internet and American Life Project. Available at: *www.pewinternet.org.*

Rasmussen, T. A. (2004) Interactive television – social use or individual control? Available at: *www.csd.abdn.ac.uk/njmasthof/EuroITV04/P13* (accessed 5 February 2010).

Rasmussen Reports (2009, 2 July) 46% say TV news more reliable than Internet, 35% disagree. Report at *www.rasmussenreports.com* (accessed 24 November 2009).

Reuters (2009, 17 June) Internet most popular information source: poll. Available at: *http://www.reuters.com/article/lifestyleMolt/* (accessed 24 November 2009).

Rice, R. (1992) Contexts of research on organizational computer-mediated communication. In M. Lea (ed.) *Contexts of Computer-Mediated Communication*, London: Harvester Wheatsheaf, pp. 113–44.

Rice, R. (1993) Media appropriateness: Using social presence theory to compare traditional and new organizational media. *Human Communication Research*, 19, 451–84.

Rice, R. and Haythornthwaite, C. (2002) Perspectives on Internet use: Access, involvement and interaction. In L. A. Lievrouw and S. Livingstone (eds) *The Handbook of New Media.* London: Sage, pp. 92–113.

Robertson, M. R. (2009, 17 February) Online video viewing in Germany – 77% of German Internet users watch video online. Available at: *www.reeelseo.com* (accessed 28 August 2009).

Robinson, J. P. (1981) Television and leisure time: A new scenario. *Journal of Communication*, 31, 120–30.

Robinson, J. P., Barth, K. and Kohut, A. (1997) Social impact research: Personal computers, mass media and use of time. *Social Science Computer Review*, 15(1), 65–82.

Robinson, J. P., Kestnbaum, M., Neustadtl, A. and Alvarez, A. (2000) Mass media use and social life among Internet users. *Social Science Computer Review*, 18(4), 490–501.

Robinson, J. P., Kestnbaum, M., Neustadtl, A. and Alvarez, A. (2002) Information technology and functional time displacement. *IT and Society*, 1(2), 21–36.

Robinson, J.P. and Levy, M. (1986) *The Main Source: Learning from Television News*. Beverly Hills, CA: Sage.

Rogers, E. M. (1995) *Diffusion of Innovations*, 4th edn. New York: Free Press.

Roper Organization (1983) *Trends in attitudes towards television and other media: A twenty year review*. New York: Television Information Office.

Rose, B. and Roisin, L. (2001) *Internet VII. The Internet and Streaming: What Consumers Want Next*. Arbitron/ Edison Media Research, New York.

Rubin, A. (1983) Television uses and gratifications: The interactions of viewing patterns and motivations. *Journal of Broadcasting*, 27(1), 37–51.

Rubin, A. (1984) Ritualised and instrumental television viewing. *Journal of Communication*, 34, 67–77.

Ruggiero, T. R. (2004) Paradigm repair and changing journalistic perceptions of the Internet as an objective news source. *Convergence: The Journal of Research into New Technologies*, 10(4), 92–104.

Salwen, M. B. and Dupagne, M. (1999) The third-person effect: perceptions of the media's influence and immoral consequences. *Communication Research*, 26, 523–49.

Schramm, W., Lyle, J. and Parker, E. (1961) *Television in the Lives of Our Children*. Stanford, CA: Stanford University Press.

Short, J., Williams, E. and Christie, B. (1976) *The Social Psychology of Telecommunications*. New York: Wiley.

Silverstone, R. (1994) *Television and Everyday Life*. London: Routledge.

Simply/Work (2008, 27 March) Online Video: What the Statistics Can't Tell You. Available at: *www.ignoretvatyourperil.tv* (accessed 27 November 2009).

Slocombe, M. (2006, 27 November) UK online video viewing bites into TV viewing. Available at: *http://www.digital-lifestyles.info/2006/11/27* (accessed on 28 August 2009).

Sparkes, V. M. (1983) Public perception of and reaction to multichannel TV. *Journal of Broadcasting*, 27(2), 163–76.

Stanger, J. and Gridina, N. (1999) *Media in the Home 1999: The Fourth Annual Survey of Parents and Children*. Pennsylvania: Annenberg Public Policy Center of the University of Pennsylvania.

Stanley, H. and Niemi, R. (1990) *Vital Statistics on American Politics*, 2nd edn. Washington, DC: Congressional Quarterly.

Stelter, B. (2009, 14 May) Hulu questions count of its audience, *The New York Times*. Available at: *www.nytimes.com/1009/05/15/business media* (accessed 27 November 2009).

Stoneman, P. (2006) Exploring time use: A methodological response to 'web-use and net-nerds,' Chimera Working Paper, 2006–11, Colchester: University of Essex. Available online at: *www.essex.ac.uk/chimera/publications.hmtl.*

Strangelove.com (2009). U.S. online video market soars in July. Available at: *http://www.strangelove.com/blog/2009/08/online-video-market-soars-july* (accesed on 28 August 2009).

Sundar, S. (1999) Exploring receivers' criteria for perception of print and online news. *Journalism and Mass Communication Quarterly*, 76, 373–86.

Swedlow, T. (2000) 'Interactive enhanced television: A historical and critical perspective'. Whitepaper, commissioned by the American Film Institute-Intel Enhanced Television Workshop for distribution to participants of its 2000 activities and on its website, *http://www.itvt.com.*

TalkTalk (2008, 16 January) British Consumers Demand TV Freedom in 2008. Available at: *http://www.talktalk.co.uk/presscentre/pressrelease/2008/January* (accessed 12 March 2010).

The Bridge (2008, 26 February) Video's Migration: From TV to Internet: Growing Popularity, New Programming and Trends of 2008. Available at: *http://www.thebridgedatagroup.com.*

Towler, R. (2003) *The Public's View 2002*. London: Independent Television Commission.

Tsao, J. C. and Sibley, S. D. (2004) Displacement and reinforcement effects of the Internet and other media as sources of advertising information. *Journal of Advertising Research*, 44(1), 126–42.

Veenhof, B. (2006) The Internet: Is it changing the way Canadians spend their time? *Connectedness Series* No. 13, Statistics Canada Catalogue No. 56F0004MIE. Available at: *www.statcan.ca/bsolc/English/bsolc* (accessed 12 February 2010).

Veenhof, B., Wellman, B., Quell, C. and Hogan, B. (2008) Isolation, cohesion or transformation: How Canadians use of the Internet is shaping society. *Connectedness Series* No. 16. Statistics Canada Available at: *www.statcan.ca/bsolc/English/bsolc* (accessed 12 February 2010).

Waller, E, (2008) Crank call or market ready to explode? *The Guardian*, TV Today supplement, 3 March, p. 5.

Whelan, S. (2008) Something just clicked, *The Guardian*, TV Today supplement, 3 March, p. 3.

Williams, C. (2001) Connected to the Internet: Still connected to life? Canadian Social Trends. Statistics Canada, Cat. No. 11-008, Winter. Available online at: *http://www.statcan.ca.*

Williams, T. M. (1986) *The Impact of Television*. New York: Academic Press.

www.redorbit.com (2007, 18 June) Huge growth occurs in online video use. Available at: *www.redorbit.com/news/technology/972120.*

Wood, M. (2004) Sky+ presentation at 'Tomorrow's Media World', 21 September, 2004, the British Museum, London. Available at: *http://www.carat-events.co.uk/download.htm* (accessed 1 September 2009).

Yahoo! (2004, September) The Internet Deprivation Study. Yahoo! and OMD. Available at: *http://www.docs.yahoo.com/docs/pr/release1183* (accessed 20 August 2009).

Youman, R. J. (1972) What does America think now? *TV Guide*, 30 September.

Zamaria, C., Caron, A. H. and Fletcher, F. (2005) Canada Online: A comparative analysis of Internet users and non-users in Canada and the world: Behaviour, attitudes and brands. Canada Internet Project/Project Internet Canada. Available online at: *www.cipic.ca*.

Index

American Life Project, 81, 119–20
AOL News, 90, 101
Arbitron and Edison Media
        Research, 155
audience, 1–33
    access, diversity and quality, 26–31
    changing patterns of consumption,
        10–14
    competition or synergy, 25–6
    future television viewing, 144–63
        enhanced applications, 153–4
        mobile television viewing,
            160–3
        near video-on-demand
            systems, 145–6
        online content reporting, 159–60
        online television catch-up
            services, 146–50
        use of video recorders, 150–3
        watching via the Internet, 154–9
    growth of the Internet, 4–7
    magnitude of consumption, 19–25
    self-attributed media habit
        changes, 20–1
    self-reported media use, 21–5
    media expansion implications, 7–9
    media supply and television
        viewing, 3–4
    models of displacement, 16–19
    television in society, 9–10
    television marketplace competition,
        14–16

audience share, 11–12
audio streaming, 122, 155

BBC, 44, 46–8, 57, 96–7, 117, 130,
        147–8, 157, 163
    importance of news brands, 110–11
    standards, 49–52
    viewing time, 97–8
BBC-GFK Pulse survey, 57
BBC/IPSOS survey, 60–1
BBC News Online, 100–1
BBC Trust, 4
Bebo, 80
Big Research, 104
bio-ecological theory, 17
Blinkx, 124, 142, 147
Blogger, 82
brand popularity, 71–4
broadband technology, 3, 25, 94, 142
Broadcasters' Audience Research
        Board, 61
BT Vision, 148, 157
Burst Media, 94

cable/satellite television systems, 3
Centre for the Digital Future, 104
Changing Media, 4, 71, 81, 117
Channel 4, 44, 46–8, 57, 97, 117,
        146, 147, 157
    importance of news brands, 111
    standards, 49–52
    viewing time, 97–8

Channel Five, 44, 46–8, 57, 117, 147
  importance of news brands, 111
  standards, 49–52
  viewing time, 97–8
channels, 139
  see also specific channels
  importance, 44–8
  satisfaction, 48–52
children's channels, 46
computer games, 114
ComScore, 125–6
conditional displacement, 74–6
content archive
  enhanced, 141–2
  online, 142
content attractiveness, 41
credibility, 107–10
cross-media, 69
cross-section analyses, 29

DAB broadcasting, 163
Deloitte, 131
Demand Five, 148
Department for Culture, Media and
  Sport research, 46–8
Digital Consumer Survey, 129–30
digital divide, 27
Digital Dividend Review, 38
digital technology, 36–44, 140–3
  choices, 140–1
  different perspective, 142–3
  enhanced content archiving, 141–2
  online content archives, 142
Discovery Channel, 163
DVB-H standard, 163

EastEnders, 146
electronic games, 114
enhanced television, 69
entertainment channels, 46
Entertainment Media Research, 64–5

entertainment source
  Internet, 117
  perceived importance, 114–17
equipment practicality, 41
European Interactive Advertising
  Association, 23

Facebook, 80, 127
film channels, 46
Flickr, 82
4oD, 156
Freeview, 148
functional displacement, 18, 86
  non-overlapping between television
    and Internet, 79–83
  gaming and virtual worlds, 80–2
  online social networking, 79–80
  user-generated content, 82–3
  overlapping between television and
    Internet, 76–9

gaming, 80–2
General Social Survey, 22
G.O.L.D., 146
Google News, 101
Google Video, 119, 156
Guardian Unlimited, 101

Hulu, 125

Independent Television
  Commission, 48
Institute for Business Value, 131
instrumental media, 77
Internet, 2
  entertainment source, 117
  functional overlaps with
    television, 67–84
  conditional displacement, 74–6
  importance of media motives,
    68–70

non-overlapping functional
  displacement, 79–83
  qualities, 70–4
future audiences and services, 137–65
  continuing distinctions, 138–40
  digital technology, 140–3
  future audiences, 143–63
  growth, 4–7
  importance to media consumers,
    35–66
  users vs non-users, 95
  vs television, 89–90
Internet protocol television services,
    32, 139, 147, 154
Interpret LLC, 123
Inuk, 147
iPlayer, 146–7, 149, 156
Ipsos MORI, 4
ITN, 96
ITV, 44, 46–8, 57, 97, 117, 146,
    147–8, 157
  importance of news brands, 110–11
  standards, 49–52
  viewing time, 97–8

Kaiser Family Foundation, 104

Livestation, 147

Magid Media Futures, 123
MARILYN – see Multimodal Avatar
    Response Live News caster
media consumers, 2
  importance of television/Internet,
    35–66
  channels, 44–8
  digital technology, 36–44
  Internet, 63–5
  media consumer behaviour, 61–3
  programme genres, 58–61
  programme service values, 52–8

satisfaction with television
    channels, 48–52
media richness theory, 75
mobile television, 160–3
MTV, 157
Multimodal Avatar Response Live
    News caster, 153
MySpace, 80, 125

near video-on-demand systems, 145–6
news aggregators, 101
news brands, 110–11
news channels, 45
news consumption, 97–9
news sources
  credibility of offline vs online news,
    107–10
  displacement, 102–7
  receptivity to new sources, 102
Newsround, 105
niche theory, 75
Nielsen NetRatings, 6, 71, 81, 120
NielsenWire, 126

Ofcom, 11, 36, 41–2, 53–5, 59, 60–1
Office of National Statistics, 5
online news, 96, 99–101
online social networking, 63, 79–80,
    158
online video viewing, 118–28
  continuous measurement, 124–8
  self-report measurement, 119–24
  vs television, 128–32
Oxford Internet Institute, 5

personal video recorders, 150–3
personalised television, 69
Pew Institute, 92, 105
Pew Internet, 81, 119–20
Pew Project for Excellence in
    Journalism, 104

platform symbolism, 40, 42
Pop-Up TV, 151
programme genres, 58–61
    audience shares in UK
        multi-channel TV homes, 62
    perceived importance, 60
Project Canvas, 148, 158–9
PSB – *see* public service broadcasting
psychographic research, 39
public service broadcasting, 13, 56–7,
    88, 151
public service broadcasting
    principles, 9

reception technologies, 2
reverse causation, 30–1
ritualistic media, 77

Second Life, 81
shopping channels, 46
Sky, 147
Sky+, 142, 151
Sky Anytime, 150–1
Sky by Mobile, 162–3
Sky News, 96
Sky One, 45
Sky Player TV, 148
Sky Sports, 163
socio-economic status, 39
sports channels, 45–6
Sun, 101

Telephia, 163
television
    competition, 14–16
    ensuring access, diversity and
        quality, 26–31
    entertainment source, 113–35
        Internet as entertainment
            source, 117
        perceived importance, 114–17

video game playing, 132–3
video viewing online, 118–28
    vs online video viewing, 128–32
functional overlaps with Internet,
    67–84
    conditional displacement, 74–6
    importance of media motives,
        68–70
    non-overlapping functional
        displacement, 79–83
    qualities, 70–4
future audiences and services,
    137–65
    continuing distinctions, 138–40
    digital technology, 140–3
    future audiences, 143–63
future information source, 85–112
    different information sources,
        90–4
    future of television news, 95–7
    importance of news brands,
        110–11
    Internet users vs non-users, 95
    news source displacement,
        102–7
    offline vs online news
        credibility, 107–10
    receptivity of new news
        sources, 102
    time devoted to television
        news, 97–9
    use of online news, 99–101
    valued attributes of television
        news, 86–9
    vs Internet, 89–90
importance to media consumers,
    35–66
increase in viewership, 3–4
magnitude of consumption, 19–25
    self-attributed media habit
        changes, 20–1

self-reported media use, 21–5
models of displacement, 16–19
patterns of consumption, 10–14
  audience shares for PSB
  channels, 13
position in society, 9–10
synergy or competition, 25–6
television catch-up services, 140,
  146–50
television news, 86–9
  future trends, 95–7
  viewing time, 97–9
Times Online, 101
Tiscali TV, 148
TiVo, 152

UCLA Internet Project, 95
user-generated content, 82–3

video game, 132–3

video streaming, 122, 155
Virgin Media, 147–8
VirginMobile/BT, 163
VoD services, 146–7
Vodaphone, 162–3

We Media/Zogby Interactive, 92
Widgets, 160
Wikipedia, 82
World Internet Institute, 91

Yahoo!, 64
Yahoo! News, 101
YouGov, 131, 148
YouTube, 64–5, 82, 118, 125, 127,
  131, 156

Zattoo, 147
zero-sum relationship, 17
Zogby Interactive, 93

DATE DUE
